The Martyr's Oath

Mohammed Mansour Jabarah at Niagara Falls, Canada, April 2002.

The Martyr's Oath

THE APPRENTICESHIP
OF A HOMEGROWN TERRORIST

By Stewart Bell

John Wiley & Sons Canada, Ltd.

Library and Archives Canada Cataloguing in Publication

Bell, Stewart, 1965-
    The martyr's oath : the apprenticeship of a homegrown terrorist / Stewart Bell.

Includes index.

ISBN-13   978-0-470-83683-5

ISBN-10   0-470-83683-0

    1. Jabarah, Mohammed. 2. Qaida (Organization) 3. Terrorists—Canada—Biography. I. Title.

HV6248.J22B44 2005   303.6'25'092   C2005-903172-7

Production Credits:

Cover design: Mike Chan
Interior text design: Pat Loi
Printer: Tri-Graphic Printing Ltd.

John Wiley & Sons Canada, Ltd.
6045 Freemont Blvd.
Mississauga, Ontario
L5R 4J3

Printed in Canada

10 9 8 7 6 5 4 3 2 1

"The fanatic is not really a stickler to principle. He embraces a cause not primarily because of its justness and holiness but because of his desperate need for something to hold on to."

—Eric Hoffer, *The True Believer*

Contents

Author's Note

THIS book tells, for the first time, the true story of Mohammed Mansour Jabarah, a young Canadian who was recruited into terrorism, and the international intelligence operation that brought him down. It is about the radicalization of one man, but at the same time it is the story of the thousands of other youths who are being lured into terrorist groups in much the same way. When I embarked on this project, I felt that by looking closely at how a seemingly ordinary high school graduate from Canada was transformed into a trained killer for his God, I could understand what was motivating so many others, especially in North America and Europe, to fall under the spell of Osama bin Laden, Abu Mussab Al Zarqawi and their murderous peers.

Because Jabarah traveled so much during his brief but stellar Al Qaeda career, I thought it was important to follow in his footsteps to experience the world he passed through on his way to becoming a full-fledged terrorist. I retraced his journeys across three continents, from Canada to the Middle East to Southeast Asia, and drew upon my reporter's notebooks from assignments in Pakistan in 2004 and Afghanistan in 2001 and 2002. The book is therefore not only about Mohammed Jabarah and his fellow recruits, but also the people, places and ideas that shape their dangerous outlook on the world.

Much has already been written in the press about Jabarah. Some of it was accurate. Some of it was not. In all of these journalistic fragments, however, Mohammed was never more than a disembodied name. I wanted to know who he was and why he did what he did. This was not an easy task. It is challenging to write a book about someone you have never met, especially a terrorist about whom little information has ever been officially released. This was the hardest story I have investigated in more than 15 years as a journalist. I wrote letters to Mohammed in prison, asking him to tell me his story, but I never received a reply. Likewise, phone calls and a letter to his lawyers went unanswered. I also sent many requests to the Canadian government asking for the disclosure of documents about Jabarah under the *Access to Information Act*. With a few minor exceptions, all were denied for reasons of national security and personal privacy.

Although I was never able to interview Jabarah, when I followed him around the world I did find his trail. I was also able to find out what Mohammed had told the Canadian Security Intelligence Service (CSIS) and FBI investigators, who documented what he said in various intelligence reports. I interviewed people involved in the Jabarah investigation and studied the statements that those who worked most closely with him—Khalid Sheikh Mohammad and Hambali—have given to interrogators since their capture. Finally, I spoke at length with the Jabarah family, who shared with me some of Mohammed's personal effects: report cards, family photos and letters from prison. While some may question the veracity of interrogation reports, especially following the recent concerns about the treatment of U.S. detainees, the version of events reported by the FBI is identical to the one documented independently by CSIS, and both accounts are consistent with the other available information on Jabarah. Since intelligence leaks are a politically charged topic for some, I note that none of the CSIS or FBI documents I obtained were leaked to me by either CSIS or the FBI.

They were either released under the *Access to Information Act* or obtained from trusted third parties who had access to them.

In addition to finding out how Mohammed was recruited, I also wanted to know how he was brought to justice, which, it turns out, is one of the most misunderstood parts of the Jabarah case. The story told here is unusual—it is an account of a successful intelligence operation. This is not to say that such successes are rare, but that they are rarely told. One of the realities for intelligence agencies is that their successes are hardly ever known, while their failures become common knowledge. This helps feed a commonly held public perception that those who work in the field of security and counter-terrorism are incompetent. My experience, both in Canada and abroad, is that this is far from the truth.

The book can be divided roughly into three sections. The first, chapters 1 to 5, tells the story of Mohammed's childhood in Kuwait and Canada, and Al Qaeda's early efforts to recruit him. The second section, chapters 6 to 12, chronicles his Al Qaeda training and operational assignments. The final section, chapters 13 to 18, deals with the aftermath of Mohammed's capture.

Jabarah was not the most important person in Al Qaeda, but that is partly why his story is so compelling. High-ranking leadership figures like bin Laden are no longer the only worrisome part of the international jihadist movement. Equally frightening are the mostly young men like Mohammed, who are volunteering to fight and die for the global jihad. People like bin Laden and Al Zarqawi are nothing without their dedicated foot soldiers. While counter-terrorism agents are rightly pursuing the leaders, Jabarah's story shows us that they must also ensure they are paying close attention to the significant pool of recruits. If terrorism is to be stopped, the incitement, indoctrination and recruitment of the Mohammed Jabarahs of the world must be disrupted.

The names, dates, places and events in this book are real, and I have presented them as accurately as possible. Some of the written source material I relied on was translated from Arabic, as were many of the interviews. Dollar figures are in U.S. currency unless otherwise stated. Finally, any references to the religious, ethnic, national or other attributes of terrorists are obviously not meant to suggest that all members of these groups are terrorists.

I want to thank Don Loney, my editor at John Wiley & Sons in Toronto, who encouraged me to write this book and skillfully saw it through all stages of development. Thanks also to Robert Harris, Meghan Brousseau and the rest of the team at Wiley Canada, as well as Pat Cairns at Creative Connections. The photojournalist Jeff Stephen of *Global National* accompanied me on most of the journeys described in the book and I appreciate his contributions, energy and companionship. Thanks also to George Browne and Kevin Newman. I would like to thank all those who saw the value of telling the Jabarah story properly and completely, especially those who shared with me the pieces of the puzzle in their possession and trusted that I would put them together responsibly.

The travels described in the book would not have been possible without the assistance of the diplomats, soldiers, civil servants, journalists, fixers, drivers and others who guided me when I was abroad, particularly Stewart Innes in Kuwait City, Rahimullah Yusufzai in Peshawar and Rohan Gunaratna in Singapore. I appreciate the cooperation of Mansour Jabarah, who was, if nothing else, a gracious host. Many thanks to Rita Katz and her staff at the SITE Institute, who found and translated some of the documents. Thanks also to Michael Elsner at Motley-Rice and the United States Marine Corps Base Camp Pendleton for sharing their documents. Maha Talkah translated some of the Arabic documents and provided valuable insights into their meaning and context.

I am grateful to my *National Post* colleagues, notably Michael Friscolanti, Adrian Humphreys and Doug Kelly, as well as our owners, CanWest, for their continuing support. Many journalists and editors have taught me a great deal, in particular

Rick Ouston, Larry Pynn, Patricia Graham, Jeff Lee, Harold Munro, the late Moira Farrow, Alex Rose, Barbara Yaffe, Martin Newland and Ken Whyte. Professor Martin Rudner has been a constant source of guidance and wisdom. Michael Berk at the Canadian Institute of International Affairs has been helpful and kind. Thanks to Richard Landry and the police officers who have watched out for my safety when necessary. Thanks to Bob and Anne, and John and Kay. Above all, thanks to Laura and the girls.

Stewart Bell
Toronto
June, 2005

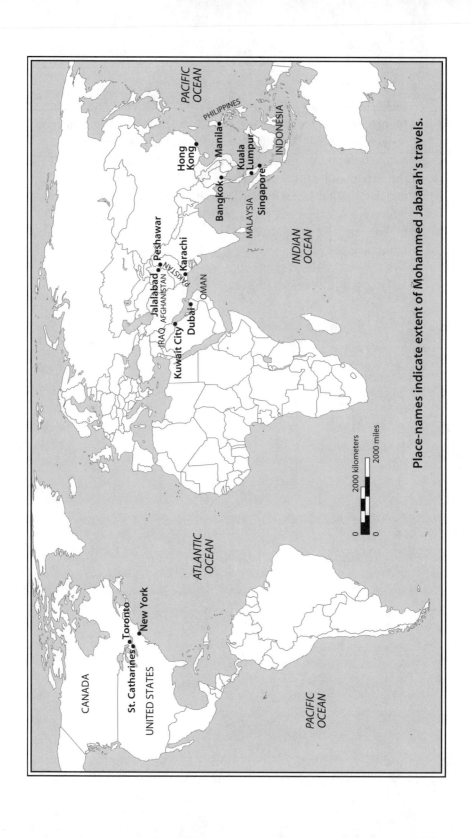

Place-names indicate extent of Mohammed Jabarah's travels.

List of Central Characters

Antara Ibn Shaddad Ancestor of Mohammed Jabarah. An Ethiopian slave born in pre-Islamic times. Accounts of his battlefield exploits form part of classical Arab literature.

Mansour Bin Moussa Al Mazidi Maternal grandfather of Mohammed. A two-term elected official in Kuwait who raised money for Algerian fighters during their war of independence against France.

Mansour Jabarah Father of Mohammed. An Iraqi citizen, he is a realtor in Kuwait City and immigrated to Canada in 1994. He was vice president of the Masjid an Noor mosque in St. Catharines, Ontario.

Abdul Rahman Jabarah (alias Abu Tulha) Older brother of Mohammed. He was also a terrorist operative involved in the Al Qaeda cell that bombed Western housing complexes in Riyadh. He was killed in 2003.

Anas Al Kandari (alias Hamza) Best friend of Mohammed. He first went to Afghanistan to train in 1999 and returned for a second time the following year with Mohammed and Abdul Rahman Jabarah. He led a terrorist cell in Kuwait until his death in 2002.

Sulayman Abu Gaith   A Kuwaiti school teacher and radical Sunni cleric who indoctrinated and recruited Al Kandari and the Jabarah brothers. He later became Osama bin Laden's official spokesman and is reported to have been captured in Iran.

Ayman Al Zawahiri (alias The Doctor, The Teacher)   The Egyptian doctor who is bin Laden's right-hand man and ideological muse. The leader of the Egyptian Al Jihad and the second-in-command of Al Qaeda, he treated Mohammed when he came down with hepatitis.

Osama (Usama) bin Laden (alias UBL, the Prince, the Emir, Abu Abdallah, the Most Wanted)   Al Qaeda leader and mastermind. Mohammed met him four times and pledged an oath of allegiance to him.

Mohammed Atef (alias Abu Hafs)   Al Qaeda's military commander. He personally viewed the surveillance tapes of targets in Singapore and approved the operation. He was killed in a U.S. missile strike in 2001.

Khalid Sheikh Mohammad (alias Mohammad the Pakistani, KSM)   Trained Mohammed at his apartment in Karachi and sent him to Southeast Asia to oversee bombings. KSM is the mastermind of most of Al Qaeda's deadliest plots, including the 9/11 attacks. He was captured in 2003.

Nurjaman Riduan Isamuddin (alias Hambali, Azman)   Worked with Mohammed to organize bombings in Southeast Asia. The Indonesian-born terrorist was the only non-Arab in the leadership of Al Qaeda. He was a leading figure in Jemaah Islamiyah until his capture in 2003.

Fathur Rohman Al-Ghozi (alias Mike the Bombmaker, Saad)
Worked with Mohammed to plan bombings in Singapore. An Indonesian and a leading figure in the Moro Islamic Liberation Front, he was killed in 2003.

Mike Pavlovic The Canadian Security Intelligence Service officer assigned to get Mohammed to talk upon his return to Canada. A former RCMP officer, he joined the Sunni Islamic extremist desk in Toronto in July, 2001.

James B. Comey The U.S. Attorney for the southern district of New York. He arranged to bring Mohammed to the U.S. and later brought terrorism charges against him. A veteran of several terrorism prosecutions, he was later appointed Deputy Attorney General of the United States.

PROLOGUE

HE called himself Sammy.

He arrived on a coach bus over the bridge spanning the Straits of Johor, the choppy emerald slough that separates Malaysia from Singapore. It is a long, low bridge that, in the space of a few kilometers, links the Third World with the First, transporting travelers from the chaos of the rough Malaysian border region of Johor to the order and stunning wealth of Singapore's high-tech miracle. After the grit and dysfunction of Kuala Lumpur, Singapore seems like it has somehow dropped out of the sky, a tiny island of gleaming office buildings and manicured parks surrounded by the verdant jungle of Southeast Asia.

At the Tuas border checkpoint, Sammy filled out an immigration landing card using his real name, Mohammed Mansour Jabarah, citizen of Canada, age 19. Under the heading Occupation, he wrote: Student. Under Purpose of Visit, he wrote: Tourism. Both answers were lies, but nobody bothered to ask. He flashed his blue and gold Canadian passport and was waved into the Republic of Singapore. He rented a room at the Royal India Hotel, a $50-a-night guesthouse in a three-storey building in Little India. There was an Internet terminal in the lobby, and the Mustafa shopping center was just across the street, a few blocks from the Abdul Gaffoor Mosque. The souvenir shops sold plastic lions, mementos of the Lion City, and miniature Buddhas—tiny versions of the obliterated ancient statues he had seen in Afghanistan a few months earlier, after the Taliban had shelled them with mortar bombs.

Near his hotel, Sammy met his contacts, members of local terrorist cells whose names and telephone numbers he had been given in Pakistan prior to his departure two days before September 11, 2001. He explained that he had come to plan Al Qaeda's next big strike after 9/11. The Al Qaeda leadership had sent him to blow up embassies in Singapore and Manila. He was the envoy, he explained, of Khalid Sheikh Mohammed, the Kuwaiti engineer behind Al Qaeda's deadliest attacks. They talked about targets and how to purchase the explosives they needed. Money was no problem. Al Qaeda had given Sammy $10,000 cash for start-up costs, and there was more where that came from.

They bought a video camera and went out to film the buildings they intended to bomb. They sat at a bus stop on Napier Road opposite the American embassy and zoomed across the eight lanes of traffic to the guard post, then panned up to the U.S. flag. Next was the Israeli embassy on Dalvey Road. Sammy sat in the back seat and aimed the camera out the driver's side window as they rolled past the embassy at moderate speed. When they were opposite the guard post, Sammy quickly lowered the camera. The targets were just as bin Laden would have wanted, for in the doctrine of Al Qaeda, the Israelis and Americans have joined together in a conspiracy to invade, occupy and control the Muslim world. "The Jews manipulate America and use it to execute their designs on the world," bin Laden had said in one of his recruiting videos.

During their reconnaissance outings, they behaved like tourists, sometimes posing in front of the camera while recording images of their targets in the background. Sammy played the part of the tourist with remarkable skill for someone who had spent the better part of the past year immersed in the austere other-world of terrorist training camps. Although still a few weeks shy of his 20th birthday, Sammy already had a thick Omar Sharif mustache that made him look older than he really was. His brown eyes were shaded below eyebrows that joined at the bridge of a hawkish nose and were so thick they looked like they had been drawn there with a black felt marker. His grin expressed quiet confidence. He bore a resemblance to the flamboyant rock singer Freddie Mercury. He sometimes wore a baseball cap and big aviator sunglasses. The overall effect was that he looked like just another tourist, out to videotape the sights of the city. And that was exactly what he wanted.

Singapore was Mohammed Jabarah's first assignment as a terrorist. During his training, he stood out as an exceptionally bright recruit. He was a particularly talented sniper, deadly accurate with an AK-47. He placed first in the Al Qaeda sniping competition. Another bonus: He had a Canadian passport, which allowed him to cross borders without problems, as his easy entry into Singapore demonstrated. He also spoke fluent English and, having grown up in Canada, he knew how to talk and behave like a Westerner. He could fit in. And he was cool and steady under pressure. With his skills, he should have been working for the good guys. Had he not been recruited into Al Qaeda, he would have made an excellent addition to the Canadian military, intelligence service or police. He was on the wrong side of the war on terror.

In Canada, he had been by all accounts a quiet student with good grades, the son of hard-working immigrants from Kuwait who had moved to Ontario after the Gulf War to escape the perpetual insecurity of the Middle East and to give their four sons a better life, a better future. Mohammed had been accepted into university and talked about becoming an engineer or a doctor. Instead, he turned his back on his adopted home and joined a cause devoted to the destruction of Western society. He became, in his eyes, a *mujahedin*, a holy warrior, a soldier of God. Stripped of its romantic euphemisms, he became a terrorist. In ruling in a terrorism case, a Canadian judge, Pierre Blais, once quoted the saying, "Tell me who your friends are, and I will tell you who you are." Mohammed Jabarah's friends were the most bloodthirsty, fanatical murderers in the ranks of Al Qaeda.

Mohammed Jabarah was at the vanguard of a disturbing trend that intelligence agencies throughout the Western world were then just beginning to notice. The type of people joining terror networks was changing. Radical Islamic groups were no longer made up of just Saudis or Pakistanis; they were increasingly the sons of middle-class immigrants living in North America and Europe. Intelligence officers started calling them "homegrown terrorists," those who were either born in the West or had immigrated at a young age, and yet were still somehow subscribing to Al Qaeda's jihadist ideology.

There were the Lackawanna Six in upstate New York, just a short drive from where Mohammed grew up in Ontario. There were the Moroccans in Spain involved in the Madrid commuter train bombings and the Britons arrested for planning an ammonium nitrate bombing in the United Kingdom. The core of the 9/11 terror squad was recruited in Germany. Following the "7/7" bombings in London, which killed more than 50 people, a leaked Cabinet dossier described how British youths were being recruited into extremism. The "factors which may attract some to extremism" were listed as anger, alienation and activism. "A number of extremist groups are actively recruiting young British Muslims. Most do not advocate violence. But they can provide an environment for some to gravitate to violence. Extremists target poor and disadvantaged Muslims, including through mosque and prison contact. But they also target middle-class students and affluent professionals through schools and college campuses. Others get recruited through personal contact, often by chance, and maintain a low profile for operational purposes."

One of the jihadis believed to have gone to Syria to help the Iraq insurgency is a French-born 13-year-old. There were no training camps in his neighborhood on the outskirts of Paris, but he didn't need them. He had the Internet, Arabic satellite TV and a radical Algerian preacher who told the local boys about the abuse of Muslims and asked what they were going to do about it.

"Europe is gradually, but surely, rivaling the Middle East and Afghanistan as a recruiting hub of Islamist terrorists," Michael Taarnby of the Center for Cultural Research in Denmark wrote in a paper commissioned by the Danish Ministry of Justice. Dennis Richardson, the Australian Security Intelligence Organization chief, said that, "While small in absolute terms, the number of Australians confirmed or assessed to have undertaken terrorist training courses continues to grow."

Canada's intelligence service is now reporting the emergence of a "new generation of jihadists." Some were born in Canada; others immigrated as children. They are young, educated and computer-literate. In many cases, they were raised in households where radical Islam was the norm. "Canada is home to a number of young men who are the sons of known Islamic extremists and have adopted a jihadist mentality," says a "secret" Canadian Security Intelligence Service (CSIS) report.

The first person charged under Canada's *Anti-Terrorism Act* was a Canadian-born Muslim, accused of taking part in a bombing plot in the United Kingdom. In October 2004, Russian troops claimed to have killed a young Canadian from Vancouver, who they said was an armed fighter with Chechen rebel forces. It later emerged that he was a follower of a Canadian sheikh who had said in a recorded lecture, "It is inconceivable that a true believer will not desire martyrdom." In Israel in late 2004, a young Palestinian-Canadian pleaded guilty to charges he was recruited into Hamas. And then there are the Khadr siblings, all Canadians, raised by Ahmed Said Khadr, a close associate of bin Laden's. One of the boys was sent to Guantanamo Bay for allegedly killing a U.S. soldier; another said his father tried to recruit him to be a suicide bomber; a third was wounded in the gun battle in Pakistan that killed his father.

"The presence of young, committed jihadis in Canada is a significant threat to national security for a number of reasons," says another "secret" CSIS study. "These individuals are very familiar with Canadian customs and morés and have no difficulty fitting into Western society. They have excellent English-language skills and can pass as average Canadians, thus evading more rigid scrutiny by security officials. Their knowledge of Canadian—and by extension Western—society renders them a valuable resource for international Islamic extremists who need individuals to infiltrate our countries to carry out terrorist acts. Young Canadian extremists also have bona fide Canadian travel documentation. The possession of a valid Canadian passport facilitates international travel." Yet another CSIS study reports, "Some of these individuals . . . [such as] Jabarah . . . have engaged in terrorist operations. For terrorist recruiters, these young men's idealism, hatred, language skills and cultural familiarity with the West renders them valuable potential resources in the international Islamic extremist movement."

When he trained at Al Farooq camp near Kandahar, Mohammed Jabarah met Frenchmen and Americans. Two of the men who trained with him were Australians with blonde hair. Another spoke with a distinctly British accent. These were not the despondent, poverty-stricken revolutionaries that conventional wisdom says join terrorist causes out of despair and lack of hope. All had joined the jihad out of comfortable homes in the West. They had thrown it all away for the brotherhood of martyrdom, and that trend has only worsened as Iraq has emerged as the new land of jihad. "They are, for all intents and purposes, elitists, much as Hitler's youth were," Saudi columnist Dr. Mohammed T. Al-Rasheed wrote in the *Arab News* about young, Western-educated jihadis. "Like the Nazis, they believe in their own superiority of moral and racial origins."

Since the Soviet War in Afghanistan, Al Qaeda and the other Sunni Islamic extremist groups that share its ideology have become expert at bringing such young men into their organizations and making them the cannon fodder for the advancement of their international agenda. The recruiters know just the right buttons to push. They play off current world events, portraying them as yet another example of the repression of Muslims. They use friends and clerics to approach potential recruits, and they couch their recruiting in the unquestionable authority of religion. Terrorists are recruiting through four frameworks: friendship, kinship, worship and discipleship.

Jabarah is a classic case.

Mohammed's journey to the dark heart of Al Qaeda was guided by all four influences until, at the age of 19, he formally swore the martyr's oath to die for bin Laden. And now, weeks after the 9/11 attacks, he was walking the streets of Singapore, posing as a tourist while orchestrating a day of holy terror. The plan was typical of Al Qaeda. He would rent a *godown*—a warehouse. He would buy six trucks and hide them in the warehouse while Mike the Bombmaker, his Indonesian explosives expert, rigged each with three tons of fertilizer and TNT. On the chosen morning, Arab suicide bombers would detonate the bombs-on-wheels outside the targeted buildings. Hundreds were going to die. Al Qaeda was counting on it.

The mechanics of Al Qaeda bombing operations are by now well known, owing to their nauseating repetition from New York to Bali. What remains elusive is perhaps the more fundamental question: How could someone possibly reach this level of fanaticism? How does a man like Sammy get here from there? How does he reach the stage where he is not only willing, but eager, to kill masses of innocent people? As a little boy, Mohammed never wanted for anything. His father was a businessman, his mother a lawyer, his grandfather an elected Kuwaiti official. One of the Jabarah family homes had an indoor swimming pool. There were bad times, for sure, but for the most part, Mohammed lived a life of privilege. He had money, family, friends, security and a good education. He had deep and proud roots in the Arab world, and he had the gift of Canadian citizenship. He could have done anything with his life.

So, how did he become a terrorist?

I

SON OF THE DESERT

THERE is a sandstorm in Kuwait City the day I arrive.

The early winter winds have sent clouds of fine grit swirling around the city. I can taste it and feel it stinging my eyes the minute I step off the plane with a group of European soldiers in desert camouflage. The arrivals board at Kuwait International Airport lists the inbound flights from London, Mumbai, Colombo, Delhi and Chennai that import the foreign laborers and professionals who account for almost two-thirds of Kuwait's population, and the Western soldiers bound for the hell of Iraq.

The highway to Kuwait City has six smooth lanes, packed with Jaguars and BMWs. My taxi is a Mercedes. The cabbie wears a navy blue uniform with gold epaulettes. Along the edge of the highway, sprinklers are performing life-support on patches of yellow and orange flowers. Perfectly squared hedges line the road and chilly gusts bend the palms. A road sign suspended from an overpass proclaims, like the voice of God, "Young man, your freedom ends where you start to bother other people."

Beyond that, I can see nothing but blowing sand.

"Dust," complains the taxi driver, a Bangladeshi. "Very dust."

The Liberation Tower soon comes into focus through the beige haze. The Kuwait cityscape consists of sharp projectiles stabbing at the sky: the space-age Kuwait Towers, which look like they belong at Disneyland; the minarets of the city's eight hundred mosques; and the construction cranes busily erecting a modern city out of the remnants of a Bedouin trading post. There is not much left of historic Kuwait. The old city is being bulldozed block by block to make way for the new Kuwait—gleaming office towers, shopping malls, beaches and elegant boulevards.

Driving through Kuwait City, it is easy to forget that an hour to the north, an ugly war is being fought. It is also easy to forget that, not long ago, Kuwait was itself invaded, plundered and torched by Saddam Hussein's army, only to be liberated by the U.S.-led coalition after seven months of occupation. Kuwait's expression of gratitude to the Gulf War coalition is painted on the face of a building near the seaside Royal Palace. Beneath a giant Kuwaiti flag, it reads: "Thanks Allies."

There is another conflict brewing to the West, in Saudi Arabia, where jihadists are waging a terrorist campaign against Westerners and the House of Saud. Compared to its neighbors, Kuwait is an oasis of calm, but still, the borders have not stopped the influences of Iraqi or Saudi unrest from spilling into Kuwait. For all its brand-name shops and shiny SUVs, its Starbucks and Virgin Records, Kuwait is no more than a tiny patch of inhospitable land in a bad neighborhood. It is peaceful and modern, but the desert is rough and resilient, and every now and then you can see that there is a struggle going on between the city and the forces of nature that are determined to return this place to its natural state, which is sand.

In my hotel room, I am greeted by a glossy coffee-table book called *Welcome to Kuwait*, which features portraits of the royal family and a lengthy tract on the true meaning of jihad, which it says may bring to mind "images of fanaticism and bloodshed" but actually refers to "the constant struggle to submit to the will of God, and to make the principles of Islam the guiding factors in the life of the individuals, family and community."

I look out the window and see a country dominated by two types of structures: refineries and minarets. The former are the source of Kuwait's material wealth; the latter are the source of its spiritual wealth. The mosques are said to be arrayed so that, no matter where you are in the city, you can always hear the *muezzin*'s call to prayer, five times a day, seven days a week.

Kuwait, the land of oil and Islam.

* * *

Sheikh Mansour bin Nazem bin Jabarah bin Saqr Al Abousi arrives at the Sheraton Hotel in a cherry-red Chevrolet Lumina. He hands the keys to the valet and steps through the metal detector positioned at the front door as a pretext to security. His wife Souad Al Mazidi, a lawyer, follows close behind, a scarf draped over her head.

Mansour is tall. He jogs to stay in shape, and it shows. He is slim and agile. He is well groomed, with a short, trimmed beard. He is a handsome man, with a long nose and fine features, and he is dashing in his white *gutra* headscarf and *agal*, the black ring of braided rope that secures it to his head. He wears a brown winter *dishdasha*, the loose robe that is the national costume of Kuwait. His smile is serene, and I notice that he holds his chin high, with pride. Under his arm, he cradles a bundle of worn scrapbooks.

The Jabarahs sit on a couch in the sunlit lobby, order coffee and leaf through their photo albums, remembering happier times.

There's their son Mohammed as a toddler, standing at the front door of the house with his older brother Abdul Rahman, both in striped shirts and brown short pants. Their dad is kneeling beside the boys with his arm curled protectively around Mohammed's waist.

Mansour turns the page.

There's Mohammed, a little older now, a broad smile on his face, riding a green amusement park dragon, the kind that goes around and around on a moat of stagnant brown water. Mohammed's hands clasp the wooden seat in front.

Mansour turns the page.

The three Jabarah boys are posing on the grass outside their house in Kuwait City, wearing identical dress shirts, black pants and belts. Abdul Rahman has his arm slung around Mohammed's neck.

Mansour and Souad have not seen Mohammed, their third-born, since he left their home in Canada in June 2000. They have tried to follow his case, but that has not been easy since the court proceedings in the case, *United States of America v. Mohammed Mansour Jabarah*, have been held behind closed doors. In fact, the U.S. Department of Justice will not publicly acknowledge it is holding Mohammed. Mansour and Souad keep abreast of developments through Canada's Department of Foreign Affairs, but consular officials can only do so much.

The Mohammed described by Mansour is a son any father would be proud of—a bright student, faithful to his religion, well regarded by his community, destined for a career as a doctor, or maybe an engineer.

"Mohammed never lied to others. Mohammed did not ever drink," Mansour says.

"He's like almost an angel person."

The same goes for Mohammed's big brother Abdul Rahman, he says.

"Since they were kids, they were the most honest people. They were always open with me and their mom. They were very clever; they were very smart. All of the people who knew them in St. Catharines, they said very good things about our family."

The message Mansour is trying to convey is that Mohammed is a good boy, from a good family. The Jabarahs want me to know they raised their sons right, gave them a good life and taught them the virtues of obedience, faith and pride. To his parents, Mohammed has done no wrong.

"He did nothing. What he did?" Mansour asks.

"Well, he trained in the camps of bin Laden in Afghanistan," I reply.

"So?" Mansour says. "Thousands of people trained over there in Afghanistan."

They return to their photo albums.

There's Mohammed in a strawberry field with Abdullah his eldest brother; they're helping their father fill a basket. There's Mohammed standing in front of a statue of a sphinx in Cairo, posing after Koranic school and smiling for his school portrait. Mansour shows me photos of Mohammed hugging his little brother Youssef at a playground; posing in his soccer uniform with Abdul Rahman; holidaying in Saudi Arabia; standing on the driveway outside their house in Canada wearing a toque; smiling for his high school yearbook portrait, gawky and thin. Mohammed has a broad smile, like his father, and sharp, dark eyes. He looks like a young gentleman.

One of the pictures shows Mohammed wearing the costume of a Bedouin warrior. "Look," Mansour says, "how he dresses like his hero, Antara."

Antara Ibn Shaddad, Mansour explains, is an Arab folk hero from pre-Islamic times. He was the son of an Ethiopian black slave named Zabiba and the Bedouin king Shaddad. Because of Antara's mixed race, his father would not acknowledge him as his son, and the tribe, the Banu Abs, treated him as an outcast. He was a slave and he was *aghribat al-arab*, a "raven of the Arabs."

"His father did not want to tell others, 'He's my true son,'" Mansour says. "Antara fought for several years just to prove himself as a regular son to his father."

The story of Antara is well known in the Arab world. It was one of the favorite Arabian odes told and retold through the ages by the desert Bedouins. One common version says that Antara was tormented because he loved his niece Abla, but as he was a slave, he could not marry her. When robbers made off with the tribe's camel herds, Antara's father offered him freedom if he would catch the thieves. He refused at first, saying, "The slave is not for fighting; he is only needed to milk the camels and tie up their udders." He obeyed his father, however, and was emancipated.

Antara went on to fight in an 11-year war that started when a rival tribe accused the Banu Abs of cheating in a horse race. Antara proved himself on the battlefield through his heroics and went on to become a roaming hero on horseback, leading the Banu Abs on conquests of Arabia, Iraq, Syria and Persia. In one battle, he was credited with killing 1,200 knights. "I am Antara ibn Shaddad, the mightiest of the Arabs in zeal and the firmest in resolve," he says in *The Adventures of Antar.* "No tongue can describe me and my noble deeds. I am the mine of valor and pride, unique in this age. I have attained every goal that I have sought . . . My foe has been slain, his blood scattered in drops."

The desert people of Antara's time held three virtues in high regard: generosity, fighting skills and language. Poetry was revered among the Arabs, and so when stories of Antara's heroics began to circulate, they were woven into first-person ballads that were carried across the desert. The *Poem of Antara* was so popular it was put on display at the Kaaba in Mecca. Antara became one of the seven "suspended poets," whose words were left hanging in Arabia's most important religious shrine.

And surely I recollected you,

Even when the lances were drinking my blood,

And bright swords of Indian make were dripping with my blood.

I wished to kiss the swords,

For they shone as bright as the flash of the foretooth of your smiling mouth.

If you lower your veil over yourself in front of me,

Of what use will it be for I am expert in capturing the mailed horseman.

Praise me for the qualities which you know I possess,

For when I am not ill-treated,

I am gentle to associate with.

And if I am ill-treated,

Then my tyranny is severe,

Very bitter is the taste of it,

As the taste of the colocynth.

Scholars believe the story of Antara originated with long lost folk tales that grew and changed as they drifted across Arabia, from campsite to campsite. Antara was the embodiment of desert pride and chivalry, but perhaps most importantly he was a pan-Arab hero for the emerging followers of Islam. He was immortalized in a statue erected in Byzantium. Painters imagined scenes from his life. Even the Prophet Muhammad was said to have mentioned that there was only one Bedouin he wanted to meet, and that was Antara. In Europe, Antara inspired a symphony and an opera.

There are as many versions of his death as there are dunes in the desert. One has him falling from his horse in battle and unable to climb back on because of his advanced age. Another has him going off into the desert to collect a camel and getting trapped in a summer sand storm that ripped him to shreds. In another telling, he is struck by a poison arrow while urinating. But even at death's door, Antara achieves a final victory. The archer is tracked down and killed, and his body presented to the dying Antara so that he can have the final satisfaction of outliving his enemy.

Mohammed Jabarah knew these stories well. The Jabarahs are Al Abousis, members of Antara's tribe, and regard themselves as the proud descendents of the legendary warrior. It was part of the family folklore, told and retold through the generations. Mohammed was proud to share the Al Abousi name with Antara. To be the descendant of a great Arab warrior was a rare honor.

"Sometimes we shared it, this kind of information during our gatherings. Even this story has been taught in schools because Antara Ibn Shaddad is a very famous person in Arab culture," Mansour says.

"We belong to a family that has been established since maybe two, three thousand years ago, from both sides, from his father and his mother. The Al Mazidi family, they belong to a very, very historical, big family, either in Kuwait or Iraq."

"Everybody has to be proud of themselves. It's important for everybody, not [just] for Mohammed, even important for myself. If you stick with your roots, you are like proud, you can talk about yourself, 'I am so and so, I belong to this and that.'"

As a child, Mohammed dressed up like Antara, and wrote poetry like his great ancestor. "Mohammed has a very strong confidence about his self, about his background, about his name," Mansour tells me.

"Always he has been proud of his name."

* * *

Kuwait was, until recently, little more than a trading post on the edge of the desert, where merchants would buy and sell frankincense, myrrh, dates and pearls. It was a port where the camel caravans that crossed Arabia would meet up with the boats that ferried cargo between the Persian Gulf, East Africa and India. The city of Kuwait was not founded until 1710, when a group of families trekked east in search of water. They built a walled city out of mud, and in 1756 Abd Rahim became sheikh of the new outpost. His Al Sabah family has ruled Kuwait ever since. In 1899, the Al Sabahs allied themselves with Britain to keep out the Germans and Ottomans, and the country became a British protectorate. But Kuwait's history really began in the 1930s with the Kuwaiti Oil Company.

When oil production soared after the Second World War, Arabs flooded in from surrounding countries to find work. With a tenth of the world's oil reserves, Kuwaitis grew so wealthy they could afford to fly in outsiders to build their nation for them. They brought in so many foreigners that out of Kuwait's 2.6 million inhabitants, fewer than one million are actual Kuwaitis. The rest are Indians, Filipinos, and non-Kuwaiti Arabs such as Egyptians and Iraqis. "In Kuwait, all the hard-working people are Indian and Bangladeshi," my cab driver tells me. "Kuwaiti people just have nice cars and do telephone talking." Too often, apparently, they do both simultaneously and at high speed. Crushed luxury vehicles lie abandoned at the roadsides like broken toys. No problem. The car dealers are well stocked. Why Kuwaitis bother to drive so fast is a mystery; the country is only 170 kilometers from north to south, and a little less from east to west. Even at a moderate speed, you can get anywhere in a few hours. Maybe the breakneck pace of their country's development has left Kuwaitis addicted to speed. Maybe they're just bored.

Among those who moved to Kuwait during the boom days was Mansour Jabarah's father, who came from the Iraqi city of Basra. A commercial city which once boasted more than five hundred types of dates, Basra is sometimes called the Venice of the Orient because of its canal network. It was also at the heart of Islamic civilization, having been founded in the 7th century by a companion of the Prophet Muhammad. In the 18th century, a young theologian named Muhammad ibn Abd al Wahhab worked as a teacher in Basra, before founding the puritanical Wahhabi reform movement, which seeks to restore Islam to its former magnificence by purifying the faith from outside influences and innovations, and directing followers to live according to the original teachings of the prophet. Today such thinking forms the basis of Sunni Islamic extremist movements worldwide.

When Mansour Jabarah's mother went into labor, she was closer to the hospital in Basra than the one in Kuwaiti City, so, by circumstance, Mansour was born in Iraq. The family lived in downtown Kuwait City, in one of the many neighborhoods that has since been demolished by the government to make way for modern office towers. Just before its independence, Kuwait conducted a national citizenship campaign, inviting residents to apply to become Kuwaitis. The Jabarahs' neighbors encouraged Mansour's father to submit his paperwork, but he considered himself an Iraqi, from the cradle of civilization. What was Kuwait by comparison? Just an oasis in the desert with no history. Why would he want to become a Kuwaiti? He never got around to submitting his citizenship papers and the deadline passed. He would remain forever an Iraqi foreigner, and so would his children and their children.

"This is his destiny," Mansour shrugs.

Mansour married Souad, a lawyer from the Al Mazidi clan, which is part of the Bin Assad tribe. Souad's family had also migrated from Iraq, although they had done so two centuries ago and were well established in Kuwait. Her father, Mansour Bin Moussa Al Mazidi, had started out as a trader of food, carpets, blankets and textiles. He later owned a printing press. At independence in 1961 he nominated himself for a seat on the committee that was establishing the new nation of Kuwait, and he won. He helped draft the Kuwaiti constitution, as well as its criminal and commercial laws. Although he resigned his seat after one term, in a show of respect, his resignation was not accepted and he went on to serve a second term. During the Algerian independence war against France, he collected money for Algerian fighters, and following the Suez Crisis, he raised money to educate the children of Egyptian "martyrs." He also collected money for the Palestinian cause.

The Jabarahs' first-born was Abdullah, who was followed soon after by Abdul Rahman. Mohammed was born two years later at Kuwait City's Al Sabah Hospital on December 21, 1981. The family lived in Al Qadsiya, a suburb of well-kept, block-shaped houses and neatly trimmed trees. There is a mall with a Burger King there now. The Jabarah photo albums show the family playing at the beach, swimming in the indoor pool at their home and vacationing in London, Paris and Switzerland. Mansour had a blue van and in the summer, when the Arabian heat was reaching its inferno highs, he would take the boys to Cairo and Saudi Arabia. Mohammed "grew up with a very normal life. He had lots of friends; he had lots of family. He had a very nice living, luxury life. And I used to take them, especially during the winter time, the summer time, to different places," Mansour says.

Mansour wanted his sons to have an Islamic education. Mohammed attended Al Najat school in Salmiya from grades one to six. "His friends liked him too much," Mansour laughs. Mohammed was a little comedian. "Even if he is gathering with us and our family, he has to make jokes with his brothers, with his uncles, aunts, friends." His teacher likewise noted in a report card that he liked to have fun.

Al Najat is a Koranic school, where students memorize the Muslim holy book line by line by reciting it in a monotone rap while bobbing their heads to the rhythm of the words. The school is a collection of two-storey buildings enclosed behind green walls. There is a dusty soccer field outside, beside the parking lot where parents driving Range Rovers pull up to fetch their kids after school. The classrooms surround a large courtyard, in which the 99 names of God are written on wooden signs. "God, The Merciful, The Most Compassionate . . ." The hallways are decorated with painted images of mosque domes and minarets. A poster advertises the annual Koranic memorization competition sponsored by the *emir*. There are cash prizes totaling 100,000 Dinars, but Mohammed would have been ineligible. It is for Kuwaiti citizens only.

Mohammed's report cards describe a student who was both bright and sociable. "The child is tidy and clean, he eats well, has got good appetite," his report card from Al Basha'er Nursery School says. "We wish him progress and success in the future." In elementary school he had perfect scores in Arabic, Math and Science. The only core subject in which he did not score 20 out of 20 was Islamic Education. He got 19 out of 20. Throughout grade school he achieved an overall score of "excellent" in every term. "He likes to listen to stories," his teacher noted at the end of the 1986–87 school year. Among the stories told in Kuwait's schools was that of Antara the Black Knight, the slave who became a prince.

And many a husband of beautiful women,

I have left prostrate on the ground,

With his shoulders hissing,

Like the side of the mouth of one with a slit lip,

My two hands preceded him with a hasty blow,

Striking him before he could strike me;

And with the drops of blood from a penetrating stroke,

Red like the color of Brazil wood.

Antara's life begins and ends in the desert, and in between there are times of disillusionment, enlightenment, self-doubt, perseverance and victory. "I conquered kings in both the east and west," he says, "and I destroyed courageous equals in the day of rout." Who can say what impact family folklore has on children, but the moral of the story of Antara is not difficult to decipher: An outcast can exact his revenge; he can win acceptance and power through bravery in battle, by confronting the enemies of the tribe.

2

LIFE UNDER OCCUPATION

THE houses in Kuwait City are big and private. They reveal little to the outside world. The windows are small and curtained. The walls are sheer and thick. They are like little castles in the desert, fortified against invaders. Street addresses have the appearance of no-nonsense precision—a numbered house, on a numbered street, on a numbered block. But in reality, the blocks are not well marked, and the house numbers are not always sequential, and many do not even display their numbers, so even locals have trouble finding them.

House 417, Street 2, Block 10 is a beige block of cement inside a walled compound in a neighborhood called Salwa. There is a palm tree at the front entrance and an empty lot next door, occupied by a few cars, a rusted dumpster and a ginger cat. In January 1990, Mansour Jabarah sold his house in Bayan and moved here with his family. There was room enough for a growing family and a big mosque in the neighborhood. The beach was within walking distance. But a few months after they moved into their new home, the Jabarahs woke up one morning to find they were under occupation.

At 2 a.m. on Thursday, August 2, 1990, 120,000 Iraqi troops crossed the border into Kuwait. They formed a massive convoy of Soviet-made tanks, armored vehicles and supply trucks that came streaming down the six-lane highway to the capital, helicopter gunships hovering overhead. They met little resistance and were in Kuwait City within an hour. By morning, the royal palace was surrounded by tanks and taking fire. Kuwaitis awoke to discover that their nation was gone, that they were now the subjects of President Saddam Hussein. Kuwait had been annexed. It was a southern appendage of Iraq. "We were sleeping in our house and everybody got word through the phone," Mansour recalls. "Most of the people did not understand what's going on. We just saw the helicopters over us and many soldiers."

Although Iraq had been assembling its army at the border for weeks, most thought it no more than a bluff by a demented tyrant. Kuwait's state-controlled press had been banned from reporting the build-up, so Kuwaitis were more shocked than anybody by the sudden appearance of the Iraqi National Guard on their streets. At first, most thought the invading soldiers were Kuwaitis, Mansour says. The Iraqis seized the Sheraton Hotel, turning it into their headquarters, and fanned out across the city to make their presence known. One unit set up near the Salwa mosque. The Iraqi troops came to the Jabarah home and knocked on the door, but they did not otherwise bother the family. As an Iraqi, it must have been strange for Mansour, to be invaded and occupied by soldiers from his ancestral homeland. It is hard to say whether his nationality protected him from the brutality of the Iraqi troops, but the family certainly fared better than many during the occupation.

Within weeks of the invasion, Amnesty International was reporting widespread abuses by the Iraqi forces. Hundreds of Kuwaiti civilians, including children, were executed. Others were arrested and "disappeared." Accounts of torture and rape were common and horrific in their sadistic methods. Iraq's undisciplined soldiers were looting, raping and murdering.

By December, an estimated 300,000 Kuwaitis had left the country. The Jabarahs stayed behind but Mansour did not work, and the schools were closed. "We were inside just protecting ourselves, sometimes searching for food, sometimes for water," he says.

The Iraqis tried to return the city to some level of normalcy, but Kuwaitis resisted. Mansour's contribution was to refuse to go back to work. "Even myself and my sons, the Kuwaiti people, we made a kind of strike. We did not go to work or to school, to show the others we are not happy with what the Iraqi has done to Kuwait. The kids stayed out of school more than seven or eight months during the occupation of Kuwait."

Mohammed was eight when the occupation began, too young to fully comprehend what was going on. But the boys understood the struggle for survival and helped out as best they could. It was an adventure for them. When water became scarce, the brothers surveyed the empty lot next door and dug until they hit an underground source. When the housemaid fled, Mohammed and his brothers took over her responsibilities, helping Souad with the chores. "They were like young men taking care of the house and their mother."

It was too risky to go out for long. The only time anyone left their homes was on Fridays, when they would walk through the empty lot and along the street to the Salwa mosque for prayers. Within the sanctity of the mosque walls, they would exchange whispered information with their neighbors. Today, Hashim Al Kandari lives in the house next to the mosque; he remembers Mohammed. "We played together. He was nice." But their soccer games were tempered by the presence of the Iraqi troops who had stationed their tanks in the parking lot outside the mosque. Hashim's father Mohammed remembers Jabarah "coming to the mosque all the time. He was a nice person; he was very nice and very polite."

The Al Kandaris have a *diwan* in their house, a large sitting room where they host a weekly *diwaniyah*, a night for men to meet, talk and play games. Reached through a separate outside entrance, it has a giant screen television. Cushioned seats line the walls. Mansour Jabarah has long attended the Al Kandari *diwaniyah* every Tuesday night. On the night I drop in, two dozen men are sitting in the room, sipping sweet tea and coffee, served by an Indian servant. The TV is tuned alternatively to Al Arabiya and Al Jazeera. The arrival of a local *emir*, a title given to Arab royalty and dignitaries, causes all in the room to rise to shake his hand.

Food is an important part of the *diwaniyah*. The men take turns hosting the meal because it would be too much to expect the owner of the house to feed everybody each week. Tonight it is Mansour's turn to host, and he prepares a buffet of chicken and fish, humus and Pepsi. He once owned a restaurant in Kuwait City and he knows how to take care of his guests. He is a gracious host, and urges everyone to fill their plates, which they do. They sit at small tables and discuss politics and the war in Iraq and joke that one of their group should run for elected office. Mansour, however, never mentions the troubles involving his sons. "He doesn't like to talk about this too much," Mohammed Al Kandari says, "and we don't ask him."

The months under occupation passed slowly, as Saddam ignored international demands for the withdrawal of his troops and the United States led a build-up of forces in the Persian Gulf. On November 29, the United Nations Security Council gave Iraq six weeks to pull its troops out. President George Bush drew his "line in the sand." The United States and its coalition partners began air strikes on January 17, 1991. Iraqi troops retaliated by setting Kuwaiti oil fields ablaze, turning the skies black.

"It passed, but how it passed, it's a really good question. All the time we were inside our houses, we had to communicate with our neighbors, we had to encourage others to have patience because everybody realized this occupation will never go for a long time because of what the Iraqi government has done to Kuwait— incredible things, really terrible things. They did not come like brothers or friends. They came like criminals to Kuwait."

The neighbors helped each other as best they could. A doctor turned her house into a clinic. The women baked bread for the hungry. Some neighbors passed information to the Americans or joined the resistance. On the morning of February 24, the Kuwaiti underground opened fire on an Iraqi intelligence patrol. The Iraqis returned fire and called for reinforcements. Three tanks surrounded the house that was the source of the gunfire and blasted away at its brick walls. The exchange lasted 14 hours. By the time it was all over, three Kuwaitis were dead, seven had escaped and eight were captured, tortured and executed.

The ruins of the house still stand, one of the few reminders of the Iraqi invasion, now known as the Al-Qurain Martyrs Museum. With its Iraqi tank shells, photos of the Kuwaiti martyrs and an old Iraqi tank, the house is a keepsake of those dark days when Kuwait almost ceased to be a nation. A white mini-bus used by Iraqi intelligence units is parked outside, its sides pocked with bullet holes. A plaque says it was used to transfer prisoners to Iraq. The museum "is a reminder to us that the Kuwaiti youth, as normally thought, was not spoiled but were active and in the most difficult time, they came forward with beautiful work," says Najat, who gives tours of the house. Her husband's cousin, Jassim Mohammad, was among those killed in the stand-off. During the invasion, the Iraqis evicted Najat and her twins from their home on Faylaka Island. "They were very rough and rude," she says, which seems a grossly understated description of the soldiers' behavior.

The uniforms worn by the resistance fighters hang on the walls of the museum, white tops with "Kuwaiti Force" written on them. They look like soccer jerseys. "It is a chapter of the history of Kuwait," Najat says. Framed on the wall are the remarks of General Norman Schwarzkopf who, upon visiting the site in 1994, said, "When I am in this house it makes me wish that we had come four days earlier."

Mansour awoke to the bleep of car horns at midnight on February 26, 1991. By 3 a.m., the sounds of celebration were louder and he tuned in to the BBC and CNN. The Kuwaiti resistance was claiming to be in control of the city. The allies had launched their land assault from Saudi Arabia, and quickly overwhelmed the Iraqi forces, taking thousands of prisoners. Saddam responded by ordering his troops out of Kuwait. Mansour went outside onto Street 2 and saw his Salwa neighbors hugging and congratulating each other for surviving the occupation. It was the happiest moment of his life. The pressures of seven months of fear and uncertainty and survival were suddenly lifted.

"Nobody can forget this day."

Radio stations reported that mines and booby traps were scattered around the city, but Kuwaitis ignored the warnings. By morning the streets were filled with people waving Kuwaiti flags and pictures of the *emir*, and shooting into the air as they walked through a city strewn with the litter of war. There were burned-out cars. There were the tanks, guns and helmets that the Iraqis had cast off as they fled north for the border. And there were the blackened skies, heavy with the smoke of oil-well fires and the burning seafront hotels.

The American and Saudi troops arrived from the south in a convoy 25 kilometers in length. Kuwaitis danced and kissed the soldiers. At 9 p.m. Washington time, President Bush declared victory in a televised address. "Kuwait is liberated. Iraq's army is defeated. Our military objectives are met. Kuwait is once more in the hands of Kuwaitis, in control of their own destiny." Operation Desert Storm had lasted a mere six weeks, and the ground war just one hundred hours.

Liberation Day was muted by the realization that the war had inflicted heavy damage to Kuwait. As well as the atrocities committed against countless Kuwaitis, and the hundreds of disappeared, the Iraqis had torched the heart of the city before leaving, and looted whatever they could carry. There was no electricity and very little drinking water. The oil fields, the source of Kuwait's wealth, were ablaze. The *emir*'s palace was in ruins. Regardless, most Kuwaitis old enough to remember have fond recollections of that day, and many still feel indebted to the United States for leading the Gulf War coalition. "It was a wonderful day," Mansour says. "The most important." How is it, then, that his sons, liberated by U.S. military might, could turn so fiercely against the Americans? Shouldn't Mohammed Jabarah have felt grateful to the Americans, who made no small sacrifice to protect and free him from Saddam?

But Islamic extremists in Kuwait view the liberation much the way bin Laden did. They were offended that American troops had set foot in the land of Muhammad. They believed it was all about oil, Israel, propping up Arab royalty and expanding American military and cultural influence. They were enraged when the Saudis invited the U.S. military to Saudi Arabia, the heart of Islam, to mobilize for the war. While glad the Iraqis were defeated, they bristled at the sight of American tanks in Arabia. In the desert, borders are just lines in the sand. They shift and vanish overnight and are redrawn in the morning. To many Muslims, they are unimportant. They are boundaries only of the state; what matters is the broader Islamic nation.

If Mohammed learned anything from the Gulf War, it may have been sympathy for those who live under military occupation, which may explain his zealousness over the Chechen and Palestinian conflicts, but his father does not believe the boys suffered any ill effects from the war.

"I don't think there is any impact for their lives because at that time they did not understand what was going on," he says. "They were kids; they were playing."

Their only concern was when they would be going back to class and when they could see their friends again, he says. The boys were, in some respects, fond of the occupation because it meant they did not have to go to school, he says.

"You know the age."

During my encounters with Mansour in Canada and later in Kuwait, he is open about some things but guarded about others. He does not allow me to come to his house in Kuwait. When I ask him whether he was ever affiliated with the Muslim Brotherhood political movement, he replies cryptically that, "All Muslims are brothers." But I had been warned about this.

A member of one of Kuwait's most prominent families told me that the "people of the desert" are wary by nature. They have always been that way; it is a defense against intruders seeking their water and animals. In the desert, there is nowhere to hide, so people hide their thoughts. When questions are put to them, they listen but give nothing away.

It is, my friend says, the way of the desert.

When I first ask Mansour about Anas Al Kandari, he tells me that he and Mohammed were "not close." But later he admits they were best friends.

"Anas Al Kandari was the closest friend to him," Mansour says. "They grew up together."

Anas lived in Salwa, not far from Mohammed's house. They were roughly the same age but did not go to school together. They were neighborhood friends and attended mosque together. "His house was close to ours," Mansour says. "Then because he lived in the same area, or close, [Mohammed] built kind of a relation with Anas Al Kandari."

Anas came from what his father's lawyer describes to me as "new money." His father had been a "regular person," an activist in Islamic politics. In the 1980s, he started investing in the Souk Al Manakh, Kuwait's unofficial, unregulated stock market. When stock prices jumped, he made millions. At his peak, he was worth $300 million, making him one of Kuwait's richest men—on paper, anyway. Then the bubble burst. The stock market collapsed, and all of a sudden Al Kandari's loans were bigger than his assets. He went bankrupt.

"He lost his millions," says Ishmael Al Shatti, his longtime friend and lawyer, and also a leading figure in Kuwait's Islamist political movement. Broke, Al Kandari withdrew from public life; he ceased his involvement in politics and religion. "He became one of those people who is wanted by police because of loans," Al Shatti tells me. He became what Kuwaitis call *duyoun al sa'ba*, literally "the difficult debts people."

"He has financial problems."

Poverty is relative in Kuwait, however. The government provides generously for its citizens, and Anas does not appear to have suffered, even if he did grow up in a house that was bitter from the resentment of financial misfortune. The Kandaris are a huge clan, and in Kuwait family looks after family. "Anas is part of these young people who are influenced by the media, by the surrounding environment which is filled with anger against United States policies. Filled with anger because of the Arab-Israeli conflict and because also of what happened in Afghanistan. There is a turmoil situation in our area, and this situation influenced most of the young people," Al Shatti says. "Sometimes prosperity stops that, because Anas came from a prosperous society. In a poor society the problem is more serious [but] prosperity is not enough to satisfy your needs. This is part of your needs. But sometimes you need to realize your thoughts, your dignity."

As soon as the occupation was over, the Kuwaiti royal family imposed martial law for three months. As often happens in post-war times, soldiers and armed militias started rounding up foreigners and accusing them of collaborating with the enemy. Hundreds of Iraqis, Palestinians, Jordanians, Sudanese, Yemenis, Somalis and Bedouins were taken away, some never to be seen again. Some of those rounded up may have been guilty of nothing more than being non-Kuwaitis, but others were indeed collaborators, such as Abd-al-Basit Balushi, better known as Ramzi Yousef, the son of a Palestinian mother and a Pakistani father who worked for Kuwait Airlines. Born in Kuwait, he studied engineering at Swansea University in Wales, trained and fought in Afghanistan and was known as an Iraqi collaborator in Kuwait during the occupation. Yousef left Kuwait after the war, and moved to New York, where he made an asylum claim and helped organize the February 26, 1993 bombing of the World Trade Center. He slipped away to the Philippines on the day of the bombing and began orchestrating another plot, this one involving the bombing of 11 U.S. airliners. He also wanted to crash planes into CIA headquarters in Langley, Virginia. His accomplice in the plot was his Kuwaiti uncle, Khalid Sheikh Mohammad.

Mansour Jabarah never mentions having any troubles during this period, but it was not an easy time to be an Iraqi in Kuwait, even for one married into a prominent family. And there was the lingering fear that Saddam would return. Souad feared for her sons. If Saddam came back they could be drafted into the Iraqi National Guard. What's more, as non-Kuwaitis, they could be expelled to Iraq. "We wanted to escape from Saddam's system," Souad says. Many Kuwaitis took up residence in other countries as an insurance policy, so they would have somewhere to go, just in case.

"After the occupation, most of the people felt not in a secure situation. Many Kuwaiti people I knew, my friends, they like to have another house in Saudi Arabia or the United Arab Emirates or Oman, to have another place for any kind of circumstances."

"For myself, holding an Iraqi passport, actually we did not feel in a hard position because most of our life, most of our friends are Kuwaiti people and they were very kind until now. But we felt, to make your life more easy than before, get higher education, to have chances . . ."

They thought they should leave Kuwait.

Companies offering to facilitate immigration to Australia and Canada began showing up in Kuwait City, and their pitches intrigued Mansour. In the case of Canada, all he had to do was invest a few hundred thousand dollars in a business and employ one Canadian, and he could become a permanent resident. After three years he could become a citizen, and get Canadian passports for himself and his sons. They could get an education and live without fear.

And he was not averse to Western life. The family had vacationed in Europe. If they could do that, he thought, they could get by in Canada. Mansour's father had blown his chance to become a Kuwaiti; Mansour didn't want to make the same mistake by passing up his chance at Canadian citizenship.

"We decided, my family and myself, to not miss this opportunity," he says, "because we realized at that time we don't know what's going on in our future."

"That's why we decided to go over, to try at least."

3

STRANGER IN A STRANGE LAND

THE Jabarah house is a two-storey, red brick suburban special on a quiet street in the north end of the city. It is an ordinary house on an ordinary street, two blocks from the Welland Canal, the shipping seaway built around the same time the city was a terminus of the Underground Railroad that brought black slaves north to freedom. Today, St. Catharines calls itself the Garden City, "a city with a bright future and a proud past," with 130,000 people living on family-friendly streets like Carluccio Crescent, where the Jabarahs reside. There are two cars in the driveway and a front porch that overlooks a small patch of lawn. It is late in August, when the leaves begin to color and the crisp fall winds blow in, too soon, off Lake Ontario to chase away the southern Canadian summer.

Mansour Jabarah is unloading groceries from his station wagon. He is wearing blue track pants and a gray T-shirt. He invites me to sit in the garage, which has been transformed into a sitting room, with couches and a coffee table. It is like a little *diwaniyah*. He keeps the garage door open and every once in a while a neighbor walks by. He acknowledges them with a smile and a wave. They all know who he is and that his sons are terrorists. They don't like it, but Mansour is a decent person and otherwise a good neighbor and they respect that. The Jabarahs even have their supporters. At the annual Labour Day parade, a local union activist walked alongside the clowns and marching bands carrying a placard with Mohammed's picture on it and the one-word slogan: "Free."

Mansour had never heard of St. Catharines before he came to Canada in search of a new home. After deciding to move his family to Canada, Mansour made an exploratory trip to Toronto and drove south towards Niagara Falls. He stopped in St. Catharines and liked what he saw. It was quiet and small, like Kuwait. And unlike Kuwait, it was safe. There were good schools and a new mosque. In August 1994, they moved into a rented house on Gordon Place, while Mansour met the requirements of his business immigrant visa by opening a service station called Fairview Gas. Mohammed was 12 years old. The Jabarah boys had their pick of schools, including the nearby Canadian Martyrs School, part of the Catholic board of education. That September they began classes at Holy Cross Secondary School. Until then, they had only attended Islamic schools but Mansour thought they would be more comfortable at a religious school, even if it was Catholic, and Holy Cross had the largest English as a Second Language (ESL) program in the district.

St. Catharines is hardly a top destination for immigrants. Just one-fifth of the city's population is foreign-born, compared to more than half in Scarborough, a city suburb of Toronto. Between 1991 and 2001, only 4,300 people immigrated to the city. Census figures say there are fewer than 2,000 Muslims in St. Catharines, and about 700 Arabs. But Mansour says the boys did not find it hard to adjust. "I don't think they had difficulty adapting to the new culture because many times they went to Western countries, to Britain, to France, to Switzerland. Secondly, they can speak English. They belong to an educated family, especially from their mother's side." The boys played soccer, and Mansour coached. Youssef, the youngest, scored a steady stream of goals for the Galbraith Electrics. "I was close to them even when we went to Canada. I used to take them with me everywhere," he says. Mansour also played on an adult team composed mostly of Scots. Although Muslims were few in number in the city, the Jabarahs connected with them through the mosque. "We easily found lots of Muslim families around us."

The brothers also met other Muslims at school. The boys were part of a group of eight to ten Muslim students enrolled at Holy Cross for the ESL program. They all wore the same uniforms and blended in. Mohammed seemed to the other students to be deep inside himself. He was one of those kids who just came to school and went home. Mohammed never did anything to bring attention to himself, to stand out among the 1,500 other students.

Jim Thanos, who was in his math class, recalls him as a quiet kid. "I don't think too many people really knew him all that well." The principal, David Pihach, made a point of visiting the ESL classes; he wanted to talk to the new Canadians and make sure they felt at home. He saw Mohammed when he did his rounds but, "My recollection of him was just being a very quiet individual. He wasn't verbose or causing a lot of trouble. As principal, I get the extremes. I get the extreme good or the extreme bad. He wasn't somebody who was brought to my attention for doing something extreme," he says. "There was really nothing to suggest he was a terrorist or anything like that. He just kept to himself, quiet. In a lot of ways you look at teenagers and you wonder how certain teenagers get involved in any group or religious sect, or sometimes you hear of kids getting involved in whatever! You wonder, how could that be?" He adds, "I've been dealing with teenagers for 30 years. I still can't figure it out. And I've got four of my own. So if somebody knows that, they'll make a million dollars. How I remember him is just so different from what I read about him. I think the same thing too. How did this happen?"

People who have crossed paths with terrorists often say the same thing. They look back and they try to recall some signal, a hint that this person was destined for a life of violence, and they can't find one. But that is exactly the point. While terrorist organizations are by definition made up of extremists, they tend to recruit those who do not attract attention to themselves, people who are quiet and would go unnoticed in a crowd. They draw upon those who are submissive and compliant, who will do what they are told without question. Those who knew Mohammed in St. Catharines recall him as quiet, respectful and polite. But as the Canadian Security Intelligence Service (CSIS) points out in a classified study on jihadist youth, the young Islamic extremists emerging in Canada are "the product of a culture where respect for and obedience to parental figures is paramount." For youth who are raised in a household where Islamic extremism is accepted, the results can be disastrous. "Having a father who in turn is a jihadist leads to an atmosphere of extremism where the children are raised to see the justification of using violence to gain political ends. The duty to obey also explains why some youth have agreed to travel to Afghanistan and Pakistan for terrorist training," CSIS writes. They are "impressionable and open to suggestion and can be easily convinced to undertake acts by more experienced and senior members of the international jihad."

Mansour was not a jihadist terrorist. He was keen for his sons to become Canadians. He also wanted them to maintain their Arab culture. Each year he would send the boys back to Kuwait to visit their relatives. Mansour and Souad would stay in St. Catharines with the eldest and youngest, Abdullah and Youssef, while Mohammed and Abdul Rahman spent the summer in Kuwait City with family. During their trips, Mohammed and Abdul Rahman would meet up with their old friend from the Salwa neighborhood, Anas Al Kandari. Anas was becoming increasingly devout in his religious outlook. He was a student of Sulayman Abu Gaith, a Kuwaiti teacher and firebrand cleric who preached that fighting jihad was the duty of all Muslim men. Mohammed had first met him before moving to Canada. Since then, Abu Gaith had fought in Bosnia and returned to Kuwait with videotapes of the fighting and training that had gone on there. In 1996, he showed the videos to Mohammed and Anas. Propaganda videos have long been one of Al Qaeda's most effective recruiting tools. They stick to a simple formula. The opening will show images depicting the plight of Muslims around the world. "The wounds of the Muslims are deep everywhere," bin Laden says in one recruiting video. "The Crusaders and the Jews have joined together to invade the heart of Islam and occupy its holy places in Mecca, Medina and Jerusalem." Next, the video explains the causes of this situation, concluding that if only Muslims would return to the Koran, everything would be fine. It ends with an impassioned exhortation to fight the Jews, the Americans and their allies.

After watching Abu Gaith's videos, Al Kandari and Jabarah were hooked. They decided to join the jihad. Mohammed started going to mosques where videotaped lectures of the radical ideologue Abdullah Azzam—whose battle cry was "jihad and the rifle alone"—were played. Mohammed was moved by Azzam's call to armed jihad. He told Abu Gaith he wanted to fight. He was 14, an age when boys imagine all kinds of fantasy careers for themselves as football stars or race car drivers. Mohammed returned to St. Catharines determined to become a mujahedin, a holy warrior, a soldier of God. His Grade 10 school portrait, taken shortly after his return from Kuwait, jumps from the yearbook page. His head completely shaven, Mohammed glares unsmiling into the camera. He looks like one of the scrawny Talibs who dwell in the *madrassas* of northwest Pakistan.

* * *

The only mosque in St. Catharines is the Masjid an Noor, the "Mosque of Light," a sandstone building next to a Sunoco station, with a bulbous white dome and two small minarets. It opened the same year the Jabarahs moved to town, and had the only Islamic school in the city, as well as a sunlit prayer room where Sudanese, Pakistani, Bosnian, Somali and Middle Eastern Muslims gather for the five daily prayers. "None to be worshipped but God. Mohammed is the Prophet," reads the sign outside. Just inside the back door, past the cubbies where worshippers leave their shoes, there is a stack of pamphlets describing the suffering of Muslims and asking for donations to help. The one that catches my eye is the glossy, four-page newsletter of the Kashmir Relief Fund of Canada. The first two pages are an account of the conflict in Kashmir and a denunciation of what it calls "Indian military terrorism." It makes no mention of the horrific terrorist attacks that have been mounted against India by Islamic jihadist groups in the region—the bus bombings of soldiers' families, the assault on the parliament buildings in New Delhi. On the back page are the "images of brutality," photos of bloodied bodies, tearful women and Indian troops. It is typical of the propaganda of the Islamic world, found everywhere from state-controlled newspapers to television stations, all with a common refrain: Everywhere Muslims are under attack.

As it had been in Kuwait, the mosque was the focus of the Jabarahs' lives. They not only prayed there but also volunteered to keep the grounds clean. Mansour served as vice president of the Islamic Society of St. Catharines, the government-registered charity that runs the mosque and school. On occasion, he led prayers and helped organize an annual open house, which sought to expose non-Muslims to the Islamic faith. Mansour would cook a sheep and invite the local Member of Parliament to visit. One year at Ramadan, *The Standard*, the St. Catharines daily, sent a reporter to write an article about Mansour, who explained to readers how Muslims fast during the holy month. He was, then, just another tile in the Canadian multicultural mosaic. Another year, the speaker at the open house was the director of the Muslim World League, a controversial Saudi group. The mosque's financial books show nothing untoward, just annual donations of about $100,000, most of it spent on charitable work and the rest on courses and seminars. "We used to invite clerics from Saudi Arabia to give lessons to the Muslims of St. Catharines, and these scholars came to stay in St. Catharines," Mansour explains.

The Saudi brand of Islam, Wahhabism, can be frighteningly extreme. Even when it is not advocating jihad, it at least portrays Muslims, even those living in the West, as bound, above all, by the laws of Islam. Such preaching emphasizes the separateness of Muslims, that while they may live in Canada, the United States, Britain, France or Australia, they are Muslims first. And for those who put the laws of faith before the laws of the state, it can be a struggle to integrate into an adopted homeland. One of the Saudi-based sheikhs invited to speak at the St. Catharines mosque once wrote of Western Muslims, "You are, in many ways, strangers in a strange land." The Internet site of the St. Catharines mosque likewise provides access to literature that decries "Muslims who have been completely brainwashed by Western ideas and dogmas" and dismisses the notion that Islamic law, or *shariah*, should adapt to modern thinking, saying "shariah cannot be amended to conform to changing human values and standards; rather, it is the absolute norm to which all human values and conduct must conform." The visiting clerics who came to St. Catharines to lecture would spend time in the community. "Of course, if the scholar comes to St. Catharines, he has to stay close to us by inviting him to and visiting him in the mosque."

The Jabarah boys were taught not to smoke, not to drink, not to party, not to chase girls. Mansour wanted them to be faithful to their prayers. Around the dinner table, he talked to his sons about the issues of concern to Muslims around the world. "All the time we discussed things that affect Muslim life, in Kuwait, in Iraq, anywhere, the Muslims in Palestine."

Mansour began taking Islamic studies courses by correspondence from the American Open University, a non-profit society founded in 1996 to "spread Islamic knowledge based on the Koran and the Sunnah of the Prophet." The Virginia-based university was not without controversy. Its president, a Sudanese named Jaafar Idris, was forced to leave the United States in 2003 after federal authorities revoked his visa because the Saudis, who had sponsored his stay in the United States, withdrew their support for his lectures.

One of the students, Masoud Khan, was sentenced to life in prison for his role in the "Virginian jihad network." Prosecutors alleged that shortly after 9/11, he met with an Islamic lecturer who said the United States was "Islam's greatest enemy" and urged his followers to take up arms. He trained in Pakistan with the Al Qaeda-linked Lashkar-e-Taiba. After his sentencing, Khan said he would not have been charged "had I been a Zionist Jew or a Christian."

Mohammed was "always discussing some major things with me while I am studying," Mansour says. "The last 20 years we went through different things. Our brothers in Palestine, they have been under occupation until this time. If you ask any Muslim, they are feeling the same thing as Mohammed, as Abdul Rahman, as myself. Anywhere in the world if you look at the Muslim community, they are under need or under their foot.

"Many countries are humiliating the Muslims' community. If you go anywhere now, like if you go to Afghanistan, the United States destroyed villages, women, babies. They did not care about any humanitarian things; they just bomb anywhere. I remember their carpet bombers, they threw bombs like carpet and they just destroyed villages. The same thing happened in Iraq. They are saying by words, 'We are bringing the democracy, we are coming with freedom.' Where's the freedom? Killing the thousands of civilian people, this is the freedom we want? We don't want this kind of freedom if it kills our nation, kills our religion. We need this freedom, we need this democracy but not in the Western image. We believe in Islam."

When Mansour graduated with a degree in Islamic studies, Mohammed began calling him Sheikh, in recognition of his achievement.

Mansour worked hard to give his family a new life. Always mindful that his father had squandered his chance to become a Kuwaiti, Mansour was not going to make the same mistake in Canada. He passed the citizenship test and, in a ceremony at the citizenship court in St. Catharines, pledged the oath to "be faithful and bear true allegiance to Her Majesty Queen Elizabeth the Second, Queen of Canada, Her Heirs and Successors, and that I will faithfully observe the laws of Canada and fulfill my duties as a Canadian citizen." The Jabarahs were Canadians. For the first time in their lives, they were citizens of the country in which they lived. They were no longer foreigners. They could get Canadian passports and vote. "They were among the best citizens in Canada," Mansour says of his sons.

At the time, Mohammed was 16 and still keen to participate in jihad. He returned to Kuwait City for the summer in 1998. "During these years the idea of participating in jihad continued to grow steadily in him and his friend Al Kandari," CSIS wrote. Seeing their devotion to the cause, Abu Gaith paid increasing attention to the friends. They were both ripe for recruitment, especially Mohammed, who was separated from his parents during his visits to Kuwait. When he returned to Canada, Mohammed spent hours surfing the Internet, reading jihadist websites. He was particularly taken by the fighting in Chechnya, where Russian troops were confronting Muslim insurgents. By the summer of 1999, the Chechen rebels had embraced terrorism, staging a series of apartment bombings in Russian cities that were allegedly ordered by the rebel leader Ibn Khattab, an Arab who has been described as either a Saudi or Jordanian. The Russians responded by deploying troops to Chechnya to quash the rebellion. "In 1999, the jihad in Chechnya became the focus of his attention," CSIS wrote of Jabarah.

In September 1999, Al Kandari traveled to Afghanistan for five months. He got back to Kuwait in February, all fired up and ready for battle in Chechnya. "It was Muslims helping Muslims, nothing to do with terrorism," Adel Abdulhadi, a Kuwaiti lawyer who represents the Al Kandari family, tells me. He describes Anas as a religious and devout person, who went to Afghanistan only to do charity work. He had collected money in Kuwait and went over to distribute it, he says. But Mohammed told investigators that Anas attended bin Laden's training camps to prepare himself for war in Chechnya. When Jabarah heard what Al Kandari was doing, he wanted to go too, but Abu Gaith advised him to wait. He counseled Mohammed to finish high school first and do his training the following summer. Abdul Rahman was similarly entranced. According to an account of his life on a jihadist website, "The love of jihad took over his heart."

* * *

By the late 1990s, the Niagara region was becoming a magnet for Islamic extremists. Montreal and Toronto had long been the hubs of Canada's Sunni terrorist networks, but in 1999, Fateh Kamel, the Algerian-Canadian leader of the Montreal jihadi organization was arrested in Jordan and sent to France to stand trial. The French and Canadians began hunting down the members of the Groupe Fateh Kamel in Canada. Many were veterans of the jihads in Afghanistan and Bosnia who were supporting terrorism financially and otherwise through petty crime and passport theft. Some associates of the group sent letters to police threatening a biological or chemical weapons attack on the Montreal subway system. The Royal Canadian Mounted Police (RCMP) immigration task force arrested Kamel's right-hand man, Karim Atmani, and two of his associates, one of them an alleged gun dealer, in Niagara-on-the-Lake, Ontario. The December 14, 1999, arrest of another of Kamel's men, Ahmed Ressam, as he tried to cross the Canadian border into Washington State with explosives in the trunk of his car, put even more pressure on the cell. Some of its members left Montreal to escape the heat; a handful of them drifted to Niagara.

Those who settled in the area included Abdellah Ouzghar and a few "jihadist returnees," those who had fought in Islamic holy wars in Afghanistan and Bosnia and had come back home, where they served as role models for youngsters. Ouzghar was considered by CSIS to be an associate of the Groupe Fateh Kamel (he was convicted *in absentia* by the French for his involvement). Another was a Libyan who had surfaced in connection with a CSIS probe into Mahmoud Jaballah, a member of the Egyptian Al Jihad in Toronto who had taught at the Islamic school at the Salahedin mosque, where several Sunni Islamic extremist notables such as Ahmed Khadr worshipped. A significant extremist element was emerging in the Niagara region, and the Jabarah brothers were right in the middle of it. Mohammed and Abdul Rahman began mingling with veterans of the holy wars in Afghanistan and Bosnia. They soaked it right up, and soon they were speaking the harsh rhetoric of jihad at the mosque. Some worshippers, however, did not like what they were hearing.

* * *

Radical organizations often attract followers who somehow feel that they don't fit in. They see themselves as misfits and rejects. They are people who have lost confidence in themselves, but are not without hope—those Eric Hoffer describes as "discontented but not destitute." They attach themselves to a movement, a cause or a leader, and through the group, they find the sense of worth and purpose they thought were missing from their lives. The experience of immigration, especially for an awkward adolescent, can cause just such feelings of discontent, and the preachers of radical Islam are ready to offer them a solution.

The cycle of immigration, isolation and radicalization is becoming increasingly familiar. Some Muslims feel excluded from Western society and convince themselves they are suffering the same persecution as Muslims worldwide. In Europe, such disillusioned youths meet likeminded people at mosques and turn to Islamic extremism to restore their dignity, Michael Taarnby writes in "Recruitment of Islamist Terrorists in Europe." Immigrants in France who embrace terrorism, for example, are often "superficially integrated," deeply resentful and confused, he notes. "The first stage is brainwashing at the hands of a Salafist imam. Later they meet an actual recruiter, who offers to quench their thirst for absolutes through militant activism."

Canadian intelligence analysts have detected a similar trend on the other side of the Atlantic: children of immigrants who adopt religious extremism as an outlet. In the past, terrorists in Canada tended to be refugees. They were often already involved in terrorism before they came to Canada. After 9/11, CSIS began reporting a rising number of adherents to radical Islam who were either born in Canada or, like Mohammed, raised and educated in the country, often by fathers who are known Islamic extremists. CSIS calls them the "sons of the father."

"It's the second generation," Dale Neufeld, CSIS deputy director, told a Parliamentary hearing in Ottawa. "It's the children of Muslims who are born in this country. [They] have a very normal upbringing, according to our analysis, but at some point in their teenage years or young 20s, decide that radical Islam is the path that they want to take. I think when the Khawaja case [Momin Khawaja is a Canadian-born Muslim who in 2004 became the first person charged under the *Anti-Terrorism Act*], which concerns the young gentleman who was arrested here in Ottawa and is currently in jail, becomes public, and unfortunately at the moment there is a publication ban . . . but he was linked to a very large number of people from the United Kingdom, who fit that very same description. They didn't come from battle-hardened Afghanistan, or Iraq, or Chechnya. These were people who had pretty normal upbringings in a very democratic country, and decided at some point to go down that path.

"The other [trend] is—which is again very disturbing because it's hard to detect and hard to investigate—young Canadians who generally are quite disillusioned. They're the kids who don't do well in high school, who could do anything. They could become petty criminals. They could get involved in the drug culture. They might join a motorcycle gang. We're now seeing a number of examples where what they decide to do is take up Islam in the radical form. So those are two trends, like I say, that I couldn't have talked about before. I do think that's a real challenge for us. It's not just rhetoric. I do believe that a number of these people, when the time comes, will attempt to do something quite serious."

To an outsider, Mohammed Jabarah had little reason to feel disillusioned or discontented, and he was no more a misfit than anyone else. But all that matters in the equation of radicalism is that someone feels like an outcast; it doesn't matter whether he is right to harbor such sentiments. It is the self-image of a person as an outsider that makes him ripe for recruitment. Indeed, the preachers of extremism encourage such feelings of discontent, telling their followers they are "strangers in a strange land," that they must not adapt their behavior to Western society, that everywhere their religion is under assault, that they are not true to their God unless they do something about it, and that the thing to do is take up jihad.

* * *

Mohammed took Abu Gaith's advice and tried to stay focused on finishing Grade 12, but he could not get the jihad out of his head. "Jabarah perused mujahedin websites and was particularly taken by the videos regarding the jihad in Chechnya," CSIS wrote. He started raising money for Chechnya, much like his grandfather had raised money for the Algerian fighters and Palestinians. Mohammed held three fundraising drives that collected CDN $3,000, $3,800 and $1,000. He sent the money to Abu Gaith using an account number the Kuwaiti cleric had given him. When Abu Gaith mentioned he needed Sony video cameras, Mohammed held another fundraiser and came up with $700, which he used to buy the cameras. He says he does not know what they were to be used for, but Abu Gaith later recorded videos extolling the virtues of jihad and threatening the West with holy terror.

Raising money for jihad was an important milestone for Mohammed. Recruiters know that it is best to ease someone into terrorism, to start them out with duties that help the cause without killing. Terrorists often begin their careers as non-violent activists. Many belong to support networks or campus activist groups. They are given roles that allow them to participate without thinking they have blood on their hands. But, as terrorist leaders know full well, from there, the step into violence is not so difficult to make. Becoming a terrorist is not something that happens overnight. The radicalization of a terrorist occurs in a series of steps, each one leading deeper into the world of political violence. Firstly, terrorists must receive a basic level of indoctrination that makes them sympathetic to a violent cause and vulnerable to recruitment. This may come from the environment in which they are raised or the values passed on by their friends or families. Secondly, from there, terrorists often begin their careers by engaging in non-violent activism, such as fundraising or spreading propaganda.

Terrorists recruited out of the West often start out as sympathizers. Their involvement begins in support organizations engaged in lawful advocacy, but over time they are pulled towards a radical, violent core, often with the help of a friend or family member. Third comes indirect involvement in violence, such as attending paramilitary training camps. That is followed by some rite of passage into the world of violence. In the case of Al Qaeda, this often used to involve spending time at the frontlines of the civil war against the anti-Taliban rebels in Afghanistan. Then comes the terrorist training, followed by an oath of allegiance to the leader and his cause and finally, a mission. These are the seven steps to hell. And Mohammed Jabarah was going all the way.

In his final year at high school, Mohammed made a deal with his father. If he finished school and got accepted into university, he would get a reward. Towards the end of the school year, Mohammed was accepted into St. Mary's University in Nova Scotia. His parents were thrilled. Mohammed told his father he knew what he wanted for his reward—one last trip home to Kuwait.

Mansour bought the ticket.

4

THE RECRUITER

TERRORIST recruiters know what to look for—young men who stand out in mosques and schools, who are devout, intelligent and have skills to offer. An added bonus is a North American or European passport, which allows a recruit to operate inside Western countries and travel with relative ease. The role of the recruiter is to be a talent scout, to close the deal and make the necessary introductions. They are the gatekeepers into the inner circle of any terrorist organization. The decision to join a terrorist group is an intensely private one. Nobody can force it on someone. There are many forces that lead people to the heights of zealotry, where they think seriously about embracing violence as a tactic of change, but in the end it is a personal choice. Often it happens during the milestones in life, such as after high school graduation or a personal setback, when people pause and reflect. That said, the decision to turn violent can be meaningless unless the recruit has someone to approach, someone connected who can open the door into the underworld of terrorism.

Abu Gaith was Mohammed Jabarah's recruiter. When Mohammed arrived in Kuwait after finishing high school,

Abu Gaith had already decided to give up his teaching job and devote himself fully to bin Laden's jihad. He explained his views in a statement recorded on videotape and distributed to news organizations. Wearing a white robe and turban, a big gap showing between his front teeth, he said, "We thank Almighty God, who said in his holy book: 'Ye who believe, take not the Jews and Christians for your friends and protectors. They are but friends and protectors to each other. And ye amongst you that turns to them is of them' . . . The Islamic nation has been groaning in pain for more than 80 years under the yoke of the joint Jewish–Crusader aggression. Palestine is living under the yoke of the Jewish occupation and its people groan from this repression and persecution while no one lifts a finger. The Arabian Peninsula is being defiled by the feet of those who came to occupy these lands, usurp these holy places, and plunder these resources.

"The Islamic nation must also know that the U.S. version of terrorism is a kind of deception. Is it logical for the United States and its allies to carry out this repression, persecution, plundering, and bloodletting over these long years without this being called terrorism, while when the victim tries to seek justice, he is described as terrorist? This type of deception can never be accepted in any case whatsoever. Let the United States know that the Islamic nation will not remain silent after this day on what it is experiencing and what takes place in its land, and that jihad for the sake of God today is an obligation on every Muslim in this land if he has no excuse. God Almighty has said: 'Then fight in God's cause, thou art held responsible only for thyself, and rouse the believers.' It may be that God will restrain the fury of the unbelievers, for God is the strongest in might and in punishment. U.S. interests are spread throughout the world. So, every Muslim should carry out his real role to champion his Islamic nation and religion.

"Carrying out terrorism against the oppressors is one of the tenets of our religion and shariah. Against them make ready your strength to the utmost of your power, including steeds of war, to strike terror into the hearts of the enemies of God and your enemies . . . There are thousands of the Islamic nations' youths who are eager to die just as the Americans are eager to live. I address Muslim youths, men, and women and urge them to shoulder their responsibility. They should know that the land of Afghanistan and the mujahedin are really facing an all-out Crusader war which is aimed at eliminating this group which believes in God and fights on the basis of a creed and religion. Thus, the nation must shoulder its responsibility. It would be a disgrace if the Islamic nation fails to do so. Finally, I thank Almighty God who enabled us to engage in this jihad and fight this battle, which is a decisive one between infidelity and faith. I ask Almighty God to grant us victory on our enemy, make their machinations backfire on them, and defeat them."

Entrusting young boys to Abu Gaith was like leaving them in the care of a child molester. He exploited his position of authority over his students to fulfill his own political fantasies of an Islamist uprising. He was a recruiter in the guise of a religious teacher. Instead of feeding the souls of his students responsibly, he planted the notion of jihad and martyrdom in their pliant young minds, and then helped them join Al Qaeda. He helped them cross the bridge between radical belief and radical violence.

For some it was a death sentence.

* * *

It was no coincidence that Abu Gaith focused his efforts on youths. Terrorist groups, Al Qaeda included, have long targeted young people, hoping to engineer a generational groundswell. Radical Islamists like Abu Gaith were trying to breed a jihad generation, and to an alarming extent they succeeded. Mohammed wrote in a letter to his younger brother:

They say when you study at a younger age, it is as if you are carving on stone. This means that this carving will never go away, even if it collects dust, because you can remove dust with just a blow of air and the carving will be clear as new.

When I first ask Mansour Jabarah if he knows Abu Gaith, he replies with a riddle.

"We have a saying," he says. "Do you know the King of Egypt?"

He pauses for effect.

"But does he know you?"

Later, I ask him again and he elaborates, sort of.

"You know, Kuwait is a very small city and any popular speaker, if he delivers any kind of speech . . . everybody can hear about this person, Abu Gaith or a different guy.

"If you ask me do I know Abu Gaith, I am going to tell you, 'Yes, I know Abu Gaith.' But . . . if you ask me do you know the president of Kuwait? Yes, but he does not know about me. Abu Gaith was very popular for everybody here in Kuwait, and he has a very loud voice, he has like a kind of specific speech for young people. But I don't think Mohammed and Abdul Rahman had strong relations with Abu Gaith."

Mohammed, however, told investigators he and Al Kandari were close to Abu Gaith. By the time Mohammed returned to Kuwait in the summer of 2000, bringing with him the Sony camcorders he had purchased in Canada, Al Kandari was ready to return to Afghanistan, and Abdul Rahman Jabarah was going to go with him. Abdul Rahman had spent a year at Brock University in St. Catharines and then switched to the University of Ottawa, but he was feeling the call of jihad. He "craved martyrdom, forgetting this world" and "sought eternity, for the world is a wreck," a fellow jihadist wrote of him. For his part, Al Kandari "had chosen to walk in the footsteps of Osama bin Laden," Mohammed Al Awadi, a Kuwaiti who knew him, told the Associated Press. "To him, killing an American soldier was an act of devotion. He considered the American presence as colonialism, not protection."

To Jassim Boodai, editor-in-chief of *Al Rai Al Aam*, Kuwait's largest daily newspaper, which has reported many of the biggest stories about the country's jihadi network, Anas was a spoiled rich kid who fell victim to the preachers of radicalism.

"Al Kandari drives a Porsche. His family's a wealthy family, and five months before he was chasing girls."

"So why?"

"This is an interesting question," says Boodai, a bear of a man in a white Arab robe. "If he was a poor guy . . . " he says, not finishing his sentence. "Simply, those guys are brainwashed.

"From a religious point of view, kill an American, you go to heaven. Killing an American is a first-class ticket to heaven. Killing an American soldier is a Concorde ticket. Killing an American general, that's a rocket. Why an American? Because Americans are creating targets of themselves."

That might be true in the Middle East, I say. But why do well-off Canadian kids like the Jabarah brothers become terrorists? He answers with another question: Why do Canadian youths overdose on drugs? "The guy mixes up with the wrong group. It all starts by getting mixed by the wrong group or person. This Kandari, the same thing happened."

"They brainwashed him.

"You don't need, today, a lot of effort to brainwash a teenager against Americans. Show a couple of films about Israel. Everyone will be convinced."

Still, Kuwait seems an odd place to find jihadi terrorists. Not only is the country fabulously wealthy, it also owes its survival to the Americans, and before that the British. There are many in Kuwait who are convinced that had the United States not drawn its line in the sand and chased Saddam's troops back to Baghdad, Kuwait would now be part of Iraq. But Kuwait has long had an Islamic movement, one that is heavily influenced by the Saudis next door. The boom years in Kuwait attracted Arabs from all over the Middle East, turning the country into a cauldron of influences from places like Egypt and the Palestinian territories. Yasser Arafat's Fatah faction was born in Kuwait, where the late Palestine Liberation Organization (PLO) leader was employed for a time. Al Qaeda notables Ramzi Yousef and Khalid Sheikh Mohammad were Kuwaitis.

Although ruled by an *emir*, who appoints a prime minister, Kuwait considers itself not a Muslim state but rather a secular state guided by Islamic principles. This makes Kuwait moderate for an Arab nation, but in this part of the world, that is not necessarily saying much. On the day of my arrival, the morning newspaper had articles about Kuwaitis joining the insurgent forces in Iraq, as well as an item about a decision by the Ministry of Information to close a magazine accused of defaming the wife of the Prophet Muhammad. The publication was accused of sedition and a store that sold it was raided. Women could not vote or run for elected office (although they have been promised they will be able to do so by 2007) and there was a plaza for public hangings. Such measures are partly the work of Islamist parliamentarians in the national assembly, who are pushing to change the constitution to make shariah the law of the land. In the meantime, they have been leading a morality campaign that has imposed strict rules on social events such as pop concerts. Dancing is banned outright, both by performers and their audience, and men must sit apart from women at shows. A government official must be present at all concerts to monitor compliance. A scandal hit the front pages of local newspapers during my visit when two Lebanese singers embraced for five seconds while performing at a Kuwait City hotel. Islamist parliamentarians accused the government of promoting immorality. Islamists have forced beach clubs to adopt alternate swimming days for men and women. Female doctors can no longer operate on men, and a segregation policy has been imposed on university campuses, where the struggle between Islamic fundamentalism and democracy is perhaps most apparent.

"The extremist agenda is that we go back to what has happened during the Prophet Muhammad 2,000 years ago and redo it again," quips Abdalla Al Naibari, a former member of Kuwait's parliament who now edits a weekly newspaper that trumpets what he calls the traditional liberal Kuwaiti values. "I would say there's a dichotomy," he says. "The Islamists, of course, generally all over the Arab world . . . are becoming increasingly anti-American. The rest of the public, they are friendly toward the Americans, but at the same time they are concerned."

The government of Kuwait takes a harsh line against jihadists, but some believe the authorities have turned a blind eye to radical Islamists heading off to fight in Afghanistan and Iraq, believing that if they leave they will be someone else's problem. "They are just using these young people and using their frustrations and trying to push them [to] what I call, myself, the death culture," says Ali Al-Tarrah, dean of Social Sciences at Kuwait University. "We need the government to do something, not only send them to court, not only arrest them." Radical *imams* must be removed from their posts and the education system must be reformed, he says. "It's a long process; it's not an easy one."

Perhaps an odder place than Kuwait to find terrorists is Lackawanna, New York. The Lackawanna Six case involved young men struggling to figure out how to live as Muslims within America. They fell under the spell of Yemeni-born Kamal Derwish, a veteran of Al Qaeda camps in Afghanistan who fought in Bosnia. Like Abu Gaith, Derwish abused his religious position to preach jihadi violence to a small group of followers. The pattern of indoctrination he used was familiar. He fed their minds with the notion that Muslims everywhere are under attack, and then he exposed them to a religious interpretation that he said obligated them to go fight in defense of their faith. "Unfortunately, they probably were convinced or preached [to] by some people with certain agendas," says Mohammed Albanna, a Muslim community leader in upstate New York whose nephew Jaber was among those indicted for his alleged involvement in the group. "Most of the kids were influenced by people who were part of the mujahedin." They convinced the recruits that "to be more informed by their religion they have to make the trip to Pakistan, and then from there some of them did go and ended up training.

"That's the way it is," says the Buffalo candy store owner. "I don't think it's limited to just kids in Canada and the United States. It happens to kids all over."

Derwish, Abu Gaith and the other preachers of radicalism attract adherents by portraying the present as something to be detested and reviled. In the case of radical Islam, it is not difficult to frame the world as a disaster zone, since poverty and dictatorship are so widespread in the Muslim world. This worldview oozes from the recorded pronouncements of bin Laden and Al Zawahiri, and from the Friday sermons at some mosques. In their view, the present barely exists. It is but a grand illusion, a chaotic version of the way the world should be, and will be. Their contempt for the world as it is finds expression in the enjoyment they take in wreaking chaos and destruction.

Things are bad, they say.

And just as the young disciple is feeling enraged at an unjust world, the radical leader says: But there is a solution. The radical leader reminds his followers that there is a better world ahead. No matter that the future depicted by radicals is realistically unattainable. Things are not right, but they will be one day when balance is restored to the world. In a country like Pakistan, a nation that was supposed to be the vanguard of Islamic ideals but instead remains backward and mired in conflict, these are comforting thoughts. The same can be said, to varying degrees, in many other parts of the Arab and Muslim world.

"It is the brainwashing of all these groups," says Abdul Majeed Khuraibet, a former police colonel who is now a defense lawyer and represents two men accused of supplying weapons to Anas Al Kandari's gang of jihadis. A replica of the Statue of Liberty rests on the shelf behind his desk, near a statue of a Mountie.

"Anas Al Kandari, as came out of the investigation, he was out of Afghanistan and he was one of bin Laden's followers. He prepared to do whatever [bin Laden] asked for, especially fighting the enemies. He was the leader of this group. And they went to Kandahar and they met with that terrorist bin Laden. They met him and they told him, 'We are going to be your followers.'

"It is religious fanaticism, like this group that goes to Fallujah now. I believe it is religious fanaticism. It is easy to see them now. It is the fanaticism which has escalated after the '80s. It has nothing to do with money, being poor or being rich. It has to do with the mastering of the mind."

It is easy to understand how the students at Pakistan's *madrassa* Islamic schools are attracted to radical Islam. They have little else. They are separated from their families and raised by extremists, some of whom were paid for each child they sent to bin Laden's camps in Afghanistan. But Mohammed had everything in Canada. He had a comfortable middle-class home in a safe neighborhood, and a good school. He had soccer and freedom. He had a family that loved him. He did not want for anything. Researchers, however, have found that terrorists tend to be more highly educated than their peers, and therefore more politically-minded. Only 13 percent of Hamas and Palestinian Islamic Jihad suicide bombers are poor, compared to one-third of the Palestinian population. Half of the bombers had a higher education, more than triple the rate for average Palestinians. One of the ironies of radical organizations like Al Qaeda is that they are attractive not only to those who are discontented because they have no future, but also those who are discontented because they can have any future they want. Mohammed's opportunities were unlimited; he could have done anything with his life, anything he wanted. And people who think they can do anything in the world can just as easily get caught up in the quest for a radically better future, for extreme change, as those who have nothing. Perhaps even more so.

* * *

When Kuwaiti authorities finally got wind of what Abu Gaith was preaching, he was banned from his mosque, but his followers remained loyal to him and his ideals. Mohammed started fasting on Mondays and Thursdays. "I think after the last trip to Kuwait, Mohammed changed. He became more religious than before," Mansour says, "but at the same time he was a very good boy." Mohammed continued watching videos of jihad, now those coming out of the Israeli–Palestinian conflict. "He felt shamed about what had happened to his brothers in Palestine," Mansour suggests.

Mohammed was showing signs of intensifying belief, that he was being drawn deeper into the social isolation of the movement. It was all so clear now. He was a believer, and everyone else was an infidel. And as a believer, he was obliged to act in defense of his leader and his God. The Jabarah brothers and Al Kandari were making the transition from zealous boys; they were becoming an operational terrorist cell. Kuwait was a good place for it to happen. For Mohammed, and for his brother as well, Kuwait was a middle ground between their old life with their parents in Canada and the future that awaited them in Afghanistan and beyond. It was in Kuwait that they were conditioned by what Marc Sageman, who served as a foreign service officer in Pakistan during the Afghan jihad, describes as the three-pronged process of terrorist recruitment: social affiliation with the jihad through "friendship, kinship and discipleship," resulting in the intensification of beliefs and formal acceptance into the jihad with the help of a recruiter. The critical element, he argues, is the social bond between believers.

Anas Al Kandari decided it was time to return to Afghanistan. He left with Abdul Rahman. Mohammed was going to follow and they were to meet up in Jalalabad. Mansour suggests his sons felt ashamed that their friend had gone to Afghanistan while they were still "outside," living the easy life in Canada.

"I think he met with some type of people who were encouraging him for [this], you could name it jihad or something like this," Mansour tells me.

I reply that there are people who exploit youths like Mohammed, convince them to do things.

"These are the things that happened to Abdul Rahman and Mohammed, and also Anas Al Kandari," he says.

At the time, however, Mansour had no idea what his sons were up to. Mohammed phoned his father from Kuwait and told him he was going to Pakistan to study Islam. He had prepared a story about how he could not get an Islamic education in Kuwait because all the programs were in Arabic and he wanted to study in English. Mansour believed him. Mohammed was trying to protect his parents, and he knew if his father found out he was going to train with bin Laden, he would be in deep trouble. Abu Gaith paid for Mohammed's plane ticket to Karachi.

His jihad had begun.

5

LOSING MOHAMMED

AT dusk in the desert, the shadows grow improbably long and the heat and light fade quickly. The wind picks up and the sands begin to move. It reminds me of the way snow swirls across the surface of a frozen lake. Camels lope along a ridge. All around, there is only sand, sun and a few scattered tents. Except for our truck, there is no time reference, nothing to suggest even what century this is. It would not surprise me to see Antara himself riding astride one of the camels, his sword raised for battle.

As the sky darkens, the camel herders appear in their four-by-fours to herd the animals back to their pens for the night, and afterwards they retreat to tents and fire up kerosene heaters. I am photographing the procession of camels when a truck pulls up and the driver asks who I am. When I tell him, he invites me to visit him in his tent.

"He is probably going to offer you camel's milk," my translator warns.

"Tell him I'm lactose intolerant."

We sit on a carpet, eating dates and sesame-flavored sweets washed down with nutty Bedouin coffee. There is etiquette to drinking coffee here. The cups are tiny, like those of a child's tea set. You hold the cup in your right hand, since the left hand is for *unclean things.* Your host is obliged to continue refilling your cup until you hold it up and give it a gentle shake, which is the signal that you've had enough. In the vast emptiness of this place, such subtle mannerisms seem incomprehensibly quaint.

My guests invite me to spend the night. I decline, but it is tempting. Outside, the blackness of the desert night is intense. The landmarks have vanished and the roads and walking paths have melted away, making it difficult to navigate.

It would be easy, out here, to get lost.

* * *

At 6 p.m., Mansour calls. He will be at the hotel in a few minutes to pick me up. He is going to show me Kuwait City. He pulls up outside the Sheraton in his Chevy. Once again, he is wearing his brown winter robe and white headgear. At a downtown intersection, he points out the landmarks.

"Here mosque, there mosque, over there mosque."

We drive past the stores in the old quarter, which are open for evening shopping. All the shopkeepers are Indians, part of the boom of migrant workers.

"Cheap labor," he says. "This is the problem."

Mansour points down the road.

"When I was growing up, I lived just down there," he says, but the building is gone now, as are most of the remnants of old Kuwait. In its place a shiny condo tower has sprouted. "I think they should keep the old things, for memory."

We get out and walk into the fish market and then to Souk Al Zal, where Iranian carpets are spread out on the sidewalks for sale. I am browsing in a shop when the Iranian behind the counter holds up a carpet with a striking pattern: the twin towers of the World Trade Center with two airplanes about to ram them. Another carpet depicts a map of Afghanistan surrounded by weapons, an AK-47, RPGs, helicopters and hand grenades. It reads, "2001. Made in Afghanistan." Mansour inspects the 9/11 carpet, but when he recognizes the scene, he quickly hands it to me as if he doesn't want to be seen with it. Later, he finds a carpet with an image of Mecca on it and tells me that he has been to the Haj many times, but not since the troubles with his sons.

"I don't feel safe to go, and I don't have the desire to go any more."

We walk through an old *souq* and emerge on a sidewalk beside a busy street across from the Grand Mosque. Mansour stops in front of the Mazidi Real Estate Company. It is his wife's family's business, he tells me. I venture to ask how many wives he has, and he smiles and says he has only the one. "This is enough," he says. "I care too much." But he goes on to defend polygamy, saying it is better than the Western alternative, which is infidelity.

We walk to a brightly lit restaurant and order falafel, kebabs, Pepsis and mint tea. His real estate business has done well by the second Iraq war, he says. The market is up 30 percent now that the capture of Saddam has eased fears of another Iraqi invasion of Kuwait. But Mansour still does not like having the American troops in Kuwait.

"Nobody wants them here."

As we are leaving the restaurant, he orders another bag of falafel and hands it to me. "Just in case you get hungry later," he says. He drives back to the hotel and I tell him to drop me at the corner but he insists on taking me right to the front door.

"You are my guest. If I could take the car up to your room, I would."

* * *

A few days later, Mansour calls again and says he will be outside the hotel in five minutes. He is going to take me to his camp in the desert.

"And Bell," he says, "dress warm."

Kuwaitis love camping. They set up huge tents in the desert and retreat there in the evenings and on weekends to enjoy the outdoors and tend to their camels. Drive south along The Custodian of the Two Mosques King Fahad bin Abdul Aziz Road, and you can see, opposite the oil refineries of Shuaiba, hundreds of tents. The Ministry of Information tells me the camps are supposed to be closed "for security reasons," but Kuwaitis ignore the order.

Mansour meets me at the hotel and we drive through the city in his red sedan, around a traffic circle decorated with the flags of the countries that fought to liberate Kuwait from Saddam. He is in good spirits. He has just received another letter from Mohammed, written two weeks ago. Mohammed wrote that at the end of Ramadan he was allowed to have a special meal. The prison guard told him that next Ramadan, he might have the same meal with his family. All he has to do is cooperate.

We drive north on the highway towards Iraq, through the desert and scrub. A few times a day, an American military convoy made up of humvees and supply trucks streaks down this road, shadowed by a helicopter gunship. Kuwait is not as friendly to U.S. troops as it used to be. At the plain known as the Turkey Shoot, where allied aircraft picked off Iraqi troops as they retreated in 1991, their cars stuffed with loot, the road forks and he turns right, towards the Gulf.

"Why they burn them inside their cars?" Mansour asks. "This is illegal."

Mansour asks if I have ever written about Islam, and I tell him my writing concerns those who use religion to justify violence.

"Believe me," he says, "in Islam there are no terrorists."

He says the U.S. is on a crusade against Islam. Jihad, he says, means only defense and Muslims must adhere to the pillars of their faith. The problem is that there are unbelievers who don't want Muslims to go back to their roots, he says.

"There is no terror in Islam," says Mansour.

"What about those who invoke Islam to incite the killing of innocent people," I ask, "those who declare jihad by claiming that the West is at war with Islam?"

He responds that North Korea has a weapons program, but Bush did not attack there. Everywhere there is conflict involving the West, it is Muslims who are suffering and dying, he says. Why, I ask, would the United States want to destroy an entire religion?

"They are crazy," he says.

On our left is a Kuwaiti military base, opposite the tall stacks of a refinery. He points into the desert to a place called Kathmah, where he would take his sons camping when they were young. I glance at it in the dying light and see a dun-colored slope and a plateau. It looks exactly like Afghanistan, and it occurs to me that anyone who spent his childhood out here would feel right at home in the camps in bin Laden.

Mansour turns the Chevrolet off the road at a black sign with Arabic script, passes through a berm and we are off-road. We come eventually to a collection of canvas tents surrounded by wire fencing. The Kuwaiti and Omani flags swing from a pole. Two dogs rush out to greet us. There are sofas and plastic lawn chairs outside, and two satellite dishes wired to the main tent. The men shake hands and kiss. The sun evaporates into the desert and a man with a big belly cups his hands to his mouth and sings the call to prayer, *Allah Akhbar*. Inside the tent, Mansour leads the sunset prayers, and then tends to the fire, making tea and coffee in the embers.

In the tin shed that serves as the camp kitchen, Mansour cooks a sheep. He boils the meat, then fries it and plants the morsels in a bed of saffron rice. At 6:30 p.m., the men pray again. Without the sun, the temperature sinks quickly and the men drape brown camelhair blankets over their shoulders. Every Wednesday they come here to relax and talk. Mansour turns off his mobile phone when he arrives, so as not to be disturbed.

"Bell, don't be shy," Mansour says, handing me a box of sweets. When I reach with my left hand, someone corrects me, saying, "You must only eat with the right hand."

This is not like camping in North America, where you enjoy the natural surroundings, the forest, the lakes and mountains. Here there is nothing but open space. The desert camp experience takes place *inside* the tent: the prayer, the food, the camaraderie and the sense of history that comes from living the way Arabs did 1,200 years ago. That connection is important to Arabs, particularly those who believe that the way forward is to go back to the original teachings of the Prophet Muhammad. This very place, on the north shore of Kuwait Bay, was where Muslim soldiers fighting under one of Muhammad's successors, Abu Bakr, defeated the Persians in battle before turning against Syria.

Plastic tablecloths are laid on the tent floor and platters piled with rice and lamb are placed in the center. The men hand out bowls of hot sauces and bottles of water.

"Today, you will be really Arabian," Mansour says. "Put your camera away; go to the fight!"

The men wash their hands and sit around the feast.

"Say *Bismillah*," Mansour instructs me, and I repeat the term, which means "In the name of Allah."

The men scoop the rice and meat with their hands and shovel it into their mouths. I quickly get full but Mansour urges me on, telling me to loosen my belt and clean the plate.

"Bell, we slaughter the sheep for you because we know you are coming."

There is fruit and more tea, and the men play cards in a circle on the floor, and by 10:30 p.m. they start trickling back to the city. The cars leave camp in a convoy because the route back to the highway is so hard to follow in the dark. Mansour loses his way and, skidding and sliding over the dunes, reaches a dead end and has to retrace his way back. But he knows this place well, and he finds the way out on his second try.

"This is our real life," Mansour says on the highway home. He means, this is what his sons would do when they were growing up in Kuwait.

Mohammed just took a wrong turn somewhere, he says.

"Everybody makes mistakes."

"You can't judge somebody for one mistake he makes."

I have been talking to Mansour on and off for two years, and he has always maintained that his sons were completely innocent, but during our conversations now, he concedes "it's possible" they were recruited into terrorism.

"Maybe they have been manipulated to go over there. But I strongly believe they did not go by themselves. Somebody has manipulated them, washed their brains to go over to change their life because I know my sons exactly, what they were looking for, what they were planning, what they were hoping to be. That's why they went over with me to Canada, we have a house over there, they finished their school over there, they applied to get their degrees in Canada. That's why in the end some group manipulated my sons to change their style, to get another path to end it with.

"Everything's possible, especially if they have friends. He has friends, they went over before him, they convinced him, maybe."

He suggests his sons just wanted to try something different, "like if you eat everything the same meal, same meal, same meal—but if I bring you another meal than you eat, you would like to try it."

Perhaps, I say, the Jabarah brothers heard about the need to prepare for jihad and they wanted to try it, to learn how to defend their faith.

"Maybe, maybe," he says, "because you know let's talk about the jihad. Maybe they would like to get some courses or some knowledge or get some things about the jihad. Somebody maybe met with them [and said], 'Go and get some courses to participate to get some knowledge about the jihad.' This is the first step to mislead others, bring them over there, put them in a camp and brainwash them."

I ask if he is angry at those who recruited Mohammed and Abdul Rahman and he says, "of course." But he says he has not been able to confront them because they are either in jail, missing or dead.

He is quiet, and I think, this man is the father of not one, but two terrorists. What are the odds, I wonder, of two Al Qaeda terrorists coming from the same family? Two brothers, raised together. Then again, his other two boys are not terrorists at all. I look at Mansour behind the wheel of his Chevy and I imagine the hell that he must be going through. His sons were terrorists. There is no doubt the world is a better place now that they are out of business. The planet has rid itself of two trained killers for God, but Mansour has lost the little boys that fill the pages of his family photo albums. He has lost his sons to terrorist recruiters, and it hurts just as much as losing a loved one to an act of terror.

He looks through the windshield at the deep dark of the desert road.

"I'm in the middle of a tornado."

6

JOINING THE CARAVAN

THE sign at the western edge of Peshawar reads, "Welcome to Khyber Agency. Attention: Entry of foreigners is prohibited beyond this point."

It is an empty threat.

Tens of thousands of foreign Muslims have passed this sign packed inside vans, buses, taxis and pickup trucks, on their way to the training camps over the mountains in Afghanistan.

At dawn in Peshawar, the streets are already clogged with donkey carts and motor-rickshaws. They dodge each other beneath bright billboards advertising mobile phone services. Along the roadside, women in bhurkas stroll past stacks of watermelons. In the traffic median, groggy men sleep on the cool grass, one arm crooked over their faces to shade their eyes from the harsh early sun. Colorful trucks and buses exhale smog so dense that the mountains of the Khyber are no more than a faint brown outline. Along the roadside, there are blue signs with self-help slogans: "The strength of our character is determined by the depth of our convictions." A man in *shalwar khameez* angrily bends and picks up a rock, threatening to hurl it at an older man. My driver says it is probably a dispute over money. "No education, big problem," he shrugs. His car radio is blasting a B-52s song called "Bush Fire," and that's what it feels like outside. The air is dry and intensely hot. It is a heat I have not felt since I stood at the edge of a forest fire in Western Canada.

There is a romance to this city. It is a legendary den of smugglers, soldiers and spies. All three can still be found here in abundance, but for all its mystique, this is above all an urban chaos, where the dominant sound is not that of the *muezzin*'s gentle song echoing from a minaret but rather the sharp bleep of car horns. The Bala Hisar Fort is a reminder of the utter unconquerability of this place, but even it seems shrunken amidst so many rows of dull apartment blocks. One of the few places that lives up to Peshawar's reputation is the bazaar in the old city, a maze of twisting, narrow streets filled with merchants hawking tribal silver and ancient coins from shops the size of coat closets.

Peshawar is a cultural crossroads, where people's faces contain hints of ancestors from Iran, China, Afghanistan, Russia, India and Pakistan. It is also a crossroads of trade. In the smugglers' market you can buy Chinese electronics carted over the mountains from the East, Persian food from the West, and hashish and guns brought down from the North. It is an ideological crossroads as well. Tens of thousands of Arabs have transited through here on their way to The Base, or in Arabic, Al Qaeda.

It seems a casual name for the world's deadliest terrorist network, until you understand that what its founders set out to do was create a base that would foster terrorist violence around the world. Its goals are grand, if ill-conceived: To serve God by combating those that do not rule by their interpretation of ancient Islamic laws, because to the rigid ideology of radical Islam, only God can make laws, and those who believe otherwise are infidels, unbelievers, enemies of faith who deserve to die. It's a harsh vision, but it was born in a harsh land: Pakistan, the first modern nation founded on Islamic ideals, with 150 million people crammed into teeming cities and spread over vast barren tribal lands where the only law is the gun.

For a young man like Mohammed Jabarah, who was already hooked on the jihad, and had heard stories about it for so long but had never experienced it first hand, coming to Pakistan would have been revelatory. Here was a place where holy war was not just something talked about in study groups. Awash with weapons and steeped in radical Islamic traditions, Pakistan was where belief was put into action. There was a fight just over the border in Afghanistan, a real jihad against the rebel forces opposed to the Taliban. And there was another jihad just outside Islamabad, against the Indian occupiers in Kashmir. "He was looking for an Islamic education," Mansour replies when I ask him why Mohammed went to Pakistan. "I think somehow he went with friends or with other people to apply in Pakistan, because in Pakistan I think the first language is English." Mohammed and Abdul Rahman Jabarah did indeed fly to Pakistan in search of education, but not the kind their father imagined at the time.

By the year 2000, those hoping to train in Afghanistan, to prepare for the jihad of the sword, were being carefully screened. Bin Laden would not take just any volunteer into his camps. He was too security-conscious for that. There could be spies. He had to be selective—and he could afford to be. Some volunteers were required to fill out a "Mujahedeen Identification Form/New Application Form" and have a sponsor who would vouch for them. It was Abu Gaith who vouched for Mohammed. When Mohammed arrived in Karachi, he called Abu Gaith in Kuwait. The cleric arranged for a Libyan known as Mabrouk to meet Mohammed at his hotel. According to Mohammed, the Libyans were in charge of the transportation pipeline that brought Al Qaeda recruits to Pakistan from Kuwait. Mabrouk picked up Jabarah and took him to an apartment where he met two Saudis, Abu Muslim and Abu Obeida. Those were not their real names, but neither was Mohammed using his actual name.

From the moment he met the Libyan in Karachi, he had adopted an alias. He was Abu Hafs.

They spent the night in the apartment and the next day Mabrouk drove the three of them north over the Sind Plain, along the highway that runs parallel to the Indus River towards the Northwest Frontier and Peshawar, where they were handed over to another contact named Adnan, who was to take them on the next leg of their journey to jihad.

*   *   *

It is difficult to pin down where an idea begins, especially one as insidious and outrageous as Al Qaeda. But some believe it started in a Peshawar neighborhood called Arbab Road. When the Soviet Union invaded Afghanistan in 1979, in a brazen attempt to expand the Communist empire to the edge of South Asia, Arab volunteers began converging in Peshawar to help their fellow Muslims. One of them was an Islamic scholar named Abdullah Azzam, a Palestinian from Jordan who had taught in Saudi Arabia before moving to Pakistan. At a small mosque off Arbab Road, Azzam preached to the local Arabs.

"Dr. Azzam was a very good speaker," Malik Iftikhar, who lives next door to the mosque, tells me when I visit. Three men in dirty *shalwar kameez* are laying red bricks to rebuild the *madrassa*, which was bulldozed by Pakistani authorities after the 9/11 attacks. Sudanese donated the land, and operating funds came from the Saudis, who were "controlling" the mosque, he says. "They donated the money for the school."

"Arbab Road was famous," he says. "This place was famous. A lot of people lived here. Azzam, he was an Arabian speaker, so they came here."

"They were fighting against the Russian people," Malik says. "They were helping the Afghanistan people, to relieve them of the Russian people."

Azzam was a believer in the brand of radical Islam that teaches that jihad is obligatory for all Muslims when there are infidels in the land of Muhammad. The war in Afghanistan, he said, was holy; it was a jihad. In a seething tract called *Join the Caravan*, Azzam laid out the rules of jihad in precise detail. "No permission of parents is required," he wrote. Fighting in the jihad was not something you could avoid by donating money, he added. You had to actually fight. And you could not just fight for a while, and then go home, feeling you had done your part. Rather, jihad was a lifetime obligation. For those who were uncertain about the true meaning of jihad, Azzam was clear: "The word *jihad*, when mentioned on its own, only means combat with weapons."

"Jihad is the zenith of Islam," he said.

Azzam listed what he considered to be the stages of jihad. First, there was hijrah, which means to live righteously. Second came preparation or training. Next was *ribat*, or living on the frontline opposite the enemy, and finally combat.

"Jihad is a collective act of worship," he said, "and every group must have a leader. Obedience to the leader is a necessity in jihad, and thus a person must condition himself to invariably obey the leader, as has been reported in the *hadith* (the sayings and traditions of Muhammad and his companions), 'You must hear and obey, whether it is easy or difficult for you, in things which are unpleasant for you, as well as those which are inconvenient and difficult for you.'

"You should know that the path of jihad is long and arduous," he warned, "and that it is not easy for most people to continue the journey, even if they were very eager at the start. Desires and effusive feelings for jihad must definitely take root in the soul to enable it to bear hardships, and to rear it upon difficulties and adversaries. Many youth came here zealous, but then their zeal steadily diminished, until they began disputing the very ordinance of jihad."

But worry not, he said, because God is behind you. "Allah has undertaken to support the mujahedin, so whoever goes forth in His path, Allah will guide him, strengthen his determination, fortify his heart and make his feet firm."

Azzam ended on a practical note.

"Whoever wishes to come to Afghanistan should call one of the following telephone numbers in Peshawar. So when you reach Peshawar, call one of those numbers, and ask the person who answers the call to come to where you are. Then, somebody will come to you and take care of you."

Volunteers came from Egypt and Algeria and Saudi Arabia to answer Azzam's call. Videotapes of his speeches were circulated around the world, and played in mosques, including those in Kuwait where Mohammed Jabarah worshipped. One of Azzam's followers was a tall Saudi from a wealthy industrial family who had come to Peshawar to run a guesthouse for those heading to Afghanistan to do battle. His name: Osama bin Laden. Together, Azzam and bin Laden founded Maktab al Khidmat, the Services Bureau, which recruited Muslims for the jihad throughout the Middle East, Southeast Asia, Western Europe and North America. "It became sort of a fashion with the upper-class Arab families to send one of their sons to jihad. This was sort of a way of purification for these young people," Hamid Gul, the former head of Pakistan's Inter-Services Intelligence (ISI) tells me at his house in Rawalpindi.

Maktab funded, indoctrinated and trained these foreign fighters. And later, bin Laden led them in battle. Peshawar was their base. It was where they would come before fighting, and it was where they would go after fighting, if they survived. And it was in this cauldron that the concept of a larger jihad, a global jihad that built on revolutionary ideas emerging from Egypt and Saudi Arabia, began to take shape. "People were radicalized here," the veteran Peshawar journalist Rahimullah Yusufzai says. "These ideas were picked up by the jihadis in Afghanistan. How to make bombings, how to destroy, how to kill." By 1989, 15,000 Russian troops had been killed and the Soviets retreated. The victory was largely the work of seven factions of Afghan guerrillas, or mujahedin, not to mention the Pakistani, American, British and Saudi intelligence services, which secretly financed and equipped them in classic Cold War fashion. But bin Laden and his volunteers felt they had played a decisive role. "He witnessed the defeat of a superpower and that was his thinking—if we can defeat the Soviet Union, we can also defeat the U.S," says Yusufzai, a kindly, bearded man who has interviewed bin Laden on two occasions.

Towards the end of the war, bin Laden fell under the influence of Egyptian radicals and began turning his fighters into terrorists. Azzam opposed bin Laden, and he was soon assassinated near his mosque. A bomb went off in his car, a killing with any number of possible suspects. At first Al Qaeda targeted Muslim regimes that were not ruling according to bin Laden's extreme concept of Islamic law. From his new base in Sudan, bin Laden used his family inheritance to finance and train Islamist movements in the Arab/Muslim world. Drawing on veterans of the Afghan conflict, he assembled an Islamic army made up of terrorists from Egypt, Libya, Algeria, Saudi Arabia, Oman, Tunisia, Jordan, Iraq, Lebanon, Morocco, Somalia and Eritrea. From Khartoum, bin Laden built Al Qaeda into an international organization. He set up an advisory council and committees, one charged with issuing *fatwas*, and others responsible for training, financing and propaganda.

Bin Laden soon decided it wasn't enough just to undermine governments in the Middle East and North Africa. He had a larger plan. He wanted to go after the United States. The first anti-American terrorist attack attributed to Al Qaeda is the December 1991 bombing of a hotel in Yemen that was hosting U.S. soldiers on their way to Somalia. In February 1993 came the first attempt on the World Trade Center. That October, Al Qaeda–trained fighters battled U.S. troops in Somalia, downing two Black Hawk helicopters. Over time, Al Qaeda's plots became more outlandish. There were plots to kill the Pope and President Clinton. In 1995, a car bombing in Riyadh, Saudi Arabia, killed five U.S. soldiers. Bin Laden began seeking chemical, biological and nuclear weapons.

Bin Laden moved to Afghanistan in 1996 and in August of that year declared war on the United States. A month later, the

Taliban captured Kabul. Bin Laden quickly formed an alliance with the new rulers: Al Qaeda would defend the Taliban, and in return Afghanistan would be bin Laden's safe haven. Early in 1998, bin Laden began to merge his Al Qaeda with the most radical of the Egyptian terror factions, the Islamic Jihad, and issued yet another call for the death of Americans, Jews and their allies. Few had heard of Al Qaeda until August 7, 1998, when truck bombs exploded outside the American embassies in Nairobi and Dar es Salaam. Two hundred and thirteen people were killed. Bin Laden suddenly became the world's most wanted terrorist. The Clinton administration ordered cruise missile strikes against his bases in Afghanistan, but he escaped unscathed.

By now, bin Laden was running a half-dozen large training camps. He was preparing a new generation of terrorists. As they had during the Soviet War, Muslims came from all over the world to train with Al Qaeda. And most of them followed the same route, to Peshawar, and overland by bus through the tribal lands to Jalalabad. The 9/11 Commission in the United States concluded that Pakistani and Iranian authorities knew terrorists were transiting their countries but "turned a blind eye." Between 1996 and the fall of 2001, tens of thousands of people made the trek to train under bin Laden. Canadian intelligence says the figure could be as high as 100,000. "Peshawar remains very important. It is still the window to whatever is going on in Afghanistan," Yusufzai says.

Major General Andrew Leslie, the Canadian soldier who served as deputy commander of the International Security Assistance Force in Afghanistan until February 2004, believes this region is the nexus of world terrorism. "The epicenter is Kabul," he said in a speech in Ottawa after returning home from his mission, "within a 1,000-kilometer (600-mile) circle of Kabul, specifically the madrassas. The religious schools along the Afghanistan–Pakistan border, which still churn out thousands of potentially angry young men—that is the epicenter. That region between Afghanistan and Pakistan is the base from which international terrorists of this particular ilk either launch their operations or retreat to under times of stress. And, of course, what does Al Qaeda mean?"

It means The Base.

The young men that concern Major General Leslie inhabit schools such as Jamia Faridia on the outskirts of Islamabad, at the foot of the Margalla Hills. The towering chalk-white minarets of the Shah Faisal Mosque, the world's largest, is a short walk away. A few kilometers down the road are the smaller mosques, where every Friday after prayers Muslims emerge with banners and megaphones to chant "Death to America" and set fire to U.S. and Israeli flags. The school is shaped like a fort, with a large inner courtyard with impeccably pruned bushes and lush lawns. Dozens of pairs of black sandals are lined up outside the sweltering classrooms. There are no chairs; teachers and students alike sit on the cement floors, 90 per class. A small computer lab holds 16 terminals loaded with Microsoft Word and Excel. There are 20,000 madrassas in Pakistan and many of them teach the Islamic religion and little else. Jamia Faridia is the second largest in the country. Since 9/11, the government has tried to shut down the more radical schools and introduce a more balanced curriculum, but the madrassas continue to thrive.

There are 2,000 boys enrolled at Jamia Faridia. They come from all over Pakistan to memorize the Koran and to study to become Islamic scholars. There are so many students that some sleep in the mosque and others live in tents pitched out back along the edge of the forest beside the cook tent, which bakes hundreds of loaves of flatbread every day. Workers balanced on scaffolding made of lashed sticks gathered from the hills are constructing an extension.

Abdul Rashid Ghazi, a pro-Taliban cleric with a black turban and thick glasses, runs the school, which was started by his father 25 years ago. He took over after his father was assassinated by gunmen in the courtyard of the Red Mosque. When we meet at his home, he tells me how he sat with bin Laden in Afghanistan and found him to be an impressive man. He shrugs off concerns about the madrassas. Pakistan is only cracking down on the schools due to U.S. pressure, he claims. "They are just trying to please the Western countries . . . because you are saying that the madrassas are the breeding grounds for terrorism." But within Pakistan as well, there are people who believe the schools are dangerous and that, with their focus on jihad and Islam, they are breeding the next generation of extremists, militants and terrorists.

A "huge catastrophe" looms unless they are modernized and the "preachers of hate" who run them are stopped, the Pakistani daily, *The News*, wrote. *Dawn*, the country's largest English-language daily, argued that the madrassas have to be overhauled to overcome extremism, and should add mainstream arts and sciences to the curricula. "This alone can end the supply of robotized humans spitting venom and hatred against those they consider infidels and programmed to resort to violence and terror in the name of religion." Zubaida Jalal, the education minister who is leading the reform drive, said that, "Extremism is a barrier to development and an enlightened moderation is the key to globalization." A few weeks later, extremists fired 20 rockets at her home.

Ghazi says his madrassa will not accept such reforms and that many other schools have made the same decision, severing their ties with the state and access to government funding."The problem is that [the government] said they want to change the syllabus," he said. "That was the point from which we started resisting because the government has bowed before the pressure of America, so all policies are being made according to U.S. demand."

In particular, the schools will not stop teaching jihad, he says. "This is not possible because jihad is part of Islam. We don't have any authority to change it." Ghazi says the madrassas are not providing any military training, and I saw no evidence of it during my visits, except on one afternoon when two small boys emerged from the school holding fake life-sized rifles, painted white. They pretended to fire into the air until an older boy ushered them back inside. But the madrassas are not responsible for training. Their job is to breed youths vulnerable to recruitment for jihad. Recruiters from the major armed Islamic groups regularly sweep through the madrassas looking for the most radical and physically able students. Ghazi acknowledges that madrassa students sometimes end up on the battlefields, but sees nothing wrong with that. "Jihad does not mean terrorism; it means that you should stop the aggressor."

But the critical question is: What constitutes aggression? Muslim extremists look at the world and see a Jewish-led Crusade against Islam. Violence in defence of the faith is, in this view, fully justified. "America has attacked without any reason. I mean there was no reasoning, there was no logical rationale about attacking Afghanistan, and they have attacked. And so if somebody goes to support [the Taliban] there is nothing wrong in that," Ghazi says. I ask him about 9/11, and he says it was the work of the Americans, who staged the assault to create a pretext for attacking Muslims worldwide.

The Faridia madrassa has a satellite school a few kilometers away called Jamia Raheemia, a tiny building in a wooded park. By the time I visit, it has been reduced to rubble by Pakistani authorities, who claim it had no permit. The lessons, however, are continuing in the adjacent mosque, where a few dozen boys sit on the floor, bobbing their heads and reciting the Koran. The teacher, Shereen Khan, criticizes General Pervez Musharraf for joining the war against the Taliban and Al Qaeda. "In my mind, this is not correct because they are not terrorists, they are defenders," he says. "If defenders are terrorists, we are terrorists."

* * *

In Pakistan, it is not hard to meet veterans of jihad. I found Khalid Khawaja one day at a law office in Islamabad (or, to be precise, he found me) and later we spoke frequently, sometimes over sweet tea and cookies, as he tried to make me understand how he and his fellow believers see the world. "What we believe [is] that all of us are to be ruled by Allah," he tells me as we sit in his son's office, where several young men are working at ancient computers, managing their stock portfolios. The trouble comes, he says, when governments try to dictate to Muslims and tell them how to behave. But since Muslims obey only God, they cannot do what these dictators tell them, so the dictators resort to violence to impose their will, and so Muslims retaliate in defence, he says. And when they retaliate to protect their Islamic beliefs, that is jihad. "Jihad is our religious faith," he says. "If we do not do jihad, we are not Muslims."

Khalid looks about 60 years old, but I have been in this part of the world long enough to know that harsh living adds at least a decade to the faces of these men and women. He has a long gray beard and wears a white robe. He is annoyingly smug and, while friendly enough, makes it clear that his view is the only one that counts. A Pakistani, he served in the air force before joining the Afghan mujahedin in the 1980s. He considers himself close to bin Laden, having fought alongside him against the Russians. Even when he was fighting the Soviets, "bin Laden was sure at the time that America was the enemy also," he tells me. During the 1991 Gulf War, he recalls bin Laden saying that the final war would be against America. "So it is jihad against America now." He will not say when he last spoke to bin Laden, but lets on that he greatly admires him, as well as those in his inner circle. "You call them terrorists," he says. "They are wonderful people. They are probably the most wonderful people of the world."

In Khalid's world, the Western countries, led by the United States, are engaged in a war against Islam. They send their armies to Afghanistan and Iraq, the lands of Muhammad, to dominate, he says. "It's a question of, I do not wish to be a slave." In face of this assault, true Muslims have no choice but to defend themselves, he says. Since they lack the advanced weapons of the Americans and their allies, it is only natural that Muslims should try to level the playing field with suicide bombers and hijacked planes, he says. "Today you have the power in your hand; the other day the suicide bomber also has power. So you use your cruise missiles and atom bombs and all that, so he uses his power. So why do you cry at that time? When you say we are fighting a war against you, so better take it then! So they are also fighting a war against you. They are fighting their way. You are fighting your way. So let's be happy. But [the] only thing is, your faces are pulled down. You are scared. Sitting in America and Canada, you are scared of a man sitting in the caves who can do nothing to you probably. We are not scared of you.

"It's not a matter of weapons of mass destruction," he adds. "It's a matter of hate. If I hate you and I want to take you with me, how can you stop that?

"We don't believe in killing innocent people but we would certainly like to send you into the Stone Age the same way you have sent us into the Stone Age." He adds that he does not know any Muslims who like Americans. "A slave normally hates his master."

"For us," he says, "this life is not . . . you see we are told that this life is not a place to enjoy and a place to be very happy. This life is a place for a test with us, and we always are willing to finish this test. This life is like a cage or a prison for us. We love it like we want to live in a toilet. And we just want to get out of it. We are like a bird who wants to be out of the prison and meet his God.

"We really love death as much as you hate death. We wait for death as much as you want to get away from it, because for us dying in the way of Allah is a victory.

"So how can you fight with us?"

7

THE LAND OF JIHAD

ISLAMABAD may be the capital of Pakistan, but Peshawar is the capital of bin Laden's jihad. "I think that Al Qaeda was made in Peshawar. It was the birthplace of Al Qaeda," the local journalist Rahimullah Yusufzai tells me, as we sit in his garden in the Army Officer's Compound.

Peshawar was the gateway to the training camps in Afghanistan. Debriefings of detainees at Guantanamo Bay have underscored the importance of this pipeline in the recruiting process. According to a classified FBI report, "Potential recruits were identified internationally through their participation in extremist mosques and religious schools that emphasized Koranic memorization and Islamic indoctrination to the exclusion of nonreligious subjects. Once identified, recruits sometimes received more intensive religious instruction in Pakistan before being smuggled to Afghanistan or other regions of conflict."

The journey there, however, was not easy. The road between Peshawar and Jalalabad, the hub of bin Laden's network of camps, is only a few hundred miles in length, but it traverses the famed Khyber Pass. My trip to the Afghan border begins in the office of General Mahmoud Shah, the Pakistan Army official in charge of security in the tribal areas. He sits behind his desk in Peshawar, dressed in a safari suit and between a pair of whirring fans. There are four phones on his desk: two red, two white. A Sony television hangs in the corner of the room, opposite a portrait of Mohammed Ali Jinnah, the founder of modern Pakistan.

When I ask if Osama bin Laden is hiding in the tribal frontier, he pulls out a silver cigarette case and lights up.

"No, I don't think," he replies. "I feel that he is mostly in Afghanistan side of border. I put a 70 percent chance that he is there."

A servant enters the room, walks past a bearded armed guard in a beret, and places a tray holding a glass and a bottle of water in front of the general. The trouble is, he continues, the tribal areas along the border with Afghanistan are only nominally part of Pakistan. The government in Islamabad exerts little real authority there. The Pakistani government calls it the Federally Administered Tribal Area, but to locals it is Pashtunistan, home to more than 3 million members of the Pashtun tribes, who were granted independent status by the British and are not required to adhere to Pakistani law. Decisions are made by a *jirga*, or council of elders, and justice is meted out according to harsh tribal custom. When soldiers are needed, the tribesmen assemble a militia, or *lashkar*. The tribal lands are a world apart. The tribesmen reject outside authority, so it is difficult for Pakistani troops to operate there. The preferred option of President Pervez Musharraf is to give tribal leaders incentives to surrender the Al Qaeda terrorists in their midst.

"We want the tribe by itself to catch these people and hand them over to the government," General Shah says. But he admits his patience is wearing thin. "They are not trying," he complains.

Unless they get serious, they will face economic sanctions, the general warns. Pakistan will restrict the movement of goods and ultimately launch military operations, although he is well aware that incursions have seldom succeeded in the storied tribal lands. Many an army has fallen trying to conquer Khyber, from the Moghuls to the British, in no small part because of the landscape: a maze of valleys and sharp peaks that are ideal for ambushing invaders. After an hour, the general agrees to give us a permission slip allowing us to enter the tribal area, and we leave to prepare for the journey.

* * *

Mohammed Jabarah and the two Saudis he met in Karachi traveled from Peshawar into the tribal lands with the Al Qaeda escort Adnan. My escort is a soldier from the Khyber Khasadar Force and my traveling companions are Jeff Stephen, a television videographer, and our translator, Arshad. Arshad is a Tabligli Muslim who has a fondness for telling jokes. He keeps a *miswak*, a soft stick that Sunnis use as a toothbrush, in the chest pocket of his clean white robe. An engineering student, he wants to study in London. His father doesn't want him to go. He fears that Arshad, with his thick beard and religious garb, will become a target of post-9/11 security measures, accused of being a terrorist and locked away. Arshad is awaiting a student visa from the British High Commission in Islamabad. Until it comes, he is taking courses in Peshawar and, as the eldest son, he waits on his father, serving cold drinks and tea when guests come calling at their townhouse.

We arrive at the Khyber force headquarters early in the morning and wait in a dark bunkroom with two high ceiling fans, an ancient computer and an electric heater. A soldier comes into the room, points at a TV blasting a Bollywood movie and says, "India." The Indians may be the enemy here in Pakistan, but their prowess in the world of cinema is not questioned.

An unsmiling young soldier with a slim face and a dark mustache is assigned to protect us on our voyage. He wears a navy tunic and carries an old AK-47 that I doubt will actually fire if he pulls the trigger. He does not seem pleased with his assignment, but I cannot tell if it is because he thinks it is beneath him or whether he is genuinely frightened to be driving into one of the most lawless regions in the world with two foreigners who are going to attract attention.

A police checkpoint marks the end of official Pakistan. Once across the line, we are in the Wild West. Arshad reminds us that in the tribal lands, someone could walk up and shoot us within sight of the Pakistani police, but there would be nothing they could do. Their authority stops at the border gate. He adds that there is a good chance we will be kidnapped. "One more thing," he says. "Be careful not to film women in the tribal areas. Otherwise they can put us in prison." I do not ask what tribal prisons are like, but Arshad's tone of voice and my intuition tell me to avoid them at all costs.

I wander into a shop and sit down with a merchant reclining behind a glass counter filled with pistols. He points sleepily to the merchandise hanging from the walls around him: Chinese and Russian machine guns, rocket-propelled grenade launchers, M-16s—enough ammunition to start a war and, of course, the ever-popular AK-47, which he remarks is his personal favorite. "It's better than M-16," he says. Some of the Kalashnikovs have decorated rifle butts; one is adorned with a smiling Mickey Mouse. He reaches behind him and grabs a jar off the shelf. It is filled with sticky red chunks.

"You want some hashish?"

Outside, the afternoon heat, truck exhaust, smoke from khebab pits and the fine Khyber dust give the air a shimmering quality.

"We can get any weapon," the shopkeeper says.

His armory is a combination of leftovers from the Afghan war and the loot of smugglers. To prove his point, he waves his assistant into the back room, behind a filthy curtain. A few minutes later he emerges with an eight-inch anti-aircraft shell. The guns that flood Pakistan's lawless frontier are "mostly" for self-defence, he says.

"Everyone," he adds casually, "they are against the U.S."

But his distrust also extends to the followers of Al Qaeda who have made this region their base. "Al Qaeda, they are not locals. They come from abroad—the Arabs."

The road to Khyber cuts through empty desert toward mountains. The tribesmen live in large compounds surrounded by high walls made of mud, brick, rocks and cement. These little fortresses are everywhere, and the biggest are the homes of the most notorious smugglers. Some of the compound walls stretch for a kilometer along the road, and reach all the way back to the mountain slopes. Once in a while, through an open gate, I catch a glimpse of the houses and lush gardens inside. I have never been to South America, but they make me think of the villa estates occupied by drug barons during their heyday in the 1980s. The first town along the road is Jamrud Fort, built by Sikhs in the early 1800s.

"One thing you'll find here is everybody is standing," Arshad observes. "Even the shopkeepers are standing."

And he is right. We stop and are quickly surrounded by curious locals, so our guard shepherds us back into the car. "They'll kidnap you for money," the guide advises. The landmark we are seeking is at the far edge of town: the gate marking the entrance to the Khyber Pass, with its two turrets, cannons and the faded green and white flag of Pakistan.

From there, the road follows a dry riverbed, where young boys are playing cricket, and then climbs in a series of tight switchbacks. Arshad points to an abandoned town at the foot of a steep cliff, its mud and rock homes collapsing from neglect as if they are melting back into the landscape.

"The Village of the Ghosts," he says.

"Why is it called that?"

"The ghosts will never let you live there."

Whose ghosts he does not say, but it may well be those of the many travelers who have died on this treacherous road. Just past the village, we turn a corner and find ourselves facing an upended tanker-truck spilling a river of crude oil, its cab dangling over a cliff.

At Landi Kotal, a trading town with narrow streets and row after row of monotonous beige houses that blend perfectly with the landscape, we stop at a paint store owned by a friend of our guide. I ask the owner which colors of paint are most popular and he points to three shades of beige.

"We want to live separately," Mussarad Shinwari says. He says he prefers the system of tribal rule over the rule of law that Pakistan wants to bring to the region. Tribal justice works because it is more severe than anything handed out by Pakistan's courts, he says. If, for example, somebody kills a member of your family, you can demand anything from him—money, a woman, even his life. The Pakistani government hopes to eventually bring the tribal areas under its control through a strategy of development. Partly using Western donor money, Islamabad has been building schools, clinics and bridges. At first, the tribesmen were hesitant because they feared their unique way of life would be lost,"but now they accept it. They want the roads. They want the hospitals," Mr. Shah says. "Of course, what has not been done over the last 50 years cannot be undone in one year or two years." The Pashtuns may be warming to development, but they resent Pakistan's threat to launch military operations in the tribal areas, and are generally opposed to Pakistan's war on terror. "We have sympathies and we have love for Taliban and Osama because they are Muslim, they fight for Islam," the paint shop owner tells me.

A red square painted on a rock wall marks the narrowest point in the Khyber Pass, barely wide enough for a single vehicle. Nearby, there is a row of "dragon's teeth"— cement pyramids meant to snag invading tanks. A sign points to the city that was the destination of Mohammed Jabarah and the many other young foreign Muslims who have come this way: "Jalalabad 98 kilometers."

The road is busy. There are dozens of trucks ferrying Afghan refugees back to their homes in Kabul; Toyota pickups with men crammed in the back; and a truck full of Pakistani soldiers on their way to guard the Afghanistan border, clutching their most valuable tool—an electric fan. The temperature is climbing into the high 40s C (115°–120°F). A boy pushes a cart piled with shrinking blocks of ice. Women wear blue *burkhas* or the black head-to-toe dresses of observant Muslims.

"United We Stand Protecting the Motherland," reads the sign at Michni Post. It is the slogan of the Khyber Rifles, who defend the border. The post is high on a mountaintop and you can see the road below as it snakes to the village of Torkham and the border. "That mountain is the end of Pakistan," our guide says, pointing to the Durant Line. The *Lonely Planet* guidebook says that at the end of the Khyber Pass, you "look over at Afghanistan—which at this point looks more or less like Pakistan—and then go back."

Not so for bin Laden's recruits.

When Mohammed Jabarah reached the border, he and his two Saudi traveling companions were handed over to an Afghan named Khoudratoula. It was too risky to try to cross the border at the official crossing. If they were stopped and questioned, they could be turned back or arrested. Instead, Khoudratoula led them on a five-hour hike along a smuggler's route through the mountains to Torkham. From there, they took a taxi to the outskirts of Jalalabad. Mohammed then took a second taxi to a guesthouse where he was reunited with his brother and best friend. But Abdul Rahman and Al Kandari were no longer using their real names. They, too, had adopted Al Qaeda aliases. Abdul Rahman was Abu Tulha, and Al Kandari was Hamza.

They stayed at the guesthouse, run by a Libyan named Abu Hamad, for a week and then they moved to another in the Wazir Khan neighborhood of Kabul. Once a lovely capital, Kabul was by then a city of ruins. Twenty-five years of war had left entire neighborhoods flattened. What the Soviets had not destroyed in the 1980s had been razed later by the rival factions of mujahedin that fought for control of the city in the early 1990s. A few neighborhoods, however, had survived the onslaught and Wazir Khan was one of them; the large compounds were favored by the new lords of Afghanistan, the Arabs who had come to wage jihad with Osama.

From Kabul, Mohammed and his brother traveled by road 30 to 35 kilometers north to the Sheikh Shaheed Abu Yahya training camp. The Taliban frontline, where a war was being fought against the Northern Alliance rebels commanded by Ahmad Shah Massoud, whose stronghold was the Panshjir Valley, was another 30 kilometers to the north.

It was a small training camp. There were about 20 recruits altogether, all Kuwaitis and Saudis. The instructors were Libyans: Omar, Abdul Hakim and Faisal, the camp leader. The training regimen was intense. Morning prayers started before dawn. That was followed by two hours of physical training, mostly jogging. The recruits would shower, using well water, and have breakfast. Following the meal the students would be divided into study groups. They would sit for an hour of classroom instruction, then recline for a 45-minute nap. Prayers were at noon, followed by an hour-long lecture on the Koran. After lunch, it was chore time, which lasted until afternoon prayers.

Then the military training began.

Mohammed was trained by Abdul Hakim. The course was called Tahziri, which means the "beginning" or "preparation." It was a basic training course, Weapons of War 101. Hakim taught Mohammed how to fire an AK-47, M-16, G-3, Klinkow, RBD, RBK, BK and Uzi. He learned how to shoot a 9-mm Makarov. He learned how to operate RPG-7, RPG-22 and RPG-18 disposable anti-tank weapons. And he was introduced to the Draganov sniper rifle. He soon found he had a unique talent for sniping. He was taught how to fire an anti-aircraft gun, and received instruction on the use of Sam-7 and Stinger missiles.

There was training in explosives as well: TNT, C-4, C-3 and an array of techniques for detonating them, including matches, fuses, batteries. As part of their training, the recruits field-tested the explosives.

There was hand-grenade training, using Russian, Czech, Chinese, Egyptian and American grenades. Mohammed learned how to bury anti-tank and anti-personnel land mines. There was a two-week course on topography, in which recruits learned how to read military maps and navigate through mountains using only a compass and a rifle scope.

The military training sessions were followed by the evening meal, then "jihad teachings," and at last the weary men would say their evening prayers at 8 p.m. and collapse into their tents—except for those assigned to guard duty, who had to stay up all night.

Few places in the world are as well suited to this kind of training and indoctrination. When I first saw it from the air in a small United Nations plane, the mountains looked like folds of a never-ending camel-colored blanket. The vastness of this barren land cannot be overstated. The isolation is the perfect environment for turning young men like Mohammed into terrorists.

To be successful, radical leaders must convince their recruits to reject the present and look to an idealized future. They must make them believe that there is no joy in life, that pleasure is trivial, immoral even. This is not so simple in a Western city, where life is comfortable and good. But once the recruits were in the backward hinterlands of Afghanistan, it was easy to make the case that a better time was awaiting. The recruits—their days spent in harsh training, their nights in cold tents, all in pursuit of God's agenda—lived such a harsh existence that their lives seemed but a small sacrifice. "To lose one's life is but to lose the present," Eric Hoffer writes in *The True Believer*, "and clearly to lose a defiled, worthless present is not to lose much."

The world of the terrorist is a parallel universe. It is the world not as it is, but as it will be—at least according to the vision of the leaders of the movement. They speak as if their victory is preordained. It is only a matter of time. The present, they say, is only a temporary state that is awaiting the agents of change, those fortunate few chosen to bring about the inevitable. They ask their young recruits, "Do you have what it takes? Will you be the ones who will push aside those who stand in our way?" In the parallel universe of the terrorist, slicing off the head of a hostage is not murder; it is the "implementation of God's judgment," as one statement by the Zarqawi group in Iraq worded it. Strapping explosives around your chest and detonating them in a crowd is not an act of murder, but rather an act of martyrdom, a step along the path to an idealized place where everything will be as it should. "To the Mujahedin brothers, the advancement of tanks means the opening of the gates of Heaven, the arrival of the Virgins, and the announcement of the ultimate relief from the prison of this world," Abu Maysara Al-Iraqi, a spokesman of the Zarqawi group, said on an Islamist website.

"With the support of God, we will be triumphant, and we do not care for a materialistic victory as much as we care about having pleased our God, and having defended the land of the Caliphate against God's enemies. Heroes of Islam! Get prepared for a heroic and bloody battle, in which the heads of blasphemy will be cut off. Show the best of you to God. Iraqis! Join forces with the Mujahedin against the Blasphemers, as you have always done. Islamic Nation! Do not spare any prayers for your sons in Ramadan, when all prayers are answered, and Islamic victories are achieved."

Perhaps because of its simplicity, it is a powerful calling to youthful minds struggling to find their place in a complicated world. And it is sold to recruits as a sure bet: "Victory or martyrdom." Either way, they win. If the trainers do their jobs well, the recruits are not even aware they are becoming terrorists. As Albert Bandura writes, "Development of the capability to kill usually evolves through a process in which recruits may not fully recognize the transformation they are undergoing." Once a recruit adopts the beliefs of martyrdom and terrorism, they are difficult to dislodge. How do you convince a jihadi that there is no flock of virgins waiting for him after he detonates his suicide vest?

* * *

The Jabarah brothers would phone home every week to ten days, but they never said exactly where they were.

"Where are you?" Mansour recalls asking.

"We are okay. We are in a secure place, we are getting our courses," Mohammed would tell his father.

"Don't worry about us. We're safe."

"When are you coming back to us?"

"As soon as I finish my courses I will come back again."

Day after day, they repeated the arduous training routine until they had handled every weapon in the Al Qaeda arsenal. Basic training took two months. Next they could join the Taliban on the frontlines, take another course or just go home. Mohammed was keen to take the ten-week Urban Guerrilla Warfare course, which was available only to the top-ranked graduates of basic training. Abdul Rahman agreed to join him. While the first course was an introduction to conventional military tactics, this one was different. It focused on fighting in cities. Mohammed learned how to organize a cell and plan an assault on a building. There was instruction in hand-to-hand combat, and advanced weapons training on the AK-47.

Mohammed was mastering the AK-47. He did well at topography and orienteering as well. When he finished the course, he asked if he could go to the Taliban front. He had spent weeks training to fight. He wanted to test his skills in live combat. In December 2000, the Jabarah brothers went north to the Taliban frontlines and fought Massoud's Northern Alliance rebels, who despised the Taliban and were stubbornly clinging to a small patch of territory along the Tajikistan border. The Canadian brothers fought alongside other Arabs, such as Abd Al-Hadi Al Iraqi. Their commander was an Egyptian known as Abdul Wakil, but his real name was Mustafa Mohamed Fadhil. Two weeks in the trenches was enough. Abdul Rahman left for Kuwait while Mohammed returned to Kabul to study the Koran and take a course on Islam.

Mohammed's time in the camps caught up with him, however, and he fell seriously ill with hepatitis. Fortunately for Mohammed, Al Qaeda had its own in-house doctor, Ayman Al Zawahiri, the Egyptian who commanded the Al Jihad and served as Osama bin Laden's second-in-command. Mohammed spent a month in bed recovering under the care of Dr. Al Zawahiri. As soon as he was better, he teamed up with Al Kandari and they made their way north. Rumor had it that there was fighting up in Bamiyan. They drove there with a group of Arabs, mostly Saudis and Yemenis. They brought a lot of weapons with them but once they arrived, they saw there was no fighting at all. The trip was not a complete loss, though. Before returning to Kabul, Mohammed visited the site of the ancient statues of Buddha that the Taliban had just blasted into dust. The Taliban leader Mullah Omar had deemed them anti-Islamic.

When he was back in Kabul, Mohammed ran into Hakim, the Libyan who had been his basic training instructor. Hakim told Mohammed he should take the advanced course in Guerrilla Mountain Warfare at the Al Farooq camp near Kandahar. Mohammed was keen. His intent was still to fight in Chechnya. It was the cause that had so moved him in Canada and the reason he had ventured to Afghanistan in the first place. And there were mountains in Chechnya; mountain warfare training could come in handy. The Libyan gave Mohammed a letter of introduction and took him to a guesthouse in Kandahar next to the Haj Habish mosque. Mohammed had impressed the Al Qaeda trainers. He was earning a reputation in Afghanistan, but his name was also beginning to surface in Canada.

* * *

Early in 2001, the Canadian Security Intelligence Service was paying increasing attention to the Niagara and Hamilton regions as more and more suspected Islamic extremists were moving in. Intelligence agents knocked on doors and tried to recruit sources. It was what CSIS Intelligence Officers, or IOs, did. They went out into the communities and talked to people. Sometimes the door would get slammed in their faces. But more often than not, they were invited in. From time to time, they would strike gold. They would come across an insider who wanted out, someone who was part of the movement but, for whatever reasons, had become disaffected and was willing to talk and perhaps even to become a human source. Maybe they needed the money. Maybe they had grown out of it and wanted to go straight and become good citizens. Maybe they had been mujahedin who had fought Serbs or Russians in the trenches, but could not bring themselves to support the terrorist tactics of their more extreme associates.

In February 2001, CSIS got its first tip about two Kuwait-born brothers who had been doing a lot of talking about jihad, hanging out with veteran Muslim fighters and raising money for Chechnya. CSIS started making preliminary inquiries about the Jabarah boys. One of the tasks of an intelligence service is to look into these types of leads. Before police can start an investigation, they must be able to show that there are reasonable and probable grounds that a crime is about to be committed, or has already been committed. CSIS can start investigating sooner, if it suspects a threat to Canada's national security. Since the aim of counter-terrorism is to prevent terrorist acts before they happen, such early detection of potential threats is vital. Agents started asking around about the Jabarahs, but they could not find them. Then by chance, a month later, one of them turned up in Toronto.

After leaving Afghanistan, Abdul Rahman had flown to Kuwait City to visit his parents. While he was there, Mansour asked if he wanted to go on the pilgrimage to Mecca. Haj is one of the five pillars of Islam, along with the five daily prayers, fasting, charity and the belief that there is "no God but God." Every Muslim aspires to complete the Haj once in their lifetime. Mansour had already been to the Haj but he was planning a return visit with his wife. Abdul Rahman was eager to go. So the three of them, Mansour, Souad and Abdul Rahman, flew to Saudi Arabia. They had a "lovely time" and then returned to Kuwait. Afterwards, Mansour asked Abdul Rahman if he would go to Canada to see his brothers Youssef and Abdullah. Upon his arrival at Toronto's Pearson Airport, an immigration officer noticed the Pakistani visa in his passport and asked him to explain.

The next day, Canadian intelligence agents came to Mansour's home in St. Catharines. They wanted to know what Abdul Rahman and Mohammed were doing in Pakistan. Had they crossed into Afghanistan? Did they attend any training camps? CSIS had awoken to Canada's role as a potential staging ground for terrorists following the arrest of Ahmed Ressam. Agents were watching for other potential jihadists, studying travel patterns to discern which Canadians were following the worn path to bin Laden's base. But Abdul Rahman assured them he had only gone to Pakistan to study Islam and that he had never been to Afghanistan. The agents left, but they returned repeatedly.

"Where are they?" Mansour recalls one of the agents asking.

"Why," Mansour replied, "are you looking for my sons?"

8

AN OATH TO OSAMA

THE pickup trucks came to a stop beside the mosque and a team of armed bodyguards clambered out into the crowd of young men waiting for a glimpse of their hero. For hours, word had spread through the camp that an important visitor was coming. Nobody would say his name; there could be spies. They just called him "The Most Wanted." The camp instructors told the recruits to cover their faces, since there would be video cameras accompanying the visitor. By the time the two four-door trucks arrived, everyone in the camp had assembled on the plain, their heads wrapped in scarves. All you could see were their eyes. The recruits were excited about seeing their leader; one wrote him a poem. When the tall visitor at last emerged from his truck, camp guards positioned atop the surrounding hills fired into the air in an apocalyptic salute.

Osama bin Laden lived for such showmanship.

The visit was intended as a morale-booster for the recruits, who had come from all over the world to join Al Qaeda—young men from Yemen and Saudi Arabia, but also a number of Western Muslims from countries like the United States, Britain,

Germany, France, Australia and Canada. For weeks they had punished themselves in the arid Afghan landscape, living in the most austere manner imaginable, training for bin Laden's great global jihad. They needed to be reminded what they were doing it for, and that was where bin Laden excelled. The camp instructors could preach jihad all day, and they often did, but the recruits looked up to bin Laden like no one else. He was the man who had shunned his wealth and privilege to defeat the Soviets, and they trusted that he would soon bring down the world's other superpower as well. It was only a matter of faith and proper training, and bin Laden would provide both.

Bin Laden had brought Ayman Al Zawahiri with him. Their appearance together was another bit of stagecraft. Bin Laden's Al Qaeda and Al Zawahiri's Al Jihad had been formally merging their organizations for the past two years, with the common goal of fighting the "enemies of Islam." This would be their coming out. Inside the mosque, bin Laden read from a letter signed by the Al Jihad stating that it had joined cause with Al Qaeda. Then bin Laden spoke about the obligation of Muslims to train and fight for Islam. He railed against America and Israel, and said U.S. troops had to be driven out of Saudi Arabia. Without giving details, he said there were 50 men willing to bear their souls in their hands for the jihad. They were on a mission to attack America, he said. After he had finished, it was the camp trainers' turn to speak, and they explained that suicide was not only justified, it was the path to martyrdom. The Al Qaeda philosophy, they said, was: One God and Jihad.

The Al Farooq training camp was a busy place when bin Laden gave his address there in May 2001. It was the main base for thousands of foreigners seeking to join Al Qaeda, a booming terrorist factory that produced jihadis as fast as it could manufacture them out of the youth of the Muslim world. The curriculum mixed religious, physical and military instruction with indoctrination. Groups of young Muslim men were arriving steadily to undergo the six-week training courses. Both basic and advanced training were offered at Al Farooq. The recruits included John Walker Lindh, the American Muslim convert who, according to U.S. prosecutors, "reported to the camp with a group of approximately twenty other trainees, mostly from Saudi Arabia" and studied "explosives and battlefield combat, which included the use of shoulder weapons, pistols, and rocket-propelled grenades, and the construction of Molotov cocktails." Mohammed Jabarah says there were hundreds of Arabs at the camp but also some "white guys," including two blonde-headed Australians, a man from Britain, a Jamaican and a Frenchman.

Al Farooq was a new camp. In 1998, the Americans destroyed the central Al Qaeda training facility near Khost with Tomahawk missiles in response to the bombings of the American embassies in Nairobi and Dar es Salaam. The following year, Al Qaeda re-opened the camp, called Mes Aynak, at an abandoned Russian copper mine near Kabul, and then the Taliban gave bin Laden permission to open another camp near Kandahar. It was called Al Farooq. The camp director was Abdullah Ahmed Abdullah, an olive-skinned Egyptian in his late 30s with a scar on his right lip. Abdullah was himself a hardened terrorist, wanted by the Americans for his role in the African embassy bombings. Al Farooq was not a permanent facility, but a moving caravan of tents that changed locations when necessary. But even if it shifted locales, its purpose was consistent; in the words of U.S. prosecutors, who charged some of the trainees, it was "run and maintained by the Al Qaeda terrorist network and financed by it," and "dedicated to producing and training terrorist fighters for the Al Qaeda cause."

Those recruited from around the world to attend Al Farooq began their training program at one of the guesthouses in Kandahar run by Arabs who would give lectures on jihad and the justification of suicide attacks. The recruits were handed green uniforms and invited to watch videos that mixed footage of Al Qaeda attacks with the speeches of bin Laden. There were long discussions about Pakistan and Kashmir, Israel and America. Bin Laden's writings were left out for reading, including a book that showed a map of the world with U.S. and British flags marking foreign military bases in the Middle East. Local Afghans did the cooking and cleaning, but were not involved in the indoctrination process. That was left to the Arabs. Nobody was allowed to leave. Bin Laden himself would sometimes drop by to meet the trainees and ask them questions about their well-being, the treatment of Muslims in their home countries and the Western view of "martyrdom operations."

It was while he was living at the guesthouse in Kandahar, waiting for a place at Al Farooq camp, that Mohammed Jabarah first met bin Laden. Anas Al Kandari had a friend who was a secretary to bin Laden's military chief Abu Hafs. The friend was, in turn, on good terms with bin Laden's secretary. Through this connection, Jabarah and Al Kandari were invited to meet bin Laden. When he found out that Jabarah and Al Kandari were from Kuwait, bin Laden was keen to learn about the situation in the country. He asked about Abu Gaith, and suggested he should come to Afghanistan. They talked about the bombing of the USS *Cole* in Yemen, and bin Laden said he was "glad the attack struck the center of the ship rather than the front, which is where the nuclear weapons are stored . . . this would have caused too much damage in the Aden harbor and to the city itself. This would have angered the Arab world."

The guesthouses of Kandahar were just an introduction; the real training took place at Al Farooq. When 20 or so fresh trainees had assembled at a guesthouse, they were loaded into a bus, pickup truck or minivan for the drive west to a secluded sea of tents. "It was in the middle of nowhere," Sahim Alwan, a Yemeni-American who trained there at the same time as Jabarah, said in an interview with the television program *Frontline*. The isolation did more than conceal the camp from attackers; it also helped the instructors mould their young pupils into indoctrinated radicals by keeping them free from outside distractions and focused on the task at hand: training to fight. In the empty plains of Afghanistan, miles from nowhere, in one of the world's least-developed countries, the extremist preachings of the instructors would go unchallenged. There was nothing to contradict the harsh message of Al Qaeda. Indeed, in most of the country, there was nothing at all.

Coming to the camp was exciting for the young men. "It was an adventure," Alwan says in his television interview. "We were gonna learn how to use weapons. That part of it was the exciting part. You're gonna be able to shoot and this and that." For the recruits, it was the fulfilment of their religious obligation. At least that's what the recruiters back home had told them. "There's a verse in the Koran," Alwan says, "that says you have to learn how to prepare. Like, you gotta be prepared just in case you do have to go to war. If there is a war, then you would have to be called for jihad. And that was the aspect of the camp itself, for going and learn how to use weapons, and stuff like that . . . "

There were so many recruits coming to prepare for jihad that the camp was bursting. And so when they first arrived at Al Farooq, the recruits sometimes had to wait for several days outside the main gate until someone left. Only then could they enter. It was like waiting for a table at a popular restaurant. There was, to put it another way, a waiting list to join Al Qaeda. Although the camp was in the wilderness, there were guards all around, and nobody was allowed to enter or leave without permission. There was no escaping, and even if someone tried to flee, they were too far from civilization to get away and were most likely to end up hopelessly lost. In addition, the recruits were required to surrender their passports and other identity cards upon entry, as well as their money, which was counted in front of them and placed in envelopes with a promise it would be returned upon completion of the program.

Giving up their passports and ID was more than a security measure. It was an important psychological step. It underscored that the recruits were not who they used to be. They were about to make a great transformation, and to emphasize this, each was given a new name, an Al Qaeda name. For the duration of their stay with Al Qaeda, they would be known only by that name.

That was done "in order to conceal their identity," according to U.S. prosecutors, adding that " . . . once they left the camp, they were free to continue on with their given names." But there was another strategy behind the system of aliases: As well as protecting the identities of the recruits, it helped the instructors begin to mould the minds of their young trainees by giving them new identities that combined the names of the Al Qaeda leadership and other well-known terrorists and historical figures with the recruits' countries of origin. Jabarah was now officially Abu Hafs Al Kuwaiti.

The camp routine revolved around the five daily prayers. Morning wake-up was at 3 a.m. and dawn prayers were at 4 a.m., followed by an hour of physical exercise such as running and push-ups. Breakfast was at 6:30. After a morning nap, the military and tactical training began at 8:30. There were lectures on battlefield combat strategy as well as weapons instruction. Recruits were taught how to assemble and fire 9-mm handguns, long-range rifles, RPGs, M-16s, and, of course, the Kalashnikov AK-47. They learned about explosives such as TNT and C-4, as well as land mines. Instructors taught them mountain-climbing, orienteering, topography and navigation. They learned communications and surveillance techniques.

A training manual recovered by the Americans at Al Farooq after it was destroyed detailed one of the additional streams of instruction: What to do if you get caught. If you are taken prisoner, it said, don't say anything for the first 24 hours, so your colleagues will have time to go into hiding and adapt their plans. It said the Americans were unlikely to physically harm their captives, but if they did so prisoners were to complain immediately to the authorities. Showing a bruise or a scar to the Red Cross can cause an international scandal, it added. The manual went on for 60 pages but the theme was consistent: Terrorists held in Western jails have nothing to worry about. They can make up stories and withhold information that could save lives, but the human rights culture of the West will ensure they suffer nothing worse than jail time.

The morning class lasted three hours. Lunch was at noon, then more prayers and camp cleanup time, followed by another hour of military training in the afternoon, and then everyone was free until sunset, when they would eat and pray once again. Every recruit had to perform guard duty from time to time. The trainees were required to wear their green uniforms every day except Friday, the Muslim holy day, when they were allowed to wear civilian clothes while their fatigues were laundered.

There were 40 people enrolled in the Mountain Warfare Course along with Mohammed Jabarah. The instructors, Saudis and Yemenis, taught the recruits how to fight a guerrilla war. There was instruction on ambush tactics and how to move through mountains and open areas in large groups. There were courses on communication techniques such as dead-letter boxes and anti-aircraft and anti-tank weapons. There was a one-month course on explosives, but Mohammed did not take it. A portion of Jabarah's training was captured on film, which was later distributed by Al Qaeda in a propaganda video called *Destroying the American Destroyer*. It shows a troop of dirty men covered in brown rags kicking up a cloud of dust as they march in the Afghan hills, their fists raised in the air. But their faces are covered and they are too far from the camera to make out Jabarah in the crowd.

Throughout this exhausting regimen, the instructors reinforced the indoctrination process by repeating their message—that the West was at war against Islam and that it was their duty as Muslims to defend the faith. Some of the Western recruits found the extremism shocking. Among them was Alwan, who had been recruited from his hometown near Buffalo. He faked an ankle injury and begged to leave. The camp instructors relented, after warning him not to tell the others he was going, fearing they would want out as well. Had he not been so radicalized, Jabarah could have done exactly the same thing, but he didn't. Instead he stayed and completed his mountain warfare course, and then decided to commit himself, fully, to the cause.

Mohammed was just finishing his course in June 2001 when Abu Gaith showed up at the camp with bin Laden, who had a house nearby and would sometimes stop in to congratulate his graduates. Abu Gaith gave a speech to the recruits, telling them to support Osama. And then bin Laden himself spoke, hinting that "hits" were coming that would make the United States forget about Vietnam. Until then, Jabarah had wanted to train in Afghanistan and fight in Chechnya, or join a Palestinian armed faction and fight Israelis. But now, after listening to bin Laden, he thought about becoming an Al Qaeda terrorist. "According to Jabarah," CSIS wrote, "this was the first time the idea of joining Al Qaeda entered his mind."

Mohammed returned to Kandahar with Al Kandari and stayed at a guesthouse next door to the Arabic Islamic Institute. Abu Gaith always stayed at the Institute when he was in town, and one day he dropped by the guesthouse to lecture the residents on Islam. It was just like old times in Kuwait. Towards the end of June, Abu Gaith asked Jabarah whether he was a member of Al Qaeda. Jabarah said he wasn't, but asked whether Abu Gaith thought he should join. "Abu Gaith told Jabarah that this decision could only be made by him but that it might be a good idea," CSIS wrote.

Kandahar was the Taliban base of power, where its leader Mullah Omar lived. It was also where Mohammed Jabarah first met Tawfiq Al Attash, a one-legged Yemeni whom Jabarah judged to be about 30 years of age. They met casually, and Jabarah would later tell Canadian intelligence agents their discussions had nothing to do with Al Qaeda operations, but Al Attash, better known as Khallad, was a serious, hard-core jihadist. It was in his blood. After his father was expelled from Yemen due to his radical views, Khallad had been raised in Saudi Arabia. His father knew the most extreme of the Saudi and Egyptian extremists—Abdullah Azzam, bin Laden and the "blind sheikh" Omar Abdel Rahman. At age 15, Khallad left for Afghanistan but in 1997 the lower part of his right leg was blown off during a clash with against the anti-Taliban Northern Alliance rebels. His brother died in the same battle, prompting Khallad to formally join Al Qaeda.

Khallad was described by the 9/11 commission as a "run boy" for bin Laden. He was involved in the 1998 bombings of the American embassies in Kenya and Tanzania, and the following year was assigned to travel to Yemen to help obtain explosives to blow up an American warship, the USS *Sullivans*. While in Yemen, he was also instructed to apply for a visa to visit the United States so he could take part in an emerging Al Qaeda plan to hijack American airplanes and crash them into buildings, but the visa was denied and Khallad was caught driving the car of a man wanted for his alleged role in the Yemen ship-bombing plot. His father, as well as bin Laden, intervened with the Yemeni authorities and Khallad was set free in the summer of 1999. He returned to the base, Afghanistan.

By then, Al Qaeda had adapted the airplane plot to changing circumstances. Experience had shown it was easier for Saudis to get U.S. visas than it was for Yemenis like Khallad. So Al Qaeda decided to mount two separate, but coordinated, operations, one inside the U.S. and the other outside, targeting U.S. planes in Southeast Asia. Khallad was to take part in the latter mission. The hijackers trained rigorously near Kabul before traveling to Karachi in December 1999 for more advanced urban terrorist instruction with Khalid Sheikh Mohammad, who taught them basic English, the Internet, and how to use codes and make travel reservations. They practiced on flight simulator games.

After two weeks, Khallad flew to Kuala Lumpur, then to Bangkok, where he took a test-run to Hong Kong on a U.S. airliner. He carried a box-cutter with him, just to see if he would be caught. He wasn't. He then made his way back to Kandahar to report on his scouting mission. Always a pragmatist in his deadly calculations, bin Laden decided the airplane plot was too complicated and cancelled the Asian part of it so that Al Qaeda could focus on the strike inside America. Khallad, however, continued with his jihad, helping orchestrate the bombing of the USS *Cole* in Yemen. It was a few months later that he would first meet Mohammed Jabarah at his base in Kandahar.

Khallad's experience in Al Qaeda, his combat training in Afghanistan, frontline fighting against the Northern Alliance, urban training in Karachi with KSM and clandestine mission to Southeast Asia are noteworthy because Jabarah would later follow the exact same path. It says something about Jabarah's level of indoctrination that he would not only strike up a relationship with someone as extreme as Khallad, but that he would also mimic his career path as a terrorist. Did Jabarah look up to Khallad as a mentor? Perhaps, but in the end both men would meet the same fate.

* * *

In July 2001, Jabarah took an advanced sniper course at an Al Qaeda camp at Kandahar airport. It lasted only a week, and focused exclusively on the AK-47. An expert sniper requires unique talents. He must be able to move stealthily through enemy terrain. He has to be able to camouflage himself, to blend into his surroundings. Only then can he get close enough to get off a shot. In many ways, it is like organizing a bombing attack. At the end of the course, the instructors gathered the trainees together for a competition. The snipers fired on targets and when the blasts subsided, the winner was declared. It was Mohammed Jabarah. Everyone who took part was later invited to bin Laden's house in Kandahar. When Jabarah got there, Osama was watching a video of an Al Jazeera report claiming that bin Laden was more popular than George W. Bush. The item made Osama "very proud," Jabarah noted.

Mohammed and Abu Gaith were both chosen to take a course to become bin Laden's personal bodyguards. Jabarah considered it a "great honor," and noted that even the envoy of Ibn Khattab, the Chechen rebel leader, had not been asked to take this particular course. The instruction focused on precision shooting with a quick reaction time using limited ammunition. Jabarah and Abu Gaith took the course, but they never worked as bodyguards. That summer, Jabarah was asked to become a camp instructor, but he turned down the offer. He "wanted to fight, not train," he said.

The recruits left Al Farooq and the other training camps the same way they arrived, by truck to Kandahar. From there they spread out in all directions to assume their assigned positions in Al Qaeda. Some, such as Lindh, stayed to fight with the Taliban. Others joined the jihads in Kashmir and Chechnya, or returned to their own countries to ignite homegrown Islamic movements in Algeria, Indonesia or Libya. Those from Western countries, like Richard Reid, were perhaps the most valuable to Al Qaeda since they could return to Europe and North America to conduct operations inside enemy territory, to go after what bin Laden liked to call the "head of the snake." They could exploit the rights and freedoms of Western democracies to undermine them from within. Some would just go underground and lie low, marry a local woman and get a job, and await the call to action. Others would be actively engaged in operations from the moment they got home, raising money, stealing passports, scouting targets, amassing explosives, building bombs and seeking out even more recruits. If they got caught, they would simply claim innocence and accuse Western security agencies of picking on them because of their religion.

At some point, the recruits had to make a critical choice: Were they willing to go all the way, to give themselves to Osama? If so, they would have to pledge *bayat*, the secret oath of allegiance. The concept of *bayat* dates back to the 6th century but was co-opted by Al Qaeda in the late 1980s. When Al Qaeda was created, bin Laden set out what he called the "requirements to enter Al Qaeda." They were: "listening and obedient, good manners, referred from a trusted side" and "obeying statutes and instructions of Al Qaeda." A final requirement was that prospective members had to read "the pledge" of loyalty, or *bayat*. The Mafia have a similar ritual called *omertà*. It is an act of personal surrender, in which an individual places himself entirely in the hands of his leader, organization and cause. Sometimes *bayat* was a signed statement, a contract of sorts; sometimes it was a spoken word of honor. The original *bayat*, found by U.S. investigators in Bosnia, reads:

> *The pledge of God and His covenant is upon me, to listen and obey the superiors, who are doing this work, in energy, early rising, difficulty, and easiness, and for his superiority upon us, so that the word of God will be the highest, and His religion victorious.*

To outsiders, *bayat* seems like nothing more than quaint words, uttered in barren conditions in the unpeopled loneliness of the training camp world. But an intelligence official who interviewed some of those involved in Jabarah's terrorist plots told me that those who have taken the pledge take it very much to heart. To them, *bayat* is a sacred rite. By the time recruits make *bayat*, they have been so deeply indoctrinated by their instructors, so thoroughly infused with the idea that Al Qaeda is the army of God, the last line of defense of the true Islamic faithful, that they believe their oath to Osama is a religious undertaking. Breaking *bayat* is like breaking a promise to God.

For the Al Qaeda trainees, it was not a decision to be taken lightly. It meant being willing to kill and die for the ideals of bin Laden. Neither was it a simple decision for Al Qaeda. Paranoid about infiltration by intelligence agencies, Al Qaeda took pains to ensure that only those with proven records were granted admission to the inner circle. And with so many volunteers willing to become martyrs, they could afford to be choosey. But there was only so much Al Qaeda could do to vet its perspective members. Joining the ranks of Al Qaeda likewise required a leap of faith. But the recruits were too far gone to notice. Although they were making a life-and-death decision, by the time it came to this, they had been so thoroughly indoctrinated that it hardly seemed like such a big step.

In Kuwait, Abu Gaith had been the one to see Jabarah's potential in the movement. It was Abu Gaith who had convinced him to go to Afghanistan to experience jihad for himself. And so it was natural that he would be the one to urge him on to the next level. What did Abu Gaith see in Mohammed? A manual seized by police in Manchester, England provides some clues. On the cover is a sketch of the Earth pierced by a sword and the Arabic words: "Military Studies in the Jihad against the Tyrants." The manual, later used as evidence in the prosecution of the African embassy bombers of 1998, spells out the military doctrine and strategies of the Arab Afghans who went on to form Al Qaeda. It is organized into sections, and the second section is titled, "Necessary Qualifications and Characteristics for the Organization's Members." Fourteen such characteristics are listed, beginning not surprisingly with Islam. "The member of the organization must be Muslim," it says, adding, "How can an unbeliever, someone from a revealed religion, a secular person, a communist, etc. . . . protect Islam and Muslims and defend their goals and secrets when he does not believe in that religion?"

It goes on to say that members of the "organization" have to be committed to the group ideology, that they must be mature, obedient and willing to make the ultimate sacrifice. "He has to be willing to do the work and undergo martyrdom for the purpose of achieving the goal and establishing the religion of majestic Allah on earth." Recruits must be able to keep secrets; they must be in good health and patient. "He should not abandon this great path and sell himself and his religion to the enemies for his freedom." A member has to be intelligent, as well as cautious, prudent and honest, it says. He must be good at observing and analyzing. And he must have the "ability to act." He must also possess "tranquility and unflappability," it says. "The member should have a calm personality that allows him to endure psychological traumas such as those involving bloodshed, murder, arrest, imprisonment, and reverse psychological traumas such as killing one or all of his organization's comrades. He should be able to carry out the work."

Jabarah was all of this and more. He was smart, devout and obedient. He had excelled at his military training, and he was committed to the cause. The year he had spent preparing himself for jihad was a testament to that.

Now he was ready.

The last time Jabarah met bin Laden was at the end of July 2001. Jabarah initiated the meeting through Abu Hafs' secretary. He wanted to meet with Osama privately. An appointment was arranged and Jabarah had an audience with the "Most Wanted" in Kandahar. They sat together, and Jabarah told bin Laden that he was ready to join Al Qaeda. He explained that he had excellent English language skills, a "clean" Canadian passport and that he had done well at his Al Qaeda training courses. Bin Laden was impressed. He told Jabarah that he must be ready to fight the "enemies of Allah, wherever they are," and specifically mentioned the United States and the Jews. Osama then asked him to swear an oath to Al Qaeda, which Jabarah did.

He swore the martyr's oath.

Canadian intelligence has estimated that as many as 100,000 men passed through bin Laden's training camps. Although only a fraction made *bayat*, the figure speaks to the depth of Al Qaeda's recruiting operation as well as bin Laden's remarkable ability to appeal to young Muslims from all over the world despite offering them nothing but death by martyrdom. A corporation so successful at recruiting would never want for skills. Nobody knows for sure how many of those who trained actually pledged *bayat*. One captured bin Laden loyalist told the FBI it was about 5,000 but "because *bayat* was secret, the number of Al Qaeda members can only be speculative," the 9/11 Commission reported. Khalid Sheikh Mohammad claimed that only a few hundred had pledged *bayat*, making Jabarah one of the small number of hardcore terrorists admitted to Al Qaeda's inner circle.

Perhaps when they met, bin Laden saw in Mohammed a bit of himself. Bin Laden was, like his young Canadian disciple, in his early 20s when he came to Peshawar to join the

The terrorist as a boy: Mohammed Jabarah (*right*) in Kuwait with his father Mansour and older brother Abdul Rahman.

Mohammed at an amusement park.

A Kuwaiti school portrait. Mohammed's teachers noted in his report card that he liked listening to stories. "We wish him progress and success in the future."

Mansour Jabarah with Mohammed.

Mohammed helps his father pick strawberries. The face of the other boy was cut out by the family to protect his identity.

PHOTO BY STEWART BELL

Mansour at his camp in the Kuwaiti desert, 2004.

The Kuwait Towers.

The Jabarahs' house in Kuwait City's Salwa neighborhood, where the family lived during the Iraqi occupation of 1990–91.

Mohammed in Canada: Outside his house in St. Catharines, Ontario (*top right*). In his school uniform at Holy Cross Secondary School (*below*). Masjid an Noor, the mosque in St. Catharines where the Jabarahs worshipped (*bottom*).

Sulayman Abu Gaith, the Kuwaiti teacher who recruited Mohammed and Anas Al Kandari.

Anas Al Kandari, Mohammed's best friend, who murdered a U.S. Marine in 2002 before being gunned down.

Abdul Rahman Jabarah in a school portrait in Canada.

Mohammed in his 1997 yearbook photo, taken shortly after he decided to become a mujahedin.

A member of the Khyber Khasadar Force, at a lookout above the spot where Mohammed crossed the border into Afghanistan in 2000.

A Pakistani boy memorizes the Koran at a radical madrassa in Islamabad, 2004.

PHOTO BY STEWART BELL

A young rebel soldier guards a Northern Alliance trench in Afghanistan during a lull in fighting against the Taliban and Al Qaeda, October 2001. Mohammed spent two weeks at the front fighting the rebel forces.

Two images taken from an Al Qaeda propaganda video called "Destroying the American Destroyer." Mohammed later told the FBI that the video shows his mountain warfare training group.

Dangerous company: During his training in Afghanistan, Mohammed contracted hepatitis and was treated by Ayman Al Zawahiri, Al Qaeda's second-in-command (*top left*). He met Osama bin Laden (*top right*) four times. Mohammed was later trained in Karachi by Khalid Sheikh Mohammad (*bottom left*). Bin Laden's military chief Mohammed Atef (*bottom right*) approved the Singapore bombing operation.

Plotting terror: Mohammed worked closely in Southeast Asia with terrorists Nurjaman Riduan Isamuddin, aka Hambali, aka Azman (*top left*), and Fathur Rohman Al-Ghozi, aka Mike the Bombmaker, aka Saad (*top right*). Below are images from Jabarah's CSIS file, taken from a surveillance camera.

Singapore. Mohammed orchestrated the attempted bombings of the American and Israeli embassies, as well as other commercial and public buildings. The attacks were thwarted but could have killed as many as 3,000 people.

PHOTO BY STEWART BELL

PHOTO BY STEWART BELL

The Malaysian-Thai border (*center*), and the bus station in Kuala Lumpur (*bottom*). When the Singapore police moved against Jabarah's cell, he fled north to Thailand by bus.

PHOTO BY STEWART BELL

Through the eyes of a terrorist: A sequence of images taken from a surveillance video filmed by Mohammed when he was scouting the Israeli embassy in Singapore in 2001. Three tons of explosives were to be used to destroy the embassy.

The airline tickets that Mohammed used to return to Canada in the
company of two CSIS agents, following his capture in Oman.

PHOTO BY PETER REDMAN/*NATIONAL POST*

Mike Pavlovic, the CSIS Intelligence Officer assigned to get Mohammed to talk.

James B. Comey, the New York prosecutor who convinced Mohammed to surrender to the United States and cooperate with the FBI in exchange for unspecified benefits.

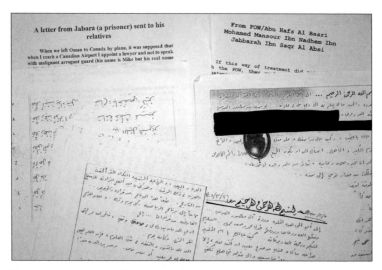

Some of the letters Mohammed has sent home to his parents and brothers from the Metropolitan Correctional Center in New York.

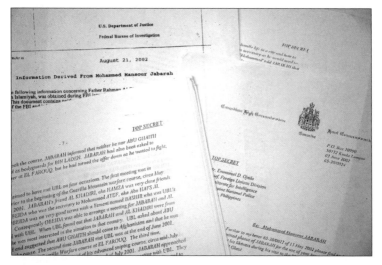

Top Secret: A sample of the intelligence documents describing Mohammed's exploits.

Abdul Rahman Jabarah, in the photo distributed by the Saudi government when he was a wanted man. He was killed in a stand-off in 2003.

jihad against the Soviets. Both came from established Arabian business families from the same part of the world, and both were articulate, smart and ideologically and religiously devout. Maybe as he sat with Mohammed and heard him pleading for an assignment, offering his services for the cause, bin Laden was reminded of himself so many years ago, a naïve but impassioned youngster at the side of his own idol, Abdullah Azzam.

After Jabarah had made his pledge, bin Laden told him to go to a place in Kandahar called the Media House to "exercise" and await further instructions. Mohammed had always wanted to fight in Chechnya, but he never did meet Ibn Khattab, although he did meet his representative in Afghanistan, Dahak, at the Chechen guesthouse in Kandahar. But the meeting had been discouraging. Dahak had told Jabarah they were not allowing any more Arabs to travel to Chechnya because they were having difficulties "hiding them." Mohammed had spent more than a year training, and if he wasn't going to Chechnya, he had to do something else.

He would give himself to Osama instead.

Bin Laden had come to think of the United States as an "octopus with many arms." The way to kill an octopus, he told Mohammed, was not to strike at its arms, but to hit its head. Osama wanted Al Qaeda's efforts to focus on continuous blows to the head of the octopus.

Jabarah's assignment came within days. He was told to travel to Karachi to meet Mohammad the Pakistani, who would give him instructions and money for "an operation."

Jabarah said goodbye to Al Kandari at the guesthouse in Kandahar and left for Karachi to meet Mohammad the Pakistani, who was just then finalizing plans for a spectacular strike against America.

9

KARACHI

MOHAMMAD the Pakistani, it turned out, was actually a
Kuwaiti, although he traced his roots to Pakistan's Baluchistan
region and chose his alias accordingly. His real name was Khalid
Sheikh Mohammad and he had been a wanted man since 1996,
when he was indicted in Manhattan for plotting to bomb U.S.
passenger planes flying out of Southeast Asia. Burly and devout,
he had come of age in the deserts outside Kuwait City, just like
Jabarah. They had something else in common as well. Khalid,
or KSM as he is commonly known, had lived in the West. He
had studied at Chowan College in North Carolina and at North
Carolina A&T State University, graduating with a Bachelor of
Science degree.

He left the United States in 1986 and went immediately to
Peshawar to join the jihad against the Soviets. He trained at an
Afghan mujahedin camp and fought for a few months before
returning to Pakistan to serve as an assistant to bin Laden's
mentor, Abdullah Azzam. After the war in Afghanistan was
won, he became increasingly radical and fought in Bosnia
before moving to Qatar to work as an engineer. In his spare
time, he dreamed up increasingly imaginative ways of killing

masses of people in the name of God. From Qatar, he helped his nephew Ramzi Yousef organize the 1993 truck bombing of the World Trade Center. The plot did not go as planned and KSM reunited with Yousef in Manila to try something else. The failure of the New York plot caused KSM to ponder other methods of attack against the United States, which led him to begin focusing on planes.

First came Project Bojinka, which envisioned the bombing of a dozen U.S. passenger planes. KSM and Yousef spent months preparing. They scouted flights and tested the security defenses they would face. Members of their underground cell were mixing explosives in a Manila apartment when a fire broke out and they were caught. Yousef was arrested in February 1995 but KSM fled to Pakistan to escape arrest. He arrived just as bin Laden was returning to Afghanistan after being kicked out of Sudan, and the two terrorists, who shared the bond of having fought the Soviets, began to conspire. While bin Laden worked out a deal with the Taliban that would allow him to use Afghanistan as the base for his global jihad, KSM forged ties with radical Islamists in Southeast Asia and continued to challenge his engineer's mind to think up a way of using airplanes as a weapon of terror. In January 1997, he moved his family to Karachi.

In the crowded Pakistani port city, KSM operated his own school for terrorists. Karachi was no substitute for the training camps that bin Laden was running in Afghanistan, but the terrorist plots that KSM was planning were not going to take place in empty terrain like the hills of Jalalabad. They were going to take place in big cities. His initial plan was to hijack ten commercial planes inside the United States and crash nine of them into buildings on both coasts. The tenth plane would land and KSM would step out to deliver a press conference. The "planes operation" was eventually scaled back but proceeded with bin Laden's blessing.

Those who would carry out KSM's missions needed to train in an urban setting. Most of them had spent months in Afghanistan, one of the most backward countries in the world, where time had all but stopped, and they needed a place where they could adjust to the chaos of the modern world. Otherwise, they risked being spotted by security officials. They also needed specialized training on how to operate in cities. As an educated man who had lived in the United States, KSM was the perfect teacher. And Karachi was the perfect place. Big enough to make it a challenge for police to keep track of what was going on and already an operational base for a variety of Islamic militant groups, the city was an ideal urban training ground. And it had an international airport with flights to the Middle East, the Gulf, Southeast Asia and Europe.

With money from bin Laden, KSM rented a safe house in Karachi for his students. Four of the men being prepared for the 9/11 attacks trained in Karachi under KSM. He gave them English lessons and instructions on how to conduct themselves once they were in the United States, such as how to rent an apartment, how to order food at popular restaurants and how to use a phone book. They watched movies about hijackings and played flight-simulator games on a computer. The training program lasted about two weeks. One of the trainees was Jabarah's friend from Kandahar, Tawfiq Al Attash, who was being sent to the United States via Malaysia to serve as a "muscle hijacker." He never made it due to visa problems and instead returned to Afghanistan, where he proposed to bin Laden a plan to hijack a U.S. plane in Malaysia, Thailand, Hong Kong or Singapore.

By the middle of August 2001, it was Jabarah's turn for urban training. He had earned it through his hard work in Afghanistan. The last time he had seen the city was when he had landed there from Kuwait on his way to Peshawar. That was over a year ago but so much had happened since then. He had not joined the Chechen campaign but he had found his calling as a secret operative. He was in the Al Qaeda elite. When he arrived in Karachi, he got a room at the Embassy Hotel and spent the next two weeks with KSM, who gave him advice on how to handle life in the city and how to prepare himself for his Al Qaeda missions. "This was necessary as he would need to become reacquainted with life 'outside' Afghanistan," notes a Canadian intelligence report. Jabarah's first assignment was to oversee a suicide bombing that was being planned. He was not going to be a suicide bomber or driver. Jabarah was far too precious to waste on a single operation. "He was considered a more valuable entity given his abilities, language capability and his clean Canadian passport," the Canadian Security Intelligence Service reported.

The attack was to take place in Manila, KSM said. Jabarah was to handle the financing of the operation and serve as a go-between, a link between Al Qaeda and the local terrorists, who were members of Jemaah Islamiyah (JI). Early in September 2001, about a week into his training, Jabarah visited the Karachi apartment of the man who had the details of the plot. He was a 37-year-old West Javanese Indonesian named Nurjaman Riduan Isamuddin. But he went by the name "Hambali." "During the course of the past decade," a report by the Canadian government's Integrated National Security Assessment Centre says, "Hambali has been linked to most of the major bombings in Southeast Asia, as well as Al Qaeda operations outside the region dating back to the 1993 World Trade Center bombing." It adds that, "He is the only non-Arab to become a high-ranking Al Qaeda member and is a conduit between the JI and Al Qaeda."

Although born in Indonesia, Hambali had left for Malaysia in the mid-1980s and became a follower of radical cleric Abdullah Sungkar. In 1986, he ventured off to Pakistan to join the anti-Soviet jihad. He trained for two months before joining a brigade of non-Afghan fighters made up of Filipino and Thai Muslims. It was during the war that Hambali first met KSM. They met again later in the mid-1990s, when KSM made two trips to Malaysia to plan his planes operation. During his last visit, in 1996, KSM noted that Hambali did not have a jihad program. He invited Hambali to return to Afghanistan to meet bin Laden. Hambali did so that year and spent four days with Osama before the two agreed to work together "on mutually beneficial targets."

In 1999, Sungkar sent Hambali to meet KSM in Karachi to discuss sending Jemaah Islamiyah recruits to Afghanistan for training. At first, Hambali was interested only in attacks against the Indonesian government, but KSM convinced him that he could better serve his cause by striking the United States and its Western allies. KSM helped out the JI by sending "operatives to travel to Southeast Asia to serve entirely at Hambali's disposal, while at other times he sent operatives to the region for his own purposes," according to the reports of his interrogators.

Hambali studied surveillance reports of the U.S. embassy in Jakarta, which were later passed on to Mohammed Atef, the al-Qaeda military chief. By 2000, Hambali was looking at such targets as the U.S. and Israeli embassies in Manila, as well as hotels and businesses in the city of Makati. Singapore was also emerging as a possible target for Hambali. "Hambali's aim was to create a situation in Malaysia and Singapore, which would be conducive to overthrowing the Malaysian government and provoking a revolution that would turn Malaysia into an Islamic state," the Singapore government noted in its white paper on Jemaah Islamiyah. "Hambali's plan was to attack key Singapore installations and to represent them as acts of aggression by the Malaysian government. Hambali wanted to provoke distrust and animosity between a 'Muslim Malaysia' and 'Chinese Singapore' and cause ethnic strife in both countries. Hambali's hope was that Muslims in both Malaysia and Singapore would then respond to calls for jihad and turn Malaysia and Singapore into another Ambon (the scene of sectarian violence between Indonesian Christians and Muslims)."

By the time Jabarah met him, Hambali was focused on the Philippines. He wanted to hit Western targets, and there was no shortage of them in Manila. The exact targets were not yet determined, but the American and Israeli embassies were on the short list. Hambali told Jabarah he would be working with several Malaysians and Indonesians: Faiz Bafana, "Azzam," and a bomb expert, Fathur Al-Ghozi, also known as Saad or Mike the Bombmaker, although the whereabouts of the latter was not known at the time, since he had gone off somewhere to fight and had not returned. Mike was going to buy the explosives. Hambali gave Jabarah a phone number to call once he reached Kuala Lumpur.

Hambali liked to communicate with his operatives by email. When he wanted to send a message to Jabarah, he would email the address Honda_civic12@yahoo.com. Messages from KSM would be sent to silver_crack2002@yahoo.com. Jabarah could contact the operatives in Malaysia using bob_marley123@yahoo.com. It was a secure system, almost untraceable. Mohammed would know who was sending the messages, but nobody else would. Just to be careful, Hambali warned Jabarah to check his messages only at cyber cafés, and to change Internet cafés often. "It is very hard to track a cyber café, and if it was identified, it would be difficult to identify the person on the computer," he told Jabarah. Whatever he did, Jabarah was not to use a cellular phone. If he had to call, Hambali cautioned, he should use a pay phone.

The next day, KSM gave Jabarah $10,000 in cash for expenses and told him to go to Malaysia, find out what was needed to bomb the American and Israeli embassies in Manila and send back a report by email. And there was one more thing, KSM said.

"Make sure you leave before Tuesday."

10

SAMMY THE TERRORIST

MANY people think radical thoughts. Some join radical movements and agitate for radical change. But only a select few enter the world of radical violence. There is no shortage of guerrillas and insurgents in the world, but becoming a terrorist is something different. The rebel is just a soldier in an improvised uniform, using the traditional tactics of warfare to fight for whatever cause has inflamed his or her passions, be it territorial aspirations, ideology or the struggle for self-determination.

The terrorist, on the other hand, seeks by definition to terrorize. To be effective, the terrorist must become someone the very thought of whom strikes fear in others. The terrorist does this by committing violence that is so indiscriminate, so random, so horrific that its practitioners seem inhuman, as if they will stop at nothing to get what they want: slaughtering school children in Russia; detonating a suicide vest on a Jerusalem bus; blowing up Spaniards commuting to work on the morning train; beheading hostages with a sword and then distributing the videotape.

Mohammed Jabarah knew he was stepping across that line. When KSM told him to leave before Tuesday, Mohammed suspected something was up. He thought a "big operation" was scheduled for that day, although he told investigators later that he did not know where or when. He left Pakistan on Monday, September 10, 2001. In a hotel room in Hong Kong the next day, he watched the looped news footage of airplanes piercing the Twin Towers and New Yorkers fleeing through streets clouded with smoke and dust. When the photographs of the hijackers were shown, he recognized four of them as fellow Al Qaeda trainees he had met at a guesthouse in Kandahar that March. He watched the television, and he hesitated. He asked himself whether he could go through with it. Could he carry out this mission of death that had been assigned to him?

It was one of those times that everyone has to confront at some point—should I or shouldn't I? But Mohammed's answer was going to affect not only his own life, but also the lives of the hundreds of innocents he had been assigned to kill.

He could have pulled back right then.

It would have been easy enough. He had the wad of cash that KSM had given him. He could have used it to buy a plane ticket to Toronto, and that would have been the end of it. He would have been just another of the tens of thousands of idealistic young Muslims who made their way to Afghanistan to pay homage to bin Laden. Others before him had done just that, and decided after meeting bin Laden that he was just an egotistical fanatic trying to get his way—someone hardly worth the sacrifice of one's life.

Except for his two weeks of combat at the Taliban front, Mohammed had not yet done any real harm. He could have flown back to Canada and left it all behind—admitted he had made a terrible mistake and moved on. He could have walked into the Canadian embassy and offered to tell everything he knew. He was only 19, and people might understand how the Al Qaeda recruiting machine had exploited him for so long and at such a young age. Had he turned back, there would have been little the authorities could have done. He had not broken any laws in Canada, at least not at the time.

But he didn't do that.

Mohammed paused, but only long enough to make sure he was certain of what he was doing. He felt that since bin Laden had personally chosen him for this mission, out of all the men in Afghanistan, he could not pull out. How could he? He had made an oath before God to bin Laden. This was about a cause that was much bigger than Mohammed; who was he to disobey? Bin Laden and KSM had given him this assignment; he was serving Al Qaeda and God. He could not question that. After all, he was Mohammed Mansour bin Nazem Al-Aboussi, the descendent of the great Antara. Even Antara had his moments of hesitation, for instance, when he watched his victims bleeding to death on the battlefield, but he got over it when he heard the shouts of "Antara, on!" Mohammed became a terrorist knowingly and willingly. He crossed the line with his eyes wide open. And once you become a terrorist, there is no going back. Mohammed knew what he was doing. What he did not know was that he was already being hunted.

* * *

A few weeks after the Canadian Security Intelligence Service first heard about Mohammed and Abdul Rahman Jabarah and their extremist talk at the mosque, intelligence officers began seeking approval to make the brothers the targets of an intelligence investigation. CSIS is not a large agency; the ongoing challenge is to decide where its limited number of agents and analysts should focus their efforts. What should be the priorities for intelligence-gathering? The trick is to make sure the various operations going on at any one time are proportional to the threat. And the rule of thumb at CSIS was that investigations had to proceed incrementally, starting with the least intrusive methods and advancing from there as required.

No investigation can begin without what is called a targeting authority. Under the *CSIS Act*, before intelligence officers can begin working a case they must get approval from management. There are three levels of authority. Level 1 allows agents to conduct background checks on the target. They can verify databases, look for police records and consult with friendly foreign partners. A Level 2 investigation allows covert surveillance, interviews and consultations with human sources in the field. The more serious cases go to the Target Approval and Review Committee, or TARC. The TARC is chaired by the Director, and includes the Deputy Director of Operations, Assistant Director of Operations, the heads of the counter-intelligence, counter-proliferation and counter-terrorism branches, and representatives from the Department of Justice and the Deputy Minister. Submissions to TARC have to describe the purpose of the investigation and how the activities of the proposed targets are a threat to the security of Canada.

The TARC deals mostly with Level 3 investigations, the most intrusive kind. A Level 3 approval gives agents the authority to recruit and task human sources against a target. It also gives CSIS the option to ask the Federal Court of Canada for a warrant authorizing covert searches and the interception of communications. If such powers are sought, a case brief is drafted and goes to the legal desk, which prepares an affidavit. The affidavit goes to a review committee, then to the minister before being presented to the court. This entire process and all its paperwork are regularly audited by the Security Intelligence Review Committee, which reports to Parliament. In the year the investigation of the Jabarah brothers began, CSIS obtained 111 new warrants, and another 155 from previous years were either replaced or renewed.

The targeting approval process is "an essential feature of how we do business," Jack Hooper, the CSIS Assistant Director, testified at an inquiry in 2004. "We are dealing for the most part with phenomena—whether they are related to proliferation issues or espionage or terrorism—that are highly internationalized. I think dealing with those threats begs a coherent response and certainly a coordinated national response for dealing with those threats. Our service is a highly centralized organization because it has to be, and TARC is simply an element of that centralization." In 2001, agents prepared a submission seeking a Level 3 authority to investigate the Jabarah brothers. The TARC, which was then headed by Ward Elcock, the longtime CSIS director, gave its consent. CSIS was going to use its most intrusive techniques to try to figure out what Mohammed and Abdul Rahman were up to.

At about 1:30 p.m., on the afternoon of September 11, 2001, two Canadian intelligence officers, one male and one female, knocked on Mansour Jabarah's door in St. Catharines. During their previous visits, the agents had been guarded, asking questions but never letting on what they suspected. They would say things like, "Maybe your sons went over to Afghanistan," and Mansour would reply, "No way. If they are going to go somewhere, they are going to tell me first." This time it was different. The agents were more direct. They started to talk more openly about their suspicions.

"We are searching for your sons," Mansour recalls them saying. "Your sons [are] over in Afghanistan. They are living over there getting courses and camping with Osama bin Laden."

"I did not know anything about this," Mansour says he replied.

That night, someone set fire to the St. Catharines mosque.

CSIS agents knocked on a lot of doors in the days and weeks after 9/11. It was part of a "we're watching you" campaign. Fears of a second wave of attacks in North America had security agencies on full alert. CSIS had more targets than it could control, so the agency decided to mount a diffusion campaign. Agents would knock on doors and let their targets know they shouldn't try anything because they were being monitored. Some of the extremists scattered or left the country, spooked by the realization that CSIS was on to them. But some of them invited the agents into their homes and provided information. CSIS was not able to find the Jabarahs, and whenever agents went to the family house in St. Catharines, they got the same response: The boys are studying in Pakistan. The agency suspected they were still abroad with bin Laden, but they were concerned the brothers might return to Canada to put their terror skills to work, so they kept working on the file. Mansour grew tired of the CSIS agents and their questions. He thought the house was being watched. He felt harassed.

"Let's go back to Kuwait," he said.

It took Mohammed three days to get his passport stamped in Hong Kong. From there he flew three hours west to Kuala Lumpur International Airport, which was to be his operations base. Malaysia was never intended as an attack target for Al Qaeda. It was a source of money and recruits, and as a predominantly Muslim nation that had experience fighting terrorism but that did not see Al Qaeda as a particular threat, it was considered a safe place for Mohammed to do his work. The books for sale at the Sultan Ismail Petra Airport in the northern Malaysian city of Kota Bahru, near the restive Thai border, offer some insights into the Malaysian perspective: two dozen copies of *The International Jew*; another book about "the Zionist conspiracy" called *The New International Jew*; a whole selection of titles claiming the 9/11 attacks were the work of the CIA and Israel. (For some reason, these are positioned near a stack of *Women's Guide to Orgasm: Pathways to Pleasure*.) I also find a copy of *The Judgment of Islam on the Crimes of Salmon Rushdie*. On the cover is a sketch of the author hanging from a noose. "It is the duty of Muslims to chase him all his life, and he will not remain out of our grasp forever . . . We can't keep silent when we are insulted." Then there is *Jihad in the Qur'an*, which details the religious justifications for taking up arms in defense of Islam.

* * *

A significant number of Malaysians have taken up arms for the jihadi cause. The border region where Malaysia meets Thailand is a lush land of palm trees, houses on stilts and songbirds in wooden cages, but it is also a perennial trouble spot. The militant groups Kumpalan Mujahedin Malaysia and Jemaah Islamiyah have used the region as a recruiting, training and operational base for many years. More recently, the border region has been the scene of a violent insurgency that seeks independence for southern Thailand's Muslims. During my brief visit to the region in February 2005, a half-dozen bombs exploded. Assassins raced the streets clinging to the back of motor-scooters and opened fire as they passed police officers. Thai soldiers patrolled in armored vehicles and waited behind sandbags and concertina wire at checkpoints on the major roads. In the town of Rangae, the bloodstains from a bombing that morning were still drying at the side of the road. A wanted poster at the police headquarters offered rewards for the leading insurgents, some of them Thai and some Malaysian.

Malaysia became a base of Islamic extremism in the mid-1980s. When the Suharto regime in Indonesia cracked down against Darul Islam, or House of Islam, a group that advocated armed struggle to impose Islamic law, some of its members fled across the Malacca Straits to Malaysia. There, they relaunched their organization as Jemaah Islamiyah (JI) and began a recruiting drive throughout the region. When one of the JI leaders, Abdullah Sungkar, ventured off to Afghanistan to fight in the anti-Soviet jihad, he laid the foundations for his group's longstanding close relations with Al Qaeda. Upon Sungkar's death in 1999, Abu Bakar Bashir assumed the role of the group's ideological leader, and over the next two years JI began preparing for terrorist attacks intended to create a pan-Islamic state encompassing Malaysia, Singapore, Indonesia, Brunei, Cambodia, the southern Philippines and southern Thailand. The first major JI attacks were the December 2000 bombings of churches in Indonesia, followed by a train bombing in Manila.

There are an estimated 5,000 members of JI, several hundred of whom are said to be "operationally oriented."

When Mohammed Jabarah arrived in Kuala Lumpur, he checked his email and found a message from KSM. It said that if the Southeast Asia operation seemed like it was going to take a long time, Jabarah should consider returning to Pakistan for the time being. Jabarah seriously thought about leaving. He even went to the Pakistan embassy to get a visa, but it was denied on a technicality. The embassy would not grant him a visa unless he had a Malaysian work permit in his passport, which he did not have. The visa request was forwarded to Islamabad for consideration, but in the end it was refused. Jabarah decided to stay in Malaysia and push ahead with the operation.

For his mission, Jabarah needed a code name. It was too dangerous to use his real name, and everybody in Al Qaeda had at least a couple of aliases. Mohammed's Al Qaeda name was Abu Hafs, but he needed something less likely to attract attention (Abu Hafs was also the Al Qaeda name of bin Laden's military chief Mohammed Atef). He needed something that would make him sound like a Western tourist. Code names "should not be odd in comparison with other names used around him," says the jihadi training manual, adding, "A brother should not have more than one name in the area where he lives."

Mohammed chose the name "Sammy."

He might have just picked it randomly. Or maybe he chose it because it was a Westernized version of the name of his leader: Osama.

Jabarah called the number that Hambali had given him in Karachi. Azzam answered and Mohammed identified himself using the code name "Mohammed Ibrahim." They met at the office of Azzam's home security business. It was about the size of a two-bedroom apartment. Azzam's real name was Zulkifli Marzuki. He looked to be about thirty-five. He was a Malaysian with a wife and a job installing home alarms and locks. He was a terrorist in the security business. Like the other members of

Southeast Asia's underground jihadi movement, he understood the security advantages of communicating by email. His address, jonathan1000us@yahoo.com, gave no hints as to his identity.

Jabarah told Azzam he had been sent by "Mohammed the Pakistani" and asked how much money would be needed to blow up the American and Israeli embassies in Manila. Azzam told him the local cell already had $10,000 to $15,000 that they were willing to "donate to the cause," as well as four tons of ammonium nitrate and 300 kilograms of TNT. Jabarah told Azzam he wanted to meet Faiz Bafana and Fathur Rohman Al-Ghozi. Bafana was a Malaysian businessman and contractor who had a civil engineering degree and was a leading figure in the JI's regional *shura* council. Al-Ghozi was an Indonesian explosives expert better known as Mike the Bombmaker, who had trained in Afghanistan and was a member of the Moro Islamic Liberation Front in the Philippines. He had already killed 22 people when he bombed a Light Railway Train in Manila in 2000. But Azzam told Jabarah that neither man was in town. Bafana was away on a "business trip" and Mike was "in the Philippines training with the rebels."

When Bafana returned to Malaysia, he met with Jabarah. Mohammed explained that he needed to go to Manila to get things going. Bafana told Mohammed to take along Ahmed Sahagi, who was to be one of the suicide bombers. (Sahagi had spent September 11, 2001, with KSM, and had told Jabarah that the plane downed in Pennsylvania was headed for the White House.) Bafana said he would contact Mike, who would contact them by email once they arrived.

They left right away.

They checked into the Horizon Hotel in Makati, and a few days later Mike emailed Jabarah with a phone number to call. They got together at the hotel. Mike's Arabic was fluent, and he knew his craft, having been trained in Afghanistan in 1995 by the infamous Abu Khabbab. According to Mike's calculations, the 300 kilos of TNT already amassed was not enough for the job. He estimated that four tons of explosives were required. He needed more time and more money.

There was another problem. Mike felt that the American embassy in Manila was set so far back from the road that it was going to be difficult to hit. To prove his point, he took Jabarah to have a look. He was right. It was a fortress. The Israeli embassy was also a difficult target because it was located in an office tower. There was a very real risk the operation would cause no significant damage. Mike wanted to go to Malaysia to confer with the others about the plot. Jabarah and Ahmed spent ten days in Manila and then returned to Kuala Lumpur separately to avoid suspicion.

When he reached Kuala Lumpur, Jabarah told Azzam to arrange a meeting with Bafana and Mike. Jabarah waited. Finally, he got an email from Azzam saying that Mike was back in Malaysia. They met and discussed the situation in Malay, occasionally translating for Mohammed. In the end, they were unanimous. The targets in Manila were no good. Jabarah and Mike, they decided, would go to Singapore to come up with a new plan of attack.

II

THE SINGAPORE PLOT

TRAVELING on separate days, Sammy and Mike made their way south by bus to Johor and crossed the Second Link Bridge into Singapore. Mike got a room for both of them at the Royal India Hotel, although he registered under the name Alih Adam Randy and claimed to be a Filipino. The key to pulling off this attack was going to be the network of local operatives who knew the city, its targets and security services. Sammy had been taught how to organize an Al Qaeda attack, and he had the cash to pay for it, but he needed the help of people who had street-sense in Singapore, who could take care of the day-to-day tasks while he kept his mind on the big picture.

Near the hotel, Sammy met with members of the Fiah Musa, an operational cell of Jemaah Islamiyah's (JI) Singapore branch. Their names were Mohamed Ellias, Adnan bin Musa, Mohamed Nazir and Mohammed Uthman. Together with two other cells of the JI, the Fiah Musa had already started to lay the groundwork for attacks in Singapore. They had videotaped the Yishun Mass

Rapid Transit station and sent a copy of the tape, along with diagrams of the train station, to Afghanistan. Al Qaeda military commander Mohammed Atef, a.k.a. Abu Hafs, had watched it and given his blessing for the bombing to go ahead.

At least five other options for bombing Western interests in Singapore had been developed as well. One target was the shuttle bus that carried U.S. military personnel and their families from Sembawang Wharf to the Yishun transit station. Another plan involved an attack against U.S. naval vessels near the Changi Naval Base using an explosives-laden suicide boat. Operatives studied the movements of navy ships from a restaurant in Johor, Malaysia and identified a narrow channel as the best spot to strike. The Paya Lebar Airbase was also considered a possible target; an operative took more than 50 surveillance photos using a digital camera. The Singapore American School and American and Israeli businesses were likewise scouted. Finally, the list of potential targets included critical infrastructure in Singapore— water pipelines, for example. The intention was to make it look like Malaysia was responsible and thereby provoke war between the two neighbors.

Mohammed Jabarah was not a lone wolf terrorist. He was not the kind who worked by himself, plotting quietly in isolation. For Mohammed, terrorism had always been a brotherhood. When he had traveled to Afghanistan for training, he had gone with his brother and best friend, and although he had left them behind when he took this assignment, he had found a new circle of brothers among the notables of Southeast Asian terrorism. Maybe that's why he felt so comfortable in this strange life: the bonds of friendship that a terrorist network offered. Mohammed was different from the others, though. For one, he was smarter. He was younger as well, and more worldly, having been schooled in the West. And while the others were affiliated with regional factions like Jemaah Islamiyah and the Moro Islamic Liberation Front, Mohammed was Al Qaeda. He was one of bin Laden's men.

Jabarah told the local operatives that his plan was to use truck-bombs to attack the U.S. and Israeli embassies. They met again in a parking lot in the upscale Marina South district and Jabarah briefed his contacts. He asked if there were any other targets they thought he should be looking at; they suggested the Australian and British High Commissions, and "soft targets" such as commercial buildings housing American companies. Then they took Jabarah on a tour of the city, to see the sites they intended to destroy.

* * *

Singapore is the vision of Sir Thomas Stamford Raffles, a British East India Company officer who set out to claim an important seaport and trading post for the Empire, but also to create an orderly, enlightened city. He laid out the streets according to a neat grid and organized the city into ethnic *kampongs*. The city boomed throughout the 19th century with the arrival of thousands of Chinese workers. Today the country has 4.4 million people of Chinese, Malay and Indian extraction who live side by side without any noticeable tension. Raffles is still revered by Singaporeans, and his name survives in the Raffles Country Club, Raffles Hospital, Raffles Culinary Academy, Raffles Museum and the Raffles Hotel, where Somerset Maugham and Joseph Conrad stayed during their literary excursions to the Far East. Although a modern Asian urban center, Singapore still retains some of its British colonial character—lovely, large homes and lush gardens. The city is a pleasant, though somewhat sterile, oasis in the chaos that is Asia. The sense of order instilled by Raffles continues as well. The laws are strict, and strictly enforced. Littering is illegal and punished severely. It is a challenge to find even a scrap of garbage on the ground. Chewing gum is banned. Anyone caught with drugs risks the death penalty. The country is among the world's wealthiest, with a boisterous shopping district along Orchard Road. Singapore is a neat, orderly, wealthy, secular democracy on friendly terms with the West. In other words, to Al Qaeda, it was an ideal place to unleash the incendiary forces of terrorism.

In Singapore, the interests of Jemaah Islamiyah and Al Qaeda converged. JI wanted to terrorize the Americans into leaving because it thought their presence was standing in the way of uniting Southeast Asia under *shariah*. For its part, Al Qaeda wanted to strike the West again to show its foes and its followers that, three months after 9/11, bin Laden was still a potent force. More importantly, it was an opportunity to kill infidels for God. The Al Qaeda leadership understands well the formula of terrorism. Terrorist attacks are about impact. The trick is to generate the most attention and panic with the least effort. Skilled terrorists like KSM know that a critical factor in the equation is the setting. An act of terrorism in an orderly city like Singapore will have a bigger impact because of the contrast between the environment and the chaos of terror.

As Jabarah toured Singapore with Mike, he might have noticed the similarities to the land of his birth. Like Kuwait, Singapore is tiny but wealthy. It endured a brutal Japanese occupation, just as Kuwait suffered under Saddam. But Mohammed's mind appeared to be more focused on the task at hand: mass killing. During his reconnaissance outings, he thought that the American embassy looked vulnerable. It was close to the street and had few barriers. It seemed an easier target than the embassy in Manila, which had heavy security and might only be damaged if a plane were used. Jabarah and his local contacts bought a video camera and recorded the targets on their list. They were careful to make it look like they were tourists. When they were filming, one of them would sometimes pose in the foreground, as if they were only sightseeing. They filmed the U.S. embassy from a bus stop across the street and then got into their car and drove past the British and Australian High Commissions. The images were later downloaded onto a diskette that was labeled, "Visiting Singapore Sightseeing."

Later, they did a drive-by of the Israeli embassy and Mohammed held the camera in the back seat, recording for the 15 seconds it took to make a pass at moderate speed.

It would have taken nerves of steel and considerable skill to videotape those buildings. Singapore is a heavily policed state, where anything remotely suspicious is reported to the authorities. When I visited the country in February 2005, with a television cameraman, photographing embassies was next to impossible. At the U.S. embassy, a man with an M-16 appeared when we started filming, and a security officer in plain clothes took our photos. Later, at the Israeli embassy, we were detained for filming a few seconds of footage. Four police officers questioned us apologetically and politely, checked our passports repeatedly and finally called in two security officers from headquarters who questioned us again. Speaking in the clipped dialect known as Singlish, they asked to see our videotape and said that, even if we weren't terrorists ourselves, we might sell our tape to terrorists. They let us go after two hours. "Please, if you see anything suspicious, report it to the police."

Embassies were understandably sensitive sites in Singapore at the time we were there, but Jabarah was there during the period just after 9/11, when governments everywhere were in a state of heightened vigilance. Mohammed, however, gave no hints he was afraid of getting caught. He had been trained well by KSM, who had taught him how to avoid detection. "The group thrived on secrecy using code-names and code-words for communication," Singapore's Ministry of Home Affairs said in its report on the plot. The Singaporeans were cautious about their security, but as the warrior Antara had said, "Caution cannot avert destiny and fate."

Mike the Bombmaker and Mohammed both studied the surveillance videos carefully. They calculated that they needed 21 tons of explosives altogether. Faiz Bafana already had four tons of ammonium nitrate hidden in Malaysia, so they told one of their local contacts, Mohamed Ellias, a 29-year-old Indian and a reservist in the Singapore Air Force, to find another 17 tons. They also needed trucks and a warehouse where the vehicles could be stored and rigged. Each truck was to carry three tons of explosives—the equivalent of the 1995 Oklahoma City bombing. Mike gave Ellias $5,500 to cover expenses and returned to Manila in November to look for TNT.

The plan was classic Al Qaeda. Six truck bombs would explode simultaneously at separate locations around Singapore. The targets were symbolic and Western, although many Singaporeans would also die. The local operatives would do the planning and preparations, but Arab suicide bombers would be brought in by Jabarah at the last minute to carry out the operation. On the morning of the attack, the trucks would be parked outside the targeted buildings and the bombers would finish the job. The attacks were scheduled to take place between 8 a.m. and 10 a.m., just as people were arriving for work. The reconnaissance work done, Mike went to the Philippines to get the rest of the materials he needed for his bombs. Jabarah took the bus back across the Tuas border crossing and returned to Kuala Lumpur to make the final plans.

"Sammy," however, had not gone unnoticed by the authorities in Singapore. After the 9/11 attacks, Singapore was one of many nations that stepped up its monitoring of Sunni Islamic extremists in anticipation of further attacks. After the horror of the World Trade Center, it was the prudent thing to do, and Singapore is a prudent nation. There were a lot of red herrings—tips about people selling Osama T-shirts, for example—but some promising intelligence also came in. One of those targeted by Singapore's Internal Security Department (ISD) was Mohammad Aslam bin Yar Ali Khan.

It began, as it often does, with a tip. A member of the public had come forward with information about Khan, a Singaporean of Pakistani ancestry. The tipster told the authorities that Khan had boasted he knew bin Laden. The ISD began a surveillance operation. Just when talk of war in Afghanistan was escalating due to the Taliban's refusal to hand over bin Laden to the

Americans, Khan suddenly left the country on a flight for Pakistan on October 4, but agents in Singapore continued monitoring some of Khan's associates, including his close friend Mohamed Ellias.

Ellias did three things that caught the attention of the investigators. First, he converted $3,500 into local currency (money Mike and Jabarah had given him to buy explosives). Second, he started asking around about buying a large amount of ammonium nitrate, even though he was not even remotely involved in agriculture. And finally, he was seen meeting with two foreigners who used the names Mike and Sammy. The investigators thought that Mike was a Filipino, but they were unsure about Jabarah. He seemed to be a Westerner but he did not look like an *ang moh*, a Caucasian. He looked Arabic. Although Sammy made every effort to appear normal, like he was just another tourist, when investigators looked more closely they began to suspect he could be someone of importance. He had to be. He was a foreigner in contact with local jihadists who were shopping for explosives. He must be connected, but who was he?

* * *

If this bombing was going to happen, Jabarah realized, he needed more cash. In late November, he got an email from KSM, with the phone number of a contact named Youssef. Jabarah was to call the number and identify himself as "Iqbal in Karachi." He met Youssef at City One Plaza in Kuala Lumpur, an apartment tower with a shopping mall on the lower floors. Inside, past the row of motorbikes parked on the sidewalk, there was a money changer, an international call center, and two Internet cafés, where messages could be sent with anonymity. There were fabric stores selling sarongs, and a vendor selling white prayer caps and framed photos of Mecca. Jabarah met his contact, who handed over two envelopes containing $50,000 in cash, all in wads of $100 bills, bound with elastic bands.

Time was running out for the Singapore plot. The logistical challenge of moving explosives into the country was pushing back the date of the operation. But Al Qaeda was in a hurry. Bin Laden was back on his heels as a result of the war in Afghanistan and the post-9/11 security crackdown. Brothers were getting arrested all over the world, and in Afghanistan the Americans were laying waste to the Taliban and Al Qaeda using precision guided weapons. B-52s had decimated the Taliban front, and in early November the Northern Alliance forces pushed south into Kabul, driving Osama and his deputies out of the capital. Al Qaeda got a lesson on the precision of U.S. air attacks and the strength of U.S. intelligence when a bomb struck the house of Abu Hafs. Bin Laden's military chief was dead. The building was not completely destroyed, however, and when American troops searched the rubble they found a stash of documents and videotapes. One of the tapes was a detailed reconnaissance film of a Singapore transit station.

The video images were accompanied by a narrative in fractured English:

This is the place where U.S. military personnels will be dropped off from a bus and they will walk towards the MRT Station, and this is one of the regular buses that carry the military personnels from Sembawang to Yishun MRT Station. Those personnels after they alighted from the bus, they will move towards the MRT Station, as you can see from the far left, the people walking towards the MRT Station, they will walk the same way as other people . . .

That is a temple with about 1.5-meter high wall, that is the entrance of the temple where many vehicles parked there so it will not be suspicious to have a motorcycle or a bicycle there. The pillars of the MRT track are very, very solid. You will notice that there is a drainage hole, it might be useful. Another drainage hole right at the junction. At this junction, the bus will turn left. This is the road along Admiralty Road East, from here you can see the residential area of the U.S. military personnels...

Now beyond this fence is a playground where normally those U.S. military personnels will gather to have recreation. We are traveling along Sembawang Road approaching the Junction of Admiralty Road East, you can see these buildings, these are the residential buildings for the U.S. military personnels. This is Dunbar Road, now this is the Eagles' Club, now we are turning into Admiralty Road East and this is the Eagles' Club located at Pakistan Road, this is Pakistan Road. This is the residential area. Eagle's Club is a mess for military personnels, this area is privately owned, owned by the U.S. government.

* * *

When word got around that Atef was dead, Jabarah met Hambali and Azzam in Kuala Lumpur and asked if it was true. They told him it was. He was gone. Hambali said that when he last talked to Atef, just days before he was killed, the Al Qaeda military commander had expressed his desire to see the operation in Southeast Asia speeded up. He wanted it to happen soon. Hambali was worried that the Singapore operation was taking too long. He thought it would be easier, and faster, to go back to the initial plan and attack the embassies in Manila. Mike had already found an illegal TNT supplier in the Philippines and bought 1.2-tons worth. He intended to get three more tons, which would allow for a two-ton blast at both the American and Israeli embassies. All he needed was money to pay for it, and that was Jabarah's job. There was another problem with Singapore: Ellias had been arrested when he tried to buy a large shipment of ammonium nitrate from a company that imported chemicals. A search of his belongings turned up a videotape titled "MP3—Rock 'n' Roll." On it was seven minutes of surveillance footage of the Sembawang Wharf and another two minutes of video of the Changi Naval Base, where the American warships docked.

In late November, Khan, the Singaporean jihadist who had gone off to fight in Afghanistan, was caught by the Northern Alliance, and the story broke in the media on December 3. The investigators in Singapore feared that once the news spread, Khan's associates would scatter and disappear underground. The Internal Security Department decided it was time to move. The operation began on December 8. During the first day of raids, six people were detained and their homes were searched. On December 14, the Americans told the Singapore authorities about the videotape they had found in Afghanistan, in Atef's bombed-out home (although it would be two weeks before the Americans handed over a copy). When Hambali heard about the arrests, he met with his operatives in Malaysia and urged them not to be discouraged and to carry on with the attack plans, if only to retaliate for the arrests. But more arrests followed in Singapore on December 15, 16, 17 and 24. Singapore called the plot "the most serious direct threat posed by any terrorist organization to Singapore's security since the days of the Communist Party of Malaya." The planned attacks threatened not only Singapore's public safety, but also its social cohesion, the government said, since its society is based on a degree of inter-ethnic trust that could have been easily undone through terrorism.

Sometimes counter-terrorism investigators outsmart their foes, and sometimes they just get lucky. Sometimes the terrorist makes a stupid mistake. Faiz Bafana had been warned by his colleagues not to travel to Singapore, but he wanted to visit his brother Fathi, so he ignored their advice. He got in without any problems, but as he was preparing to leave to return to Malaysia, he was arrested. The Singapore authorities had caught one of the few men who knew almost everything about the bombing plot.

The winter monsoon season was just beginning when Jabarah received an urgent email from Azzam in Kuala Lumpur. The subject line read, "Problem." It said that Faiz Bafana had been arrested and "that everyone was getting rounded up." Azzam told Jabarah to get out of Malaysia before someone turned him in.

Mohammed boarded a north-bound bus the very next day.

12

PRISONER OF THE SULTAN

THE bus went as far as Hatiya in southern Thailand. From there Mohammed made his way to the railway station and boarded a train. It was late in December when he arrived in Bangkok and checked his email. There was a message from Hambali. He too had fled Kuala Lumpur with Azzam, taking a circuitous route from Kuala Lumpur to Tanjung Pinang island, by ferry to Medan and then by air to Singapore, Phuket and Bangkok. Hambali sent Jabarah a phone number and told him to call.

They were reunited the next day at the Chaleena Hotel, along the banks of the Saen Saeb Canal. Mohammed noticed that Azzam had shaved off his beard. They discussed Faiz Bafana's arrest and their fears that he would talk under interrogation. Jabarah was afraid that Faiz would give police his description and that his photograph or sketch would be circulated and published in the newspapers. Hambali was not ready to call things off, though. He was still planning more attacks. But he feared for his Canadian friend. Jabarah knew so much about so many people; his arrest could endanger the entire organization. And Mohammed was the future of Al Qaeda. "It will be a very big hit for us if you're arrested," Hambali told him.

Mohammed tried to take a bus to Myanmar but he was turned back because he did not have a visa. He went instead to Chang Mai in northern Thailand. He called the United Arab Emirates embassy and asked about visa requirements, then boarded a plane to Bangkok and transferred to a flight to Dubai. He was still on the run, a wanted man in a dangerous time, but at least he was back on the Arabian peninsula. Kuwait was only a short flight away. He sent emails to KSM and Hambali, letting them know he was in Dubai and that he was safe. Hambali did not reply, but two days later KSM responded with a new contact number. Jabarah also phoned Abu Mohammed and some other old friends in Kuwait, and he called his parents as well. Mansour was furious because Mohammed's name had been in the news.

On January 11, the Singapore home ministry had issued a lengthy press statement about the progress of their investigation of the bombing plot. Thirteen of the 23 suspects under arrest had confessed they were active members of Jemaah Islamiyah (JI) and had been involved in the surveillance of targets and logistical groundwork for the attack, including stockpiling materials and finding hiding places. They were being held under the *Internal Security Act*. Eight of them admitted they had trained in Malaysia and Afghanistan, via Peshawar, and said that Hambali had taken care of the logistical arrangements for their travel to Pakistan. Their cover story was the same as the one used by Mohammed—that they were going to study at Pakistani religious schools. Some of the detainees identified the leader of the Jemaah Islamiyah as Abu Bakar Bashir.

The investigation was providing the first glimpse of the JI terror network and its links to Al Qaeda. The surveillance videos found at the office of Fathi Bafana, Faiz Bafana's brother. The original version of the surveillance video recovered in Afghanistan was found hidden in the bottom of a cabinet. Police found documents such as notes on how to make bombs and a letter sent to Taliban leader Mullah Omar, advising that, "I am glad to inform you that some of our brothers are ready to extend their help for the cause of Islam and the Muslims." A $1,000 contribution was enclosed. Ibrahim Maidin, the Jemaah Islamiyah head in Singapore, told police the fact the bombing was stopped meant that God didn't want it to happen. Another important break came when Mike the Bombmaker was about to leave Manila for Kuala Lumpur to get the money he needed to buy more TNT. He was arrested and a police search turned up the TNT he had stockpiled, as well as 300 detonators and six rolls of detonating cords. Under interrogation, he admitted it was to be used in Singapore.

"How did such Singaporeans who were by no means marginalized or ignorant wind up this way?" Wong Kan Seng, Singapore's Minister of Home Affairs, asked during a session of Parliament. "Many of the detainees now regretted their actions and attributed it to their blind loyalty to their leaders and their teachings. They were in search of religious knowledge but got sucked into a militant ideology and were infected by its hatred and radical and violent values. A few had some doubts but they felt they were too deeply involved to withdraw. Moreover, they had taken oaths of allegiance to their leaders which were sworn in the name of God and feared retribution if they should betray their vows."

The Singapore government said in a press statement that the local cell members had been approached by two foreigners who were looking for help with a bombing. One of them, the statement said, was "of Arab extraction calling himself 'Sammy' and believed to be linked to the Al-Qaeda organization." Sammy was described as "the leading and directing figure in the plan," but there was no other mention of him. The interrogations of the Singapore cell members yielded a lot of intelligence about JI, but none of the suspects had much to offer about Sammy. It was just one of the many indications of Mohammed's skill as a clandestine operative that he could spend weeks in the company of a group of men, but when they reflected under questioning, they realized that they knew almost nothing about the man.

The Internal Security Department (ISD) had only a few pieces of the puzzle; it needed to see the whole picture, so the agents did what intelligence services do—they tried to piece it together with the fragments that they had. They knew Sammy was a foreigner and that he had entered the country by road, so they got the landing cards from the border crossings and started sifting through them. That gave them a short list to work from. They entered the names into their databases and looked for hits. One of the possibilities was a Canadian passport holder named Mohammed Mansour Jabarah, age 20. He had entered Singapore at about the right time and was a Westerner of Arab ancestry, just like Sammy appeared to be. On his landing card Jabarah had listed his occupation as student and said he was coming to Singapore as a tourist. His record was clean. There was nothing in the computer system that indicated he was a threat. There was, however, some information about his father and brother. It said that Mansour Jabarah had been involved with right-wing Islamic groups. (For his part, Mansour says he was not involved in Islamist politics in Kuwait and suggests he appeared in the database because of his involvement at the St. Catharines mosque.) One of Mohammed's brothers was also listed. (I have not been able to determine which one.) There was no record of terrorism for either the father or the brother, but the information on the family told the investigators they might be on to something.

At first, the ISD thought that Sammy might actually be one of his brothers using Mohammed's passport, but they soon had it figured out. Sammy was Mohammed Jabarah. He was traveling on his own Canadian passport. It was a stroke of genius by Al Qaeda. Since 9/11, it was increasingly difficult to travel on forged documents. But Mohammed did not need a fake passport; he had a Canadian one. By the time Sammy had been identified, he had already left Singapore. The priority for the ISD investigators was to neutralize the Al Qaeda–JI cell and learn as much as they could about its operations. The agency shared its information with its security and intelligence partners around the world. "Investigations are continuing," the statement concluded. "Several suspect operations cell members have fled the country and efforts are being made, in co-operation with the authorities of neighboring countries, to locate them." Experts believe more than 3,000 people could have died had the attack succeeded. An Asian 9/11 had been averted.

The Singaporeans contacted Canada's Department of Foreign Affairs for help and, on January 17, the Canadian Press wire service reported from Washington that Sammy had been carrying a Canadian passport in the name of "Jabarah Mohd Mansur." The story ran on the front page of the *Toronto Star*. "Canadian authorities will provide Singapore with any assistance it requires in pursuing this investigation," the story quoted an unnamed Canadian embassy official as saying. When Mansour saw the article, he was angry and he told Mohammed so on the phone. Mansour says he had no idea his son was in Dubai. Mohammed was still telling his parents he was in Pakistan.

Worried, Mohammed sent KSM a copy of the *Star* article. A few days later he called KSM and told him he wanted to go to Mecca for the Haj, but the plan was scuttled when he could not get a visa for Saudi Arabia. His mood brightened when he got word that his brother Abdul Rahman was on his way. Following his brush with the Canadian Security Intelligence Service in St. Catharines, Abdul Rahman had left Canada and returned to Afghanistan in August, but when the U.S. air strikes started, he fled to Pakistan with the rest of the Al Qaeda exodus. He flew to Syria and then Dubai. Mohammed went to the airport to surprise him, he told investigators later.

The brothers spent a week together at a Dubai hotel while Mohammed awaited further instructions. Abdul Rahman told him that because of the devastating air strikes in Afghanistan, Al Qaeda members were supposed to go to Tajikistan, Iran or Pakistan "to regroup or to return to their home countries and wait for a call." Mohammed called the number that KSM had given him, but another man answered. It was Al Attash, who Jabarah knew from Kandahar. They caught up on events and Al Attash told Jabarah that Al Qaeda had another mission for him. He was to travel to Muscat in the Sultanate of Oman and then call back. Jabarah got a visa within three days and left.

The American-led war in Afghanistan had pushed hundreds of Al Qaeda members into neighboring countries, particularly Pakistan and Iran. But these were not necessarily safe places for fleeing terrorists and Al Qaeda was searching desperately for escape routes. One of the pipelines they came up with was to travel by boat from Iran to Oman and then to Yemen, which many in Al Qaeda thought would be their next operational base. Bin Laden was a Yemeni by ancestry, and the country had large tracts of wild desert where bandits and terrorists could operate out of reach of the law. And there was nothing separating Yemen and Saudi Arabia but sand dunes. Jabarah called Al Attash upon his arrival in Muscat and was told to rent an apartment for 15 to 19 men who would be arriving from Iran en route to Yemen. In code, they were to be referred to as "fifteen nice girls without papers." Al Attash said he was sending another operative from Pakistan to help out, a Saudi in his late 20s named Abu Abdelrahman. Jabarah had met Abdelrahman once at a guesthouse in Kandahar, although he did not know him well. Abdelrahman had stayed in Afghanistan throughout the fighting until the end of December 2001 or the beginning of January 2002. He arrived in Oman with $5,000 that KSM had given him to set up the transit apartment. Abdelrahman brought Jabarah up to date on what was happening inside Al Qaeda.

At the beginning of March, Jabarah spoke again by phone with Al Attash. As soon as the Oman mission was completed, Jabarah was to return to Pakistan for his next assignment. Jabarah also received emails from Al Attash asking him to come back to Pakistan. Jabarah understood that Al Qaeda had a new job for him, but he had no idea what it was. When the boat full of "nice girls" arrived from Iran, Jabarah got a call from Pakistan.

He was instructed to meet up with the transiting fighters and phone back when they were safe.

It all fell apart on a single day.

The Al Qaeda operatives who had come to Oman by boat were arrested, and so were Abu Abdelrahman and Jabarah. They were together when the police arrived on March 2, 2002. Abdelrahman was deported to Saudi Arabia and the "nice girls," who were Yemenis and Saudis, were expelled to their respective countries.

Only Jabarah remained. His was a more complicated case for the Omanis. Their first priority was to determine just what he was doing in Muscat. Was he scouting embassies for an attack? They pressed him on the matter for a week but came up empty. Some have suggested Mohammed was tortured during this time, but officials told me he wasn't. Jabarah told the Omanis he was not aware of any Al Qaeda operations in Oman. He said he had not visited the U.S. embassy and did not even know where it was.

The Omanis were satisfied that Mohammed was not a threat to them and decided to release and deport him. But to where? Kuwait was a possibility, but Mohammed said he did not want to go there. He knew that as soon as he arrived, he would be detained. Al Kandari and the other Kuwaitis returning home from jihad were all being arrested. He knew the same fate was waiting for him. He also ruled out going back to Pakistan. The Pakistanis were rounding up Al Qaeda members and handing them over to the Americans, and Mohammed knew he would be "scooped."

Mohammed suggested Iraq. He was still an Iraqi citizen and he had family in Basra. He thought he would be safe there (the U.S. invasion was still a year away at this time). But the Omanis said no. They were afraid of the damage to Omani–American relations should the United States find out they had sent an Al Qaeda terrorist to Saddam's Iraq. There was only one option left, and that was Canada. For his part, Mohammed was willing to go back, and the Omanis saw no difficulties with that. The Omani intelligence chief approved. Mohammed would be handed over to the Canadians.

The Canadian security liaison officer in charge of Muscat took the phone call. He listened as the Omani official explained the situation: Mohammed Jabarah was in custody and unless a Canadian official came to pick him up, he would be set free. CSIS knew immediately who Jabarah was, and desperately wanted to talk to him. The agency had wanted to talk to him since the first tip about his activities at the St. Catharines mosque had come in a year earlier, and the emerging intelligence about his role in Singapore made it that much more pressing.

CSIS had a couple of options. It could try to convince the Omanis to give Mohammed to the Americans, who wanted him for the Singapore plot. CSIS consulted the CIA to find out what the Americans would do with Mohammed if they got him. The answer was that he would be sent to Guantanamo Bay, and that did not appeal to CSIS.

When they found out that Mohammed had been caught, the Americans started lobbying the Omanis. In one of his letters from prison, Mohammed describes the attempts by U.S. authorities to convince Sultan Qaboos bin Said Al Said, who has ruled the country since 1970 and also serves as prime minister, to hand him over.

One of the officials of the CIA visited Sultan Qaboos of Oman during the period when I was in jail and tried to convince him that Oman must deliver me directly to them. Qaboos refused that request based on the fact that there was no agreement between Oman and the U.S. to expatriate a Canadian citizen to the U.S.

The Omanis would not give Mohammed to the Americans. On that they were firm. Another option was to ask the Royal Canadian Mounted Police (RCMP) to pick up Mohammed. This was the choice favored by CSIS. Canada had recently passed its *Anti-Terrorism Act*, which outlawed terrorist activities for the first time. The RCMP looked into the case and, incredibly, could find no grounds for arresting Mohammed. The problem was one of timing. The things that Mohammed had done for Al Qaeda were indeed illegal under the *Act*. But Parliament had only passed the law on December 24, 2001, in response to the 9/11 attacks. All of Jabarah's terrorist activities pre-dated the enactment of the legislation, and the law was not retroactive. Canada's lawmakers were so slow to outlaw terrorism that Mohammed could not be charged. The RCMP option was ruled out completely when the Omanis declared that they would not hand Mohammed over to any police force, even the Mounties. There were only two possible scenarios left: Either CSIS would bring him back to Canada, or Jabarah would be set loose. For an agency charged with protecting the security of Canadians and their allies, the latter option was no option at all.

Two CSIS agents, a senior officer from headquarters in Ottawa and another from the Toronto regional office, flew to Oman to take custody of Mohammed and bring him home. When they saw him, he looked to be in good shape. He was eager to return to Canada. They took him to the Muscat airport and boarded British Airways Flight 72 to London at midnight on April 18. At Heathrow Airport, they walked to Gate 24 and, at 9 a.m., boarded Air Canada Flight 869, destined for Toronto's Lester B. Pearson International Airport.

Mohammed writes in a letter to his brother in Canada:

When we flew from Oman to Canada, I was supposed when I first reach Canada to ask for a lawyer and not to speak to this cunning Arabic Mike, whose real name is Marlon. All security places, not only in Canada, but everywhere, usually will have strong evidence against the accused. The strongest way to arouse the anger of American detectives is to tell them during questioning, "I shall never speak in the absence of a lawyer." Saying this will be like spitting at their faces and giving them a nice slap on the cheeks.

In less than two years, Mohammed Jabarah's jihad had taken him from Canada to Kuwait, Pakistan, Afghanistan, Hong Kong, Malaysia, the Philippines, Thailand, United Arab Emirates and Oman. He had been trained by the top-ranked terrorists in the world, who had been grooming him to become a leader of the future, another Khalid Sheikh Mohammad. He had been their apprentice.

And now it was all over.

He had not achieved his goal of martyrdom, but he had served the cause of Al Qaeda like few others had. And at least he was coming home in style.

Mohammed flew Executive Class, in seat 4D.

13

THE SOURCE

GETTING Mohammed to talk was no trouble at all. He wanted to talk. Not in an arrogant, bragging way. He just wanted to tell someone about the extraordinary things he had experienced.

And CSIS wanted to listen.

It was one of the odd things about Al Qaeda terrorists. They were so devoted to the jihad that they were ready to die in a "martyrdom operation." But as soon as you took them out of that environment, they could shed their fanaticism like they were taking off a uniform. It wasn't always like that, but in many cases, it was that easy—if you played them right. You could bring a terrorist home, show him his family and he would revert to his old self. It was almost like there were three Mohammed Jabarahs. There was the Kuwaiti Mohammed, the keen young disciple of God. There was the Afghan Mohammed, the steely-eyed missile man. And there was the Canadian Mohammed, the polite student and good son. Now that he was back on Canadian soil, he went back to being the kid in the toque.

The agent assigned to get Mohammed to talk was a veteran intelligence officer named Mike Pavlovic. Self-assured, with dark hair combed straight back, "Pav" was in his 40s and spoke

Serbian. He had served in the Royal Canadian Mounted Police before joining CSIS about a year after it was created in 1984. He was what they called a "direct entry"—he left the police force one day and joined the intelligence service the next. Pavlovic is "a real competent street guy, no question about it," a former senior intelligence official says. He was a good interviewer and a great source recruiter, even if he sometimes had trouble taking direction from management. He was tenacious enough to do what he had to do. In the mid-1990s, he knew the Serbo-Croation community better than anyone. But his bosses began to fear they were over-exposing him and they pulled him back to headquarters in Ottawa. In July 2001, he was sent to the Toronto office at the foot of the CN Tower to join the Sunni Islamic extremism desk. Two months after starting his new position, Al Qaeda struck in New York and Pavlovic found himself making the rounds of those suspected by CSIS and its partners of links to violent Muslim factions.

Chasing terrorists was nothing new to Canada's intelligence community. CSIS agents had long experience at it. From the moment it was formed as a civilian agency assigned to take over from the RCMP Security Service, CSIS had been involved in counter-terrorism. The first targets were Sikh terrorists who, less than a year after the birth of CSIS, placed bombs aboard two Air India planes at Vancouver airport, killing 331 people. CSIS tried to learn from its mistakes; it needed to because terrorist groups kept coming to Canada one after another. By the late 1990s, every one of the most dangerous terrorist organizations in the world—from the Sikh Babbar Khalsa and Tamil Tigers to Hezbollah and Al Qaeda—had set up shop in Canadian cities to raise money, buy weapons, spread propaganda, lobby politicians, recruit and, occasionally, plan and execute terrorist operations. CSIS did its best to track them and help their partner agencies get rid of them, but Canadian politicians had little appetite for counter-terrorism and this did not make their job any easier. Although the country's immigration system and open borders with the United States made Canada an attractive zone for terrorist infiltration, the Liberal government slashed CSIS budgets throughout the 1990s in search of the post-Cold War peace dividend. Terrorism was only criminalized by Parliament after the attacks of 9/11, but by then, terrorists were already well-entrenched, running front organizations that collected money and provided a cloak of legitimacy to the dirty work of terrorists.

Al Qaeda had used Canada primarily as a support base throughout the 1990s, a source of money, passports and recruits. But in the late 1990s, terrorist support cells around the world began mutating into attack cells, and Canada was one of the first venues for this new era of extremism. Ahmed Ressam's arrest in 1999 showed that Al Qaeda now considered Canada an operational base as well as a logistical support base. Although Canadian politicians boasted that none of the 9/11 hijackers had crossed the border from Canada, the uncomfortable truth was that there were indeed Canadian connections to the Attack on America. Two of the 9/11 hijackers had been recruited by Mohamedou Slahi, who once lived at a Montreal mosque, according to the 9/11 Commision. Khaldun camp, where Al Qaeda trained some of the hijackers, was supported in part by a Canadian extremist named Ahmed Said Khadr, according to the testimony of his son. A kingpin of the Canadian Al Qaeda network, Khadr was close to bin Laden and held fundraising appeals at mosques across Canada. And one of the "hijacker candidates," who was trained for the mission but for unknown reasons did not take part, the 9/11 Commision reported, was a Tunisian-born Canadian citizen named Abderraouf Jdey. With American and French help, CSIS had been working to dismantle the main Al Qaeda groups in Canada, the Khadr network and the Groupe Fateh Kamel, to which Ressam belonged. Several members of Al Qaeda and its affiliates were arrested for deportation or extradition and many others were being watched.

On September 20, Mike Pavlovic paid a visit to one of them, Abdellah Ouzghar, who was then living freely in Hamilton even though five months earlier he had been convicted *in absentia* in a Paris court for his role in the Montreal extremist faction. Ouzghar had left Montreal to settle in Hamilton while the Jabarah brothers were preparing to go off to jihad. Pavlovic and Ouzghar met at a Tim Hortons coffee shop for about 30 minutes. Pavlovic said he wanted to know "where he was on September 11th . . . whether he could provide any information pertaining to September 11th." It was typical of the work done by CSIS intelligence officers. CSIS is not a law-enforcement agency. It cannot make arrests. Its function is to collect intelligence related to security threats to Canada. Those targeted for investigation, which number between 300 to 350, might be watched, their phones might be monitored and they could find their circle infiltrated by an undercover operative. But the job of intelligence agents is mostly just to get out into the community, meet people, try to recruit human sources, ask questions and generally to keep a handle on what is going on so they can advise the government and police about emerging threats.

There had never been a successful terrorist attack in Canada linked to Al Qaeda, although Canadian soldiers in Afghanistan had been hit, and bin Laden himself had publicly declared Canada a legitimate target. There was also mounting evidence that Al Qaeda was scouting targets, especially in Toronto. By 2004, CSIS began admitting openly that it was not a matter of if Canada would be attacked, but when. Approximately 100 "hard-core" Islamic extremists were known to be operating in Canada, 70 of them in the Toronto area. "While the United States and United Kingdom are priority targets for Al Qaeda operations for Sunni Islamic extremists," says a classified CSIS report, "Canada is no longer regarded as simply a safe haven for criminal and logistical support activities. Canada is a viable terrorist target." An RCMP counter-terrorism official was more blunt: "This group will kill in Canada." So when Mohammed Jabarah came to the attention of CSIS, the agency already had considerable experience with jihadists. What was new was the phenomenon of "homegrown terrorists," the increasing number of second-generation immigrants who were becoming supporters of Al Qaeda ideology. Few of these made-in-Canada extremists, however, had attempted anything as serious as Mohammed Jabarah.

CSIS wanted Mohammed at ease. They needed to take him someplace where he would feel that his jihad was over, that it was something in the past. They needed to get him somewhere he would feel safe. They decided to take him close to home. Mike Pavlovic got a hotel room near the casino in Niagara Falls and took him there. Niagara Falls is a tourist town, the Honeymoon Capital of the World. Eighteen million people visit every year to watch the water plunging over shale cliffs, draining the Great Lakes, which hold one-fifth of the world's fresh water. There are restaurants, wineries, the Ripley's Believe It or Not Museum and a casino (at the time there was one, now there are two). Niagara Falls is a fun place, and that's what CSIS wanted. It seemed to work. Mohammed was happy to be home. He knew his parents were close by, only minutes away in St. Catharines. The challenge was to get him to let down his guard so he would talk freely and honestly. They needed to establish a rapport with him. That was the task handed to Mike Pavlovic.

Pavlovic is known within CSIS as a solid intelligence officer, but also a personable guy, someone who knows how to have a good time. Everybody likes him. He likes to have fun and he knows how to get people talking. Some intelligence officers are good analysts; some are good investigators. Mike is what some call a "rounder." He can go into any setting, size it up and assume just the right role. He can wander into a pub and pretty soon people will be telling him everything. Even if they don't want to talk, they just can't help themselves. Not everyone can do that. It's not something that can be taught at spy school. It's a gift, and Mike has it.

He got Mohammed a haircut and a shave, bought him some clothes and a rain jacket at the shop in the hotel lobby, and then took him out for steak and lobster. Like a good intelligence officer, he listened, encouraged and probed as Mohammed talked. And talked. And talked. Mohammed had remarkable recall. He told Pavlovic how he had met bin Laden, how KSM had given him an assignment in Southeast Asia, how he had gone there, who he had met, what they looked like. He told him he thought KSM was "one of the masterminds" behind the 9/11 attacks. He provided email addresses and passwords. He said he had been in "casual contact" with four of the 9/11 hijackers in Kandahar. CSIS agents showed him photos and he identified the hijackers: Ahmed Al Haznawi, who was aboard Flight 93, which crashed in Pennsylvania; Abdulaziz Alomari, who crashed Flight 11 into the North Tower; and Khalid Al Mihdhar and Salem Alhazmi, who crashed Flight 77 into the Pentagon. He said they exchanged "pleasantries" and there was no mention of the upcoming attacks when they met. "According to Jabarah, he has never met any of the other hijackers, including suspected hijacker Zacarias Moussaoui," CSIS noted in a report. Jabarah added that he was "impressed" by Al Haznawi because he was so devout and could recite the Koran from memory. He said Al Qaeda had operated three main training camps. Al Farooq, where he had trained, was about 70 kilometers south of Kandahar, he said. El Matar was at the Kandahar airport, and Center Nine was 20 kilometers south of Kabul. Center Nine was for Yemenis heading to the Taliban front, he added. Mohammed explained that he had tried to train there but was turned down because he did not intend to fight at the front. At the time, his destination was Chechnya. The man in charge of all the camps was Abdullah Ahmed Abdullah, he said.

At the time, very little was known about bin Laden's efforts to acquire and develop weapons of mass destruction. Intelligence agencies knew he wanted to get his hands on them; that much was obvious. They knew he had tried, but how close was Al Qaeda to being able to use chemical, biological or even nuclear weapons? Again, Jabarah had some insights. He told CSIS he had not seen any biological or chemical weapons facilities in Afghanistan. He had also never heard of any WMD training programs, nor had he ever met anyone who had received training in such weapons. But he had overheard others talking about nuclear weapons. "According to Jabarah," CSIS wrote, "these discussions were casual in nature, amongst fellow mujahedin, and not with the Al Qaeda leadership. Jabarah had overheard that the problem with developing nuclear weapons was not in procuring the necessary material, but in holding or storing it 'after it has been heated.' Jabarah said that he had been told that Al Qaeda could easily procure material for a nuclear weapon, but did not have proper 'metals' or 'boxes' to hold it after it has been processed. According to Jabarah, this information arose from general discussions, and he did not know if Al Qaeda had actually acquired any of this material."

Mohammed told Mike that Al Qaeda had been responsible for the assassination of Ahmad Shah Massoud, the charismatic and politically moderate commander of the anti-Taliban Northern Alliance. Abdelrahman had told him so in Oman. He added that Al Qaeda was also responsible for the November 12, 2001 crash of American Airlines Flight 587 in Queens, New York. The crash had been reported in the press as an accident, but Abdelrahman told Mohammed the plane had been brought down with a shoe bomb similar to the type used by Richard Reid. Abdelrahman told Jabarah the bomber was the Canadian Abderraouf Jdey. (Although Jdey is alleged to have trained with the 9/11 hijackers, and he recorded a martyrdom pledge on video that was found in Afghanistan, the National Transportation Safety Board has found no evidence indicating the crash was the result of an act of terrorism.)

Finally, Jabarah identified 13 "leading" Al Qaeda figures, in addition to bin Laden and KSM, with whom he had been in direct contact, notably Ayman Al Zawahiri, bin Laden's number two, who had treated Mohammed when he was sick. "It was Jabarah's opinion that Zawahiri was the most likely successor to bin Laden," CSIS noted. The others were middle- and lower-level figures in the Al Qaeda network:

- Abdullah Ahmed Abdullah, who was in charge of the training camps and whom Mohammed had met at Al Farooq; he is wanted by the FBI for his role in the 1998 embassy bombings in Kenya and Tanzania;

- Muhsin Musa Matwalli Atwah, with whom Mohammed had exchanged pleasantries at a guesthouse in Kabul; he is also wanted for the African embassy bombings;

- Ali Saed Bin Ali El Hoorie, whom Mohammed met at the same guesthouse; his is wanted by the FBI for his alleged role in the 1996 Khobar Towers bombing in Saudi Arabia;

- Mustafa Mohammed Fadhil, a.k.a. Abdul Wakil, the official responsible for the Arab fighters at the Taliban frontline;

- Abu Zubeida, a.k.a. Khalden, a key Al Qaeda recruiter in Pakistan whom Mohammed had met in Kabul in 2001; he was captured and is in U.S. custody;

- Abdulrahman Mahajre, an explosives expert who taught courses for Al Qaeda;

- Mohammed Salah; whom Jabarah believed had been killed in Khost, presumably in U.S. airstrikes;

- Abu Jafar Al Jazaeri; Jabarah said he was dead;

- Ibn Sheikh Al Liby; he is wanted for the 1998 embassy bombings;

- Abd Al Hadi Al Iraqi, who had fought alongside Mohammed at the Taliban front

- Sheikh Said Bamusa, who was in charge of the Arabic Islamic Institute and was wanted by the U.S.;

- Zubeir Heli, who ran the Kandahar guesthouse with Abu Kouloud.

Some of these names appear on U.S. most wanted lists but others do not and their involvement in terrorism has not been proven.

Mohammed thought some of them had been killed in U.S. airstrikes. He said he didn't know what had happened to the rest. "He believed it to be highly likely that most of these individuals would still be hiding in Afghanistan," CSIS noted, "as their identities are now known to the world which would make it difficult for them to travel." CSIS added that "Jabarah said that he always wished to go to Chechnya but never met Ibn Khattab [the Chechen rebel leader]. He met Khattab's representative, Dahak, at a special guest house in Kandahar reserved for Chechens. Dahak told Jabarah that they weren't allowing any more Arabs to go to Chechnya at that time."

For all his bluster about jihad and martyrdom, Mohammed was singing like a bird. He became an intelligence source. The only thing he lied about was his brother. Mohammed told CSIS that Abdul Rahman was studying computers in the Persian Gulf somewhere and that he was planning to settle down and get married. CSIS bought it, at first, noting in an intelligence report that Abdul Rahman "may still be in UAE." It was far from the truth, but while Mohammed might have been willing to talk about his other Al Qaeda associates, he was not about to give up his brother.

Mohammed's reward was a phone call to his parents in St. Catharines, but he did not let on where he was. "He told me, I remember exactly, 'Hi Dad, how are you. I am close to you. I am going to see you soon,'" Mansour says. "I remember these words exactly from him. 'I am going to see you soon.'" Mike took Mohammed to the lookout above Niagara Falls and snapped a photograph of his source. The sky was clear and blue. A cloud of mist boiled up from the waterfall. Mohammed looks self-assured in the photo. He had grown up a lot in the two years since he had left home. Cleaned up with new clothes, he did not stand out among the tourists and honeymooners. In the photos that Mike took that day, Mohammed does not look at all distressed, like someone being held against his will. He looks confident and relaxed. He looks resigned to his fate.

After two days in Niagara Falls, Mike was burning through so much money showing Mohammed a good time that CSIS decided to pull them back to Toronto. The agency had a short-term lease on a condominium near the downtown office and brought him there. Mohammed spent two weeks in the company of CSIS. He talked so much the agents had trouble getting all the information down. The intelligence reports based on what he gave them fill many pages. Mohammed knew he was finished with Al Qaeda. He also knew that Canada was not going to arrest him.

Mohammed wrote in a letter home:

> *Maybe I haven't told you this, but I remember when we were in Niagara with CSIS, this cunning Mike forgot some papers in my room regarding my charges and when I read it—of course, a day after I started talking with him—I found that they wrote in it, "There is no clear evidence or enough evidence to charge him or accuse Mr. Jabarah" (i.e., me). "We at CSIS are doing our best to convince the [prosecutor to press] charges, but they said that they have no evidence to charge Jabarah."*

Mohammed was partly correct. It wasn't that there was no evidence; it was that there was no law that could be used against him. He had raised money for Abu Gaith, trained with Al Qaeda and helped organize mass casualty suicide bombings in Southeast Asia, but he had not broken any laws in Canada. The Americans were a different story. Mohammed knew he would never be able to lead a normal life until he cleared things up with them. He was young. Did he want to live his life looking over his shoulder? His bargaining chip was his knowledge. If he told the Americans what he knew, maybe they would make a deal with him. He was only 20 years old. He could serve some time and be out of prison while he was still young enough to salvage his life.

CSIS also had a dilemma. The agency wanted to keep Mohammed in Canada, but the RCMP had made it clear there was no way charges would stick. Since Canadian criminal law was incapable of dealing with Mohammed, the choices were to let loose a trained Al Qaeda terrorist or help him turn himself in to the Americans. It was not a difficult decision to make. The CSIS mission is to protect Canada's national security and the safety of Canadians. Only seven months had passed since the 9/11 attacks, and bin Laden had hardly concealed his desire to strike again. This was no game. It was a race against time to find the shards of intelligence that would prevent the next catastrophe. Mohammed didn't know the place or time or date of any future Al Qaeda strikes, but the things he did know might help in some way. They could help security forces track down people who were planning more attacks, like KSM and Hambali. Mohammed would choose his own fate in the end. But if he decided to surrender himself into U.S. custody, CSIS was not about to stand in his way.

CSIS got in touch with the Americans and explained the situation. U.S. Department of Justice lawyers were assigned to work out a plan. They drafted an agreement. The terms of the deal they were offering were written out in a two-page document. It was a straightforward proposal: If Mohammed agreed to plead guilty to criminal charges, go into detention and provide information and testimony, he would be eligible for unspecified benefits. The exact terms of the agreement would be determined following his debriefings with U.S. authorities. If Mohammed agreed to the terms, the Americans would fly to Toronto with the agreement in hand. Mohammed would sign it and he would be taken to the United States. Mohammed decided he was going to do it. He wanted to clear the books and start again.

Mohammed knew he was going to jail and prepared himself accordingly. He did his laundry at the hotel and made two final requests of CSIS. First, he wanted Mike to come with him on the plane. Second, he wanted a night on the town. He wanted to drink scotch, smoke a cigar and see the girls at Toronto's Brass Rail Tavern.

And that is exactly what he did.

The strip club on Yonge Street, which advertises its "totally nude European–style dancers," is one of those dimly–lit bars with a stage and pretty girls who ask, "Would you like me to dance for you?" Those who want "personal attention" are invited upstairs to the VIP lounge. The home of "Toronto's best all-nude ladies" and all-nude lap dances is not the sort of place you would expect to find a devout jihadi, but there were unconfirmed reports the 9/11 hijackers had done the same thing, frequenting a strip club before they set out to commit mass murder. The alcohol was a sin as well, but Antara had been a wine drinker and he rationalized it by writing, "When drinking, all I own, I spend away, though what I am, is undiminished." If nothing else, Mohammed's decision to spend his final hours of freedom boozing in the company of exotic dancers is a reminder that beneath the mujahedin's uniform, there was a human being.

The morning after Mohammed's night on the town, a U.S. government airplane landed at Toronto Island airport. The Americans handed Mohammed a copy of the parole agreement. There were spaces on the second page for the signatures of James B. Comey, the U.S. District Attorney for the Southern District of New York, and Mohammed. It was dated May 3, 2002. It was partly a legal formality. Because he was a terrorist, Mohammed could not enter the United States without the approval of the Immigration and Naturalization Service (INS). The FBI could not bring him into the country until the INS signed off on a parole agreement that spelled out the terms of his entry. Those terms were that he was to plead guilty and cooperate. The agreement did not sugar coat what was in store. It said he would be detained 24 hours a day, seven days a week. It said he had to plead guilty. It specifically said that the process would be lengthy. The unknowns were the exact criminal charges Mohammed would face, what his sentence would be and what benefits he would get in exchange for his cooperation.

Mohammed signed the agreement.

The plane flew across the border to an Air Force base in upstate New York. "With the assistance of CSIS," Canadian officials wrote in a briefing prepared for Canada's Solicitor-General, "Jabarah is currently in the United States." Mike Pavlovic stayed at the air base overnight before returning to Toronto. He gathered Mohammed's personal effects, drove to St. Catharines and knocked on Mansour Jabarah's door.

According to Mansour, "CSIS told me, 'Your son, we captured him in Oman.' They asked me, 'Why he went to Oman?'" Mansour replied, "What's wrong if he wants to go here or there?" Since Mohammed's phone call, and his pledge that he would be home soon, Mansour had been expecting to hear back from his son, but there had been nothing. And then Mike arrived with Mohammed's bag. In the bottom, Mansour found the boarding passes Mohammed had used on his flights home from Oman. Mike also gave Mansour a collection of the photographs he had taken at Niagara Falls. "Your son Mohammed is under arrest in the United States," Mansour recalls the agent telling him.

Mansour asked if he could visit Mohammed and, according to Mansour, Mike promised to take him, but it never happened. Consular officials at the Department of Foreign Affairs tried to set up a visit, but at the time of this writing, they have been unable to convince the Americans to allow it. Mansour is angry at the way Canadian intelligence handled Mohammed. He calls people who work in the intelligence business "the dirtiest people." He blames Pavlovic for his son's fate. "He is an evil person," he says. If Mohammed broke the law, he should have been prosecuted in Canada, Mansour says, not sent to the United States. "This is the worst thing that the Canadian government has done when they transferred my son to the United States," he says. In Mansour's version of events, Mohammed thought he would spend three or four hours in the United States and then return to Canada, but instead, CSIS left him behind with the FBI. Mansour is convinced his son was set up.

"They tricked him."

After Mohammed's arrest, Mansour tried to call the Minister of Foreign Affairs but he could not get through. He talked to the minister's office staff instead. "As he is a Canadian person they have to tell him his rights as an accused person, they have to give him a lawyer, they have to tell him what he has to do but just to trick him, to take him to another country . . . They have to protect their citizens." Mansour believes Mohammed was only treated that way because of his race and religion. "I strongly believe they have done [this] to Mohammed because he is Arab; he is a Muslim." John Walker Lindh, he adds, was not dealt with that way.

He sees a parallel between the way Mohammed was treated by the Al Qaeda recruiters, and the way he was treated by CSIS. "As the people misled or tricked Abdul Rahman and Mohammed if they went over to Afghanistan, the Canadian government and the official people in the United States, they did the same thing with Mohammed. They misled him. Unfortunately, we came to Canada to find a secure place, to get a shelter for our future, but unfortunately we did not find this."

Mohammed's mother Souad uses a metaphor to explain her frustration. If you invite people for dinner, she says, you have to cook them a meal. Likewise, "Canada invited us, so she has to protect us. She is a great country. Why did she take Mohammed to the U.S.? She damaged the family."

But it is hard to see, based on the parole agreement that Mohammed negotiated and signed, how he was tricked. In fact, CSIS did more to help Mohammed than it would for any ordinary Canadian arrested abroad. Canadian intelligence plucked him out of prison in Oman and brought him home at taxpayers' expense. Few Canadians who find themselves arrested in a foreign land will ever get such treatment. Mohammed was allowed to surrender himself to U.S. custody and bargain for leniency. Considering that Mohammed had already been involved in plots of terror, the agency's actions were a prudent way of safeguarding innocents. Bringing Mohammed home and helping him take responsibility for his past were akin to a cult intervention, only with much higher stakes. The lives of

Al Qaeda's future victims were at stake. Mohammed had pledged to die for Osama. CSIS just might have saved his life as well.

From the moment Jabarah entered U.S. airspace, CSIS was finished with him, but the agency still needed to make sure the things he had told them were put into circulation so they could be of use in the war on terror. On May 13, 2002, Nick Rowe, the First Secretary at the Canadian High Commission in Kuala Lumpur, sent a Top Secret CSIS report to Canada's allies, including the intelligence chief of the Philippine National Police, containing the details of the Jabarah interviews in Ontario. On June 3, Rowe followed up by sending two pictures of Jabarah, one apparently a surveillance photo and the other a snapshot that had been taken at Niagara Falls. Rowe sent out another intelligence report on June 11, filling in some of the details. "Thank you," he wrote, "for your continued cooperation in matters of mutual interest and concern."

14

THE FBI INTERROGATIONS

THE FBI interrogations began on May 7, 2002. If the Americans had not fully recognized Mohammed's value as an intelligence source before they talked to him, they realized it soon enough. He had rubbed shoulders with the entire Al Qaeda leadership. He had met bin Laden four times. Ayman Al Zawahiri had been his doctor. He had spent two weeks with Khalid Sheikh Mohammad in Karachi. He was a huge catch.

They needed an insider like him. His memory was sharp and there was no shortage of levers they could pull to keep him talking. Mohammed was still young and, unlike the Pakistanis and Yemenis at Guantanamo, he had the expectation of living a decent life in Canada. And there was his family. The more fully he cooperated, the sooner he was going home. Mohammed agreed to talk. That's why he had come to the United States in the first place, but later he wrote an angry letter decrying the tactics the FBI used on him.

There are many methods that these dog interrogators use.
In the beginning they tell you some cunning advice like,
for example, saying, "You are still young. Look at your future.

*We will forgive you and we want what is best for you. There
are many of your friends who cooperated with us and now
they live a very nice life. We are not against Muslims. Look at
your parents and their welfare. You cannot win over us"* . . .
etc. and all this kind of nonsense.

*If this style did not work, they change it by saying: you will
waste your life, you stay all your life in prison. There is another
cunning style through which they tell you the information
they know about you. At that point you think to yourself
that, "These guys know a lot about me, so why don't I talk to
them?" This is the first step towards falling into the precipice
because the information they have is either fabricated or not
confirmed, which means that all of it is built on doubts and
not conclusions. They use tricks cleverly, but by Allah's grace
I could discover these tricks just by looking into their eyes and
nasty faces.*

Mohammed told the FBI the same story he had told CSIS
a few weeks earlier. He told them about the Singapore and
Manila plots, about bin Laden, KSM, Mike the Bombmaker,
and Hambali. "Jabarah stated that there were code words
used by Al Qaeda," according to one FBI report. "These code
words were generally established by the individual cells. Some
of the code words they used in Asia were: Market = Malaysia,
Soup = Singapore, Terminal = Indonesia, Hotel = Philippines,
Book = Passport, White Meat = American." The FBI agents
asked about potential targets in Asia, and Jabarah repeated
what Hambali had told him in Bangkok. "Hambali discussed
carrying out attacks with his group. He was planning to conduct
small bombings in bars, cafés or nightclubs frequented by
Westerners in Thailand, Malaysia, Singapore, Philippines and
Indonesia," the FBI wrote. Jabarah gave the FBI names, dates,
email addresses. He gave them details he had not given CSIS. He
talked so much that the interrogation report based on what he
said stretched to dozens of pages.

He told them that Al Qaeda had 3,000 to 4,000 members. He told them that the British were now considered viable targets. He told them that bin Laden was frustrated with the Taliban and "wanted to move to Yemen." He told them about "a special explosives course" at the Al Farooq training camp. "In this course," the FBI noted in an interrogation report, "you learn how to make explosives, mix it with germs and shoot with an RPG [Rocket Propelled Grenade] or Katusha. Abu Khabbab taught the course on poisons." He also told them that his father was active in Islamist politics in Kuwait, the FBI noted, although Mansour denies this. Mohammed added that "he would not have acted in a suicide role" in an attack. There were other people willing to do that.

Just a few months earlier, Mohammed had been an operative out in the field, planning to blow up American embassies. Now he was sitting with FBI agents in New York telling them everything he knew. He continued in the letter in which he talked about his FBI interrogations:

> They have another game called "very smart," but thanks to God, I knew it before I saw their cunning faces. This game, they tell you "You are very smart, choose for yourself." Or they tell you when you start talking with them, "Oh! You are very smart." And when you give them a new information they say, "Oh! You are very smart." The whole purpose is that they praise you, so whoever doesn't know this game will think, "Yes, I am smart," but whoever knows it knows that they mean, "You are very stupid."
>
> God Almighty summarized all this for us in one verse, which we overlooked and asked for the devil. God said, "Never will the Jews or the Christians be satisfied with thee unless thou follow their form of religion. Say, The Guidance of Allah, that is the only Guidance. Wert thou to follow their desires after the knowledge which hath reached thee, then wouldst thou find neither Protector nor helper against Allah." If it appears

. . . that they are angry and confused, then you should know that "you are very smart," but if they appeared happy and satisfied, then you should know that "you are very stupid" and that you are falling into the pit, God forbid. You should know that the believer is not going to be bitten by the snake twice and God will never overpower the infidel over the believers.

* * *

Jihadists have had to contend with arrest and interrogation since the days of the Soviet War and before. The bulk of the Muslim volunteers who trekked to Afghanistan to fight with the mujahedin eventually went home, and they were sometimes detained and tortured. Faced with this threat, Al Qaeda allowed that, "Under pressure of torture in the custody of the questioning apparatus, the brother may reveal some secrets."

The more senior Al Qaeda members in captivity have revealed all kinds of secrets to counter-terrorism investigators. Khalid Sheikh Mohammad, for example, has been remarkably cooperative. But in their minds, Al Qaeda members are not criminals; they are prisoners of war, captured by the enemy during the epic battle between Islam and the infidels. For a terrorist to confess is not to admit to sins; it is the opposite, to say proudly before God that he is not only a believer but one who has acted on his faith. Besides, terrorists know full well that the more they talk, the more they will be rewarded with leniency—and maybe a spot in the witness protection program. And although Al Qaeda prepares its members for capture, interrogators can be persuasive. Before sitting down with someone like Jabarah, the FBI consults experts at their psychological unit who devise an interrogation strategy. They study their source and come up with a plan of attack, and if that doesn't work, they adjust tactics accordingly. Interrogation is a much more sophisticated art than some in Al Qaeda recognize.

The initial interrogations of Mohammed Jabarah ended after three weeks, on May 31, 2002. Mohammed called his father and said he was fine, that he was being held in an apartment-like room, and that he was eating and sleeping well and cooperating. But Mohammed had more than the FBI to contend with. In the agreement he had signed in Toronto, cooperating with the investigators was only step one of the process. He had also agreed to plead guilty to criminal charges.

Once the FBI was done with him, Jabarah had to deal with James B. Comey, the United States District Attorney for the Southern District of New York. A father of five, Comey had majored in chemistry and religion at the College of William and Mary in Virginia before studying law at the University of Chicago. He clerked for Judge John M. Walker and then joined the U.S. Attorney's Office in 1987. By January 2002, he was the U.S. Attorney in Manhattan.

As a prosecutor, he had taken on the drug trade, the mafia and corporate crime—WorldCom, Adelphia and Imclone, the downfall of Martha Stewart. He had also prosecuted his share of terrorists. He convicted those behind the 1996 Khobar Towers bombing in Saudi Arabia, which had killed 19 U.S. servicemen. He was no stranger to Canadian terrorists either. Comey had successfully fought the appeal of Mokhtar Haouari, an Algerian shopkeeper from Montreal who had conspired with Ahmed Ressam to blow up Los Angeles International Airport. It was Comey who had signed, on behalf of the U.S. government, the agreement that Mohammed had endorsed in Toronto.

The prosecutors took the statements Mohammed had given to the FBI and rewrote them into a legal case. Comey approved a five-count indictment, charging that, "From in or about January 2000 through the date of the filing of this Information, in Singapore, Malaysia, the Philippines, Pakistan, Oman, and Afghanistan . . . MOHAMMED MANSOUR JABARAH . . . together with Usama Bin Laden and other members and associates of the groups known as al Qaeda and Jemaah Islamiyah and others known and unknown, unlawfully, willfully and knowingly combined, conspired, confederated and agreed to kill nationals of the United States." It said Jabarah had "attended terrorist training camps sponsored by al Qaeda" in March 2001, and that in May 2001, he had "made 'bayat,' that is, he pledged allegiance to Usama Bin Laden."

Comey detailed Jabarah's travels through Southeast Asia, and charged him with plotting to bomb the American and Israeli embassies in Singapore and Manila. The indictment said Mohammed had conspired to kill U.S. government employees, and "to use weapons of mass destruction, to wit, bombs, against nationals of the United States." There was a fourth count of conspiring to destroy U.S. property, and to top it off, Comey charged Jabarah with lying to FBI agents when he told them the last time he had seen one of his co-conspirators was in January 2002 in Bangkok. The indictment identified Jabarah by his real name and two of his aliases, "Abu Hafs al Kuwaiti" and "Sammy."

The Americans were throwing the book at Mohammed.

They had taken the things he had told them and used them *against* him. The proceedings in *United States of America v. Mohammed Mansour Jabarah* have all taken place behind closed doors, so it has proved difficult to follow the case, but in March 2004, according to his father, Jabarah wrote a letter explaining his guilty plea.

The only reason I pleaded guilty in front of the judge was because at the time I wasn't being held in prison. I was in a special room, I have everything I want and they told me if you did not plead guilty we are going to put you right now in the prison.

The charges decided, the only outstanding question was what sentence Mohammed would face. The charges put forward by Comey were extremely serious, enough to keep Mohammed behind bars for the rest of his life. But there was still the matter of leniency. Before leaving Toronto, Mohammed had made sure that the promise of "benefits" for his cooperation was put down on paper. Mohammed was hoping he could bargain for a two-year jail term or, at most, five years, but the U.S. Attorney's office had a more substantial jail term in mind.

As the prosecution and defense lawyers argued over his fate, Mohammed continued writing letters home. In one, he tells his brother Abdullah to learn from the errors he believed he made in captivity. Indeed, he seems to regret having ever opened his mouth. He says he should not have talked to the FBI or the "cunning" CSIS agent Mike (in Mansour's translation of that particular letter, Mike is not "cunning" but "malignant" and "arrogant"). He continues in his letter:

> My brother, you may wonder, what is the use of saying all this? I'll tell you. These are all experiences that I have passed through and I am telling you the mistakes that I have made so that you can avoid them. In summary, I should not have answered them with anything, even when they asked me, "Is your name Mohammed?" I shouldn't have responded to them because if I said "Yes," then you are confirming your identity and this is something that will benefit them very much.

* * *

The story of Jabarah's capture and transfer to the United States broke in the press in July 2002. Reporters staked out the Jabarah house in St. Catharines but were greeted by a sign on the front door reading: "No Media Please." The Canadian government was ready with press lines to feed to reporters. CSIS had drafted answers to anticipated questions for the Solicitor-General that were vague but summed up the agency's take on the Jabarah case: "Counter terrorism is the number one priority of CSIS; international cooperation is critical to ensuring public safety here and abroad; I will not comment further on the details of this case as the matter is the subject of ongoing investigation." Two days later, the Minister of Foreign Affairs was briefed about what he should say if asked what Canada was doing to assist Jabarah: "The individual has not requested consular assistance from the Canadian government. The Department of Foreign Affairs is seeking further information."

As the media interest continued, the Solicitor-General was advised he could go a bit further in his answers: "I can confirm that I was made aware of this case and that CSIS provided assistance to their American counterparts. In the fight against terrorism, such cooperation amongst international security and law enforcement agencies is vital. For reasons of national security, it would be inappropriate to comment further on this case."

On August 1, the minister was given more to tell reporters. "The fight against terrorism is an intricate, cooperative and international effort. In this particular case, CSIS assisted U.S. authorities, in compliance with Canadian law."

The Singaporeans were pleased with the information that CSIS shared with them concerning Mohammed. On August 16, the Internal Security Department (ISD) conducted more raids, arresting another 21 people. Nineteen of them were members of Jemaah Islamiyah, while the remaining pair were affiliated with the Moro Islamic Liberation Front. The Singapore JI network was, by now, thought to have been "severely disrupted."

Following Mohammed's capture, Abdul Rahman Jabarah became the focus for Canadian investigators, but he was nowhere to be found. Mansour recalls having the following exchange with a CSIS officer who came to his door in St. Catharines asking about his 23-year-old son.

"Has he done anything against the Canadian rules?" Mansour asked.

"No."

"Does he have the right to go everywhere?"

"Yes."

"Why you are looking for him? You are looking for each Canadian citizen?"

"No."

"But why you are looking for Abdul Rahman?"

"There is information," the agent replied. "I have to look for it."

Abdul Rahman was still on the loose, but the other two-thirds of the Abu Gaith trio had at least been accounted for. Mohammed was jailed in New York and Al Kandari was back in Kuwait, where security authorities were monitoring him—although not nearly closely enough.

15

THE FAYLAKA OPERATION

THE Persian Gulf sun was high in the sky when Lima Company broke for lunch. The Marines had spent the morning doing urban combat training in the ruins of a school. "It was ridiculously hot," radio operator Lance Corporal George R. Simpson recalls of that day in early October 2002. The Marines had left their base at Camp Pendleton, California, in June, and sailed aboard the USS *Denver* to Singapore, Thailand, Djoubouti and Bahrain. And now they were in Kuwait to take part in Eager Mace, a joint training exercise with the Kuwaiti armed forces. After a month in the desert, they moved camp to Faylaka Island, a tiny drop of land in Kuwait Bay that had been occupied and obliterated by Iraqi troops in 1991. The soldiers pitched their tents on the beach, opposite a row of war-gutted buildings that still had Iraqi war graffiti on them, and spent the evening playing baseball.

The Marines had been led to believe that Faylaka was abandoned, but when they arrived they found there were quite a few people around. Kuwaitis had been trickling back since the end of the Iraqi invasion. The soldiers felt secure on the island nonetheless. They had been through anti-terrorism and force protection training. They knew the potential threats, but the Kuwaitis had told them Faylaka was safe. Kuwaiti military personnel and police were on the island to guard against trouble, and besides, soldiers had been training there for years and there had never been an incident. This was, after all, Kuwait, where people loved Americans. Most of them, anyway.

"All the Kuwaitis that I talked to seemed more than friendly, more than happy to have Americans there. They had malls and they seemed to mix their traditional culture with the new world that they really embraced," Corporal Simpson says.

In the morning the soldiers, part of Battalion Landing Team 3/1 of the 11th Marine Expeditionary Unit, held a promotion ceremony and then got down to training, practicing the close-range combat techniques they would need should the order come to invade Iraq. They stopped for a rest at about 11 a.m. A few of the Marines got out a baseball and a bat and tossed their helmets onto the sand for bases. They felt like they were back at Camp Pendleton. "That was kind of the attitude; there wasn't any threat," says Corporal Simpson, a 21-year-old from Ohio. "We weren't all armed. We weren't in any kind of state of readiness." Only the captain and a few others had weapons.

Corporal Simpson warmed up his arm with rifleman Lance Corporal Antonio James Sledd, who was playing third base. Sledd was a native of Tampa who drove a Mustang and had a twin brother who was a marine stationed in Japan. They were lobbing the ball back and forth when a white pickup pulled up on the road. Out of the corner of his eye, Corporal Simpson caught a glimpse of it, and as he turned for a look, two men emerged wearing long robes.

"They were dressed for battle," he says.

The men in the truck were close, so close Corporal Simpson could see one of them clearly. "I could see his face, just that second that I turned around. I could see his face and I could see what he was doing." What Corporal Simpson saw, in that split second, was a young man with a black beard raising an AK-47 into firing position. It was Anas Al Kandari. And then the bullets came whizzing in. Corporal Sledd collapsed onto the burning sand. "They shot him in the back."

* * *

Al Kandari had returned to Kuwait one week before the 9/11 attacks. The Kuwaitis detained him upon arrival, questioned him about his activities in Afghanistan and advised him he was not to leave the country, lest he cause more trouble. Many other Kuwaiti jihadists got the same treatment as they returned from Afghanistan, where they claimed to have been doing charity work for refugees, widows and orphans. Jobless, Anas resumed his studies at the Kuwait University faculty of education. After living among the austere Taliban, Anas was shocked by the behavior of his countrymen. He was outraged when a group of actors and singers visited Kuwait to perform at a festival, considering it ironic that such infidels should be warmly greeted while he, an "Islamic scholar" who had memorized the Koran, was treated as a criminal. He visited several Members of Parliament to complain about the moral corruption of Kuwaiti society. And then he decided to do something about it. Like his best friend Mohammed Jabarah, Al Kandari wanted a martyr's death. The Americans had caught Jabarah before he could fulfill his death wish. Al Kandari was not going to make that same mistake.

It was what Abu Gaith would have wanted. But the teacher and recruiter had never made it home. There were rumors of his capture in Iran, but Tehran would not confirm or deny them. His absence left a vacuum for the brothers of Kuwait City, who had grown up listening to his preachings and exhortations to jihad. Al Kandari decided it was up to him to carry on in the spirit of Abu Gaith. If the Kuwaiti authorities would not let him leave to fight his jihad, he would do it right at home. He started recruiting within the Al Kandari family. An "Al Kandari" is someone who fetches water. The families that would cross the

Gulf to bring back drinking water were called Al Kandari, even if they were not all related. Today, there are many Al Kandaris in Kuwait, and many of them are related to Anas. Some had followed him to Kandahar to train at the camps of bin Laden.

Anas began visiting the young men. He showed them videotapes of bin Laden and Abu Gaith. Come fight the Americans with me, he told them, it is a jihad. Anas gathered the recruits at his house and announced they would soon begin attacks in Kuwait. The ideology—if it can be called that—of the Al Kandari gang was that the Kuwait government was the enemy, an apostate regime because of its ties to the Western world. Therefore, the Al Kandaris would wage jihad in Kuwait by disobeying the government and attacking both the national infrastructure and the foreign troops. The Al Kandari gang was an autonomous cell of Al Qaeda, although most of its members had trained under bin Laden in Afghanistan. But the group did meet with one active Al Qaeda member.

Anas armed his men with guns left over from the Iraq war. They trained at his house in the desert at Al Wafra. Anas taught them how to conduct surveillance, and told them which targets to watch. Cell members scouted U.S. military camps, but they were scared off by the security measures. Anas assigned his members to monitor other targets as well. Two schools were mentioned; they were to be attacked "when the time is right." One of the military bases that Anas thought might make a good target was Faylaka Island. Faylaka is about twelve kilometers long and six kilometers wide, and laden with old land mines. It is the most important archeological site in Kuwait, with a history dating back to the Bronze Age. The Greeks settled the island in the 4th century BC. When Saddam invaded in 1990, the Iraqi troops turned the island into a military base and, when they retreated, they left little but rubble. A car ferry leaves Kuwait City every day for Faylaka, a 90-minute trip, but not many people embark on it. For the most part, the island is a military training ground, although there are a handful of local inhabitants.

One of the Al Kandaris who trained in Afghanistan with Anas had a family home on Faylaka, and he would visit it frequently. Anas used him as a scout to keep track of U.S. military activities on the island. Anas went to Faylaka himself a few times with his cousin. They would play soccer, drink Pepsi and catch the ferry back to the city. On September 29, 2002, Anas called his scout and asked about the exact location of the soldiers. He also asked for information about the ferry. Anas had a plan. He was going to rent a truck, take the ferry to Faylaka and kill the Americans, just as he had been taught in Afghanistan. He had a stash of weapons ready, and his cousin Jassem Al Hajeri, a 26-year-old former Ministry of Oil employee, had volunteered to go with him.

In the days before the Faylaka operation, Al Kandari fasted and prayed. He wrote a will in which he talked about the Palestinians and advised his family to give all his possessions to his brothers in the mujahedin. He asked his mother to wish him martyrdom, and she did. On the night of October 7, Anas watched the evening news at home. An item about an Israeli military incursion into Gaza enraged him. "The Almighty is generous," he told his family afterwards, "because we are going to slaughter the Americans like they do to us." He spent the night at the Al Romithiya Mosque, where Abu Gaith had preached. He cleaned his Kalashnikov, dressed himself in an Afghan robe, sat in front of a video camera and recorded his martyrdom statement. After reciting verses from the Koran, he urged Muslims to stick to their faith and to fight non-believers. In the morning, he took his little brothers to school and kissed them goodbye. Then he and Al Hajeri boarded the ferry and crossed Kuwait Bay. It was 10:30 a.m. when they reached Faylaka.

* * *

Soldiers call it "pray and spray." When the gunfire started, Corporal Simpson hit the ground and tried crawling to a concrete pavilion, but his arm was dangling and useless. A bullet had gone in the back of his arm and blown a hole in his elbow and forearm. His arm was almost broken in half and it was flopping around.

"It was probably a fluke that it hit me, just bad luck," he says.

"It's a rather strange sensation. It didn't necessarily hurt like you'd think it would. I guess it was just kind of surreal. I never really looked back, I just tried to crawl. I don't think I got very far."

Another soldier grabbed the wounded corporal's good arm and dragged him to cover. He was still lying there when he heard the marines returning fire with their 9-mm handguns. They were unprepared for this kind of assault, having been assured by the Kuwaitis that Faylaka was safe. The first sergeant and other members of Lima Company made a quick assessment and engaged the attackers with small arms and security ammunition. The attackers jumped back into the truck and began to speed away. Captain Matthew S. Reid took cover and directed a hasty counterattack. The most accurate fire, however, came from the command post, which had an M-16. The bullets peppered the truck. It swerved and came to a stop. Al Kandari got out and fell to the ground. By the time the marines got there, both shooters were dead. But the gunfire kept coming in. There was a third shooter somewhere.

And then the shooting stopped.

"It was over just like that."

Corporal Simpson was badly wounded, but Corporal Sledd was worse. He was in bad shape. He had taken four rounds to the torso, and a fifth had blown off the fingertip on his right hand. Navy hospital corpsmen rushed over to treat the injured marines. They administered first aid but it was clear the soldiers needed to get to a doctor. They radioed the U.S. Army hospital at Camp Doha and called for a chopper.

While the two attackers were dead, Captain Reid was not convinced the assault was over. He organized the troops of L Company into a defensive position and sent in a request for more ammunition. Captain Reid cleared the buildings one by one and halted all passing vehicles, detaining 31 people and handing them over to the Kuwaitis. Meanwhile, an unmanned aerial vehicle was launched to provide an eye in the sky look at the island and two British RAF Tornadoes and two U.S. Air Force F-16s took to the air to provide air support. "We never found the third shooter," says Colonel Bill Durrett, a staff advocate judge. "Nobody could find him but one of the marines actually said he thought he hit him."

The wounded marines were loaded onto a pair of medical evacuation helicopters from the 1042nd Medical Company. They flew to the Kuwait Armed Forces Hospital but Corporal Sledd went into cardiac arrest later that day, due to heavy blood loss and shock. He died at the hospital. He was 20 years old, a year younger than Anas Al Kandari. "To lose a loving kid like Antonio has been my worst nightmare," his mother Norma Figueroa wrote in a letter to President Bush, in which she asked why her son's unit was not properly protected. "Last time I talked to Tony was two weeks ago. Tony promised me that he would return home soon and not to worry about him. He told me that they were doing their best to protect our country and I wonder, did the military do their best to protect our marines while they were training?"

The press lines approved by the U.S. Marines Corps that day did not identify who was behind the attack. "It is unknown at this time who the gunmen were. The incident is under investigation." But the Kuwaitis knew right away. When Captain Abdel Aziz Saad, an officer in Kuwait's national security department, got to the scene later in the day he found the white truck and the remnants of the gunfight—AK-47s, a shotgun, ammo clips, loose rounds. When he stared into the faces of the shooters he recognized one of them immediately as Anas Al Kandari, who was well known to the State Security Department. They had been watching his gang for some time, although they were unaware of the Faylaka plot. "We could not read their minds to know what they were planning," he testified later. "It was difficult to keep pace with their movements because they were from the same family and they were well organized."

Captain Saad phoned the state prosecutor and told him what he had found. The prosecutor gave his consent for Saad to round up anyone who had "close ties" to Al Kandari and had taken Al Qaeda training in Afghanistan. The Kuwaitis questioned more than 50 people, and a dozen were charged for their roles in the attack. Most of them confessed and were convicted, but they later backed away from their confessions.

Corporal Simpson was treated in the trauma unit at the hospital in Kuwait, where a regal-looking visitor, deputy premier and defense minister Sheikh Jaber Al-Mubarak Al-Sabah, paid him a visit. "He seemed quite upset about the whole ordeal," the wounded solider said. "I don't remember much. I was kind of in a medicated daze." He was transferred to the Landstuhl Regional Medical Center, the U.S. military hospital at the Ramstein Air Base in Germany, and then to the National Naval Medical Center in Bethesda, Maryland. "I have a whole lot of hardware in my arm," he says. But he knows it could have been worse. "They could have cut it off."

The Judge Advocate General ruled that the shooting was a concerted and deliberate attack. "The investigation revealed incorrect assumptions about the safety/security of Faylaka Island, the lack of a robust force protection office in Kuwait, and mistakes in the rendering of quality trauma care. However, it is also assessed that were it not for the rapid and decisive actions of Lima Company personnel, the terrorist action could have inflicted much more serious injury and potential loss of life on those marines and sailors training on Faylaka Island." Two days after the attack, Colonel Anthony Haslam, Commanding Officer of the 11th Marine Expeditionary Unit, eulogized Corporal Sledd as "a warrior wearing the uniform of a United States Marine. He deployed without reservation during a time of great uncertainty to protect and defend his country. On the 'tip of the spear,' he came face to face with the enemy and was taken from us."

The Faylaka shooting was yet another violent outcome of the careful recruitment done by Abu Gaith. It was an attack rooted in the indoctrination that Anas and Mohammed had gone through years earlier. Al Kandari's family told reporters that Anas had acted out of his anger over the treatment of Palestinians that he had seen on television. "Every Muslim believes Americans are helping Jews, and he was burning to do something to help," his brother Abdullah told the Associated Press. "My brother was not a terrorist," the same brother told Agence France Press. "He was horrified by the U.S. Congress decision to recognize Jerusalem as the capital of Israel. My mother is proud of him."

The truth, however, was not so tidy. Anas had not erupted in anger over Palestinians. He had been programmed years earlier to explode when the time was right. He was a walking time bomb, just like Mohammed Jabarah. The funeral was held at the Sulaibikhat Sunni Cemetery the day after the attack. Hundreds of mourners shouted "Allahu Akbar"—God is Great. Radical preachers praised the actions of Al Kandari and Al Hajeri. "They were better than us," said one mourner. "They were better because they stood up against infidels bent on usurping our rights." A statement posted on a jihadist Internet bulletin board said, "May God accept them both among His martyrs."

Corporal Simpson was assigned to a reserve unit in his hometown, Dayton, Ohio, but he left the Marines in 2004. It wasn't just the shooting. He had been planning to go to college anyway. "It beats you up pretty good. You're always away from home and I don't think I like that." He married a dental surgical assistant from the local air base and they had a son. He went back to school to study political science and economics. He still has the hat he was wearing on the day he was shot. When he shakes it, sand spills out of the seams. But he hasn't given much thought to the man who shot him. "I have never really looked into it. It just doesn't interest me to look into him. All I know is, I guess they got what they were looking for." Anas Al Kandari finally got the martyrdom he had wanted for so long. "It's unfortunate that they decided to do that and Sledd died because of that.

"It doesn't seem to have accomplished a whole lot."

* * *

Four days after the Faylaka shooting, Jabarah's gang of jihadis struck yet again. After the Manila and Singapore plots had fizzled due to the arrests, Hambali had continued plotting from Bangkok. He thought about striking the American, British and U.S. embassies in Indonesia, but security was tight, and he felt the chances of success were not good. He considered bombing companies such as an Exxon facility in Mojokarto, a gold mine in Sumbawa and a Caltex facility in Riau, but in the end he decided that Western tourists were his best targets.

In May 2002, Canadian intelligence had sent the information it had obtained from Jabarah during the two weeks of questioning in April to its international partners. The initial report circulated to such nations as the Philippines, however, included the caveat that the source was "of unknown reliability," and there was no mention of any specific future targets. Australian intelligence was eager to talk to Jabarah in New York but they were not granted access to him, largely because of legal difficulties stemming from his prosecution. Nor did the FBI provide the Australians with a copy of its two-page, August 21 report detailing what Jabarah had told them about Hambali's plans to bomb "bars, cafes or nightclubs frequented by Westerners."

Countering terrorism is partly about finding a loose thread that, when pulled, unravels the whole sweater. The discovery of the Singapore plot and the interrogations of those arrested, who by now numbered several dozen, had been an eye-opener for security agencies. The questioning of Jabarah and bombmaker Fathur al-Ghozi had revealed the close links between Al Qaeda and Jemaah Islamiyah. Captured Kuwaiti Al Qaeda operative Omar Al Farouq provided information that underscored that Al Qaeda had an extensive network of extremists throughout

Southeast Asia upon which it could draw to execute attacks. With new information coming in daily, intelligence analysts were painstakingly trying to map out Jemaah Islamiyah and predict its next move.

A U.S.-sponsored seminar examined a number of imagined scenarios for future terrorist attacks, among them the possibility that local extremists would cooperate with Al Qaeda to strike tourist facilities in Bali. The interrogations underscored the threats in Southeast Asia, but specific details about upcoming attacks were lacking, although Indonesia seemed a likely venue. As symbols of "Western decadence," as well as engines of the Indonesian economy, tourist areas were clearly potential targets. Western governments issued travel advisories, warning their citizens to avoid large gatherings and places that catered to tourists. Despite the warnings, thousands of travelers continued flocking to the region, and especially to Bali, which many considered safe because of its predominantly Hindu population and its longstanding hospitality to foreigners.

In August 2002, Hambali sent $5,000 to a JI operative named Mukhlas to support the operation being developed in Indonesia, and then moved to Phnom Penh, Cambodia, and stayed in contact with his Jemaah Islamiyah operatives in the field through email. He received an email from Mukhlas in Indonesia advising that "the program is OK, still progressing." Later in the fall, he got another email. "Program OK, you will hear and read from news, will happen in weekend soon." Two weeks later, on October 12, 2002, two massive truck bombs exploded outside Paddy's Bar and the Sari Club in Kuta, on the Indonesian island of Bali. It was a Saturday night and the bars were crowded with Western tourists and local workers. More than 200 people died; more than a third of them were Australians. The dead were still being counted a week later when Hambali received a brief email from Mukhlas.

"Operation over, success."

16

FAREWELL, MARTYR

SHORTLY after Mohammed found out about the death of Al Kandari, he got word about his brother's fate. Following Mohammed's arrest, Abdul Rahman had traveled to Saudi Arabia, arriving in May 2002. He began working for a jihadi group called Maktab Al-Wathaik, the Office of Documents, disbursing financial aid to the families of captured terrorists. One of the "great deeds" with which Abdul Rahman was credited was re-establishing the flow of money to the families of mujahedin holy warriors following the arrest of the "brother" who had been doing the job previously.

"He would often mention the Kuwaiti brother Anas Al Kandari," Abdul Hadi Al-Qahtani writes on the Arab-language Internet message board afti.net, which is used by jihadists to distribute statements and the beheading videos of hostages in Iraq. He would also talk about his mother, describing her as "one of the elements contributing to his steadfastness and strength."

"And he would often mention his brother Mohammed as well, who was extradited by the renegade Sultanate of Oman to the Country of Blasphemy, Canada, and from there to America, may

God release him." It continues: "Whenever he would mention them, or other brothers who have gone on the same path, one could see the sadness on his face and the pain squeezing his heart, and he would say: 'We have been incapacitated by our sins.' Then he would set forth with words full of sorrow, agony and pain."

Abdul Rahman, a.k.a. Abu Tulha, was "disciplined by the religion," Al-Qahtani says, and "driven by a great determination." He "despised this transient and vain world, and had a lust for eternity." So did the other extremists he hung around with in Riyadh, such as a former Al Farooq training-camp instructor named Yousif Salih Fahad Al-Ayeeri, a top Al Qaeda operative also known as Swift Sword. The Saudi jihadis were angry and determined to re-ignite the conflict in the land of the two holy places of Islam. Swift Sword was an Al Qaeda propagandist, and the webmaster of some of its Internet sites. His writings reflect the ideology of the Saudi gang to which Abdul Rahman was attached. "Once the Islamic *ummah* abandoned jihad, the enemies overpowered them and it was subjected to humiliation," he wrote in one tract. "The sole escape from this humiliation and debasement is to return to jihad, to return to loving fighting for the sake of Allah and to forsaking this world and its vanities."

* * *

On March 18, 2003, an explosion destroyed a house in the Al Jazira neighborhood of eastern Riyadh. When Saudi security forces arrived on the scene, they found the body of a man they were unable to identify, since he was carrying no identity papers. As they searched the house, they stumbled upon an impressive arsenal of weapons—twelve AK-47s, three hand grenades, two rifles, a revolver plus ammunition and high explosives. It remains unclear whether the house was deliberately bombed or whether the blast was an accident, as sometimes happens when explosives are handled by amateur bomb-makers. But regardless, as a result of the discovery, police began a surveillance operation against a group of suspected extremists.

Police monitored the suspects as they made repeated visits to a house in Riyadh's Ashbiliya district. A team of security forces moved in on May 6, but the jihadists opened fire and fled in a car. The vehicle broke down but the suspects simply hijacked another. By the time police caught up with the escape car, it had been abandoned and the men had melted into a crowded neighborhood. Inside the car, however, the police officers found an arsenal: 55 hand grenades, 208 machine gun bullets, 38 9-mm bullets, seven empty machine gun magazines, 49 2.2-mm bullets and travel documents, ID cards, diaries and $5,300 in cash. A second car parked outside the house was searched, and police found more weapons, three fully loaded AK-47s, as well as wigs and other disguises. Hidden inside the house were four AK-47s, three crates of ammunition containing some 2,000 bullets, 21 boxes of ammunition and 82 loaded magazines. Most disturbingly, police found 377 kilograms of high-explosive paste. There were enough weapons to kill thousands. The jihadists were preparing for all-out war.

The weapons "were intended to carry out acts of terrorism," the Interior Ministry said in a statement. The Saudi authorities announced they were looking for 19 men, whose names and photos they released along with an appeal to Saudi citizens "to inform the authorities if they have any information on these suspects." Seventeen of them were Saudis but one was said to be a Yemeni. Number 18 on the list was described as "a citizen of Kuwait and Canada." The next morning their faces stared out from Riyadh's daily newspapers in a wanted poster. One of the men was a young Arab with small dark eyes and a full black beard, Abdul Rahman Jabarah.

The Saudis claimed they had "foiled planned acts of terrorism" when they raided the house, but the U.S. State Department remained wary and issued a travel advisory against nonessential travel based on intelligence indicating that terrorists were in the final stages of planning an attack against Americans. In an Internet posting, a group calling itself the "Mujahedin of the Arabian Peninsula" claimed that it was behind the plots and that an attack was imminent. It came soon enough, on May 12. Gunmen battled their way into three housing compounds before detonating their explosives-rigged vehicles. Twenty-five people were killed—Americans, Britons, Irish, Swiss, Lebanese, Jordanians, Filipinos and others—along with nine terrorists. Saudi Prince Bandar bin Sultan called the attacks "evil and unforgivable crimes" and said terrorists had "perverted" the Islamic faith. "We will continue to hunt down the criminals, we will continue to cut off their finances and we will bring them to justice."

In the weeks that followed, the Saudis waged what they called a "fierce and merciless war against terrorism." Sixty FBI agents were brought in to work on the case, as well as a team from Scotland Yard. It was not a good time to be a fugitive in Saudi Arabia. Mansour was understandably worried about Abdul Rahman. At one point, Abdul Rahman had called home but he did not say where he was. Mansour has caller ID, but the call was blocked.

"Please, my son," Mansour pleaded, "if you are not secure, please, Abdul Rahman, go to a Canadian embassy, present yourself as a Canadian."

Abdul Rahman responded that it was the Canadian intelligence service that was looking for him. Why, then, should he go to the Canadian embassy?

"Have you done anything wrong?" Mansour asked.

"No."

Mansour told his son to go anywhere but Saudi Arabia.

"Saudi Arabia is very close to America. They are going to act as the Americans."

* * *

During the 1980s, the Saudis played an important role in the Afghan jihad. The Saudi intelligence service financed the anti-Soviet mujahedin, Saudi charities funneled huge amounts of money to the cause and hundreds of young Saudi men went off to fight, among them Osama bin Laden. But when the war ended, and bin Laden was looking to take his jihad elsewhere, he turned against his homeland. He was particularly infuriated when the Saudis allowed Western troops to use the kingdom as a staging ground for Operation Desert Storm. His denunciations of the royal family led the Saudis to strip him of his citizenship. The presence of U.S. troops in Saudi Arabia was a source of tension between the royal family and its 20 million citizens, one that was easily exploited by bin Laden to draw people to his cause. It can be no accident that 15 of the 19 hijackers responsible for 9/11 were Saudis. The Americans withdrew to Qatar in 2003, but that only seemed to trigger a new wave of terrorist attacks inside the kingdom, and an unprecedented counter-terrorism crackdown.

The Saudis announced on May 19 that they had arrested four men in connection with the Riyadh bombings. "We are making progress in this investigation," Prince Bandar said. "Our country is still reeling from these horrible attacks and our people demand quick action. And, they will get it." Security throughout Saudi Arabia was tightened and Special Forces teams were deployed to guard against more attacks. On May 31, a security patrol came across Abdul Rahman's friend Swift Sword, who was wanted for his role in the bombings. He tried to run but was shot dead. Three weeks later, Ali Abdulrahman Said Alfagsi Al-Ghamdi, also known as Abu Bakr Al-Azdi, another suspected mastermind of the bombings, surrendered to police and underwent extensive interrogation.

As the investigation progressed, the Saudis arrested a disturbing number of radicalized youths who had joined the cause of bin Laden. Prince Nayef bin Abdulaziz, the Interior Minister, issued a surprisingly frank statement on the development, which had the air of soul-searching. "We have witnessed the criminal acts of some of our youth, who are citizens of this country. They have killed people, and have destroyed property, and have terrified families. If a person does something wrong and is convinced it is right, then we have to look at the root causes. We need to ask: Did the source of this ideology come from this land or was it imported from outside? Was it the result of fanatical ideas from people who have been brainwashed? Or is it a combination of factors, internal and external?" His own security forces seemed to offer the answer when they arrested three clerics who had urged Saudis to support those behind the Riyadh bombings.

By July 2, the Saudis had made 124 arrests in connection with the bombing, but Abdul Rahman was still out there, somewhere. Mansour called the Canadian embassies in Kuwait City and Riyadh to inquire about his son, to ask what kind of rights he had as a Canadian abroad. Mansour wanted to get him back home to safety, a task that seemed all the more urgent now that it was becoming increasingly clear that Mohammed would not be returning to Canada anytime soon. But it was too late. A consular official told Mansour he had bad news. Abdul Rahman was dead. The embassy was trying to get more information from the Saudi Ministry of Interior, but it appeared he had been caught as he was preparing to flee the kingdom. He had gone down fighting, like his friend Al Kandari.

The Saudis issued a press release that day, describing the operation in Sowair, part of the northern Al-Jawf province. Two hundred troops had been involved. They moved into position in a house opposite the mosque where the five suspects were thought to be holed up, including the man who topped the Saudi most-wanted list, 30-year-old Turki Nasser Mishaal Aldandany, one of the highest-ranking Al Qaeda operatives in the country and a mastermind of the May 12 bombings. The Saudis linked the operation to the earlier capture of Aldandany's number two, Al-Ghamdi, but never said conclusively whether he had given up his accomplices. The local press reported only that the operation was the result of a tip-off.

"A national manhunt for Aldandany had been underway and at 5:00 a.m. this morning security forces surrounded the house where he was hiding along with four other wanted individuals. Security forces evacuated the surrounding area and used loudspeakers to call for the surrender of the suspects. One of the Saudi suspects did, and he is now in custody," the statement said. "The others immediately began firing machine guns and lobbing grenades at security officers. In the ensuing gun battle, Aldandany and three others were killed. Authorities later also arrested three accomplices [two Saudi nationals and one Syrian national] who had been trying to smuggle the terrorists out of the country." One Arab newspaper reported that the four suspects had committed suicide by detonating explosives.

A second news release issued later in the day identified those killed with Aldandany as Amash Al-Subaibie, Rajih bin Hassan Al-Agjmi and Abdulrahman Gobbara, "a Kuwaiti of Iraqi origin." Although the statement misspelled his name, Abdul Rahman Jabarah was soon confirmed by Canadian authorities as one of the dead. He was 23 years old. The Saudi newspaper *Al-Riyadh* quoted Mansour as saying he had "already disowned his son for belonging to Al Qaeda." But he nonetheless tried to get his son's body to Kuwait for burial. The Kuwait government authorized the return of Abdul Rahman's remains but the Saudis would not cooperate, perhaps fearing a repeat of Al Kandari's funeral, which had turned into a rally for jihad. In fact, Abdul Rahman had already been buried in Saudi Arabia. The Saudis informed Canadian officials they would not exhume the body, and that their decision was final. They did agree, however, to grant visas to the Jabarah family so they could visit Abdul Rahman's resting place. But Mansour says he has no appetite to visit Saudi Arabia anymore. He has no idea where his son is buried.

"I believe the first person who killed Abdul Rahman? The government of Canada," he tells me. "They were looking for him, they were chasing him more than one or two years, and he was hiding himself in different places. That's why he did not know where he has to go.

"The first person made the order to kill Abdul Rahman? The government of Canada. This is what I believe. And the same thing has happened to Mohammed."

It must be difficult for a mourning father to see the harsh truth. In the aftermath of tragedy, it is natural to want to blame somebody. But Abdul Rahman made his own choices. He may have been preyed upon by religious extremists and Al Qaeda recruiters but in the end he died for just one reason: he was a terrorist. A jihadist videotape soon surfaced on the Internet, featuring clips of bin Laden wearing his camouflage jacket and talking to the camera. As he spoke, the mug shots of Al Qaeda "martyrs" flashed on the screen, among them the image of Abdul Rahman's heavily bearded face.

Those who knew Abdul Rahman and fought jihad with him penned an overwrought eulogy describing his life and martyrdom. One of them told about a dream he had about his dead friend.

"We were sitting and Abdul Rahman was in front of us. I asked him: 'Weren't you killed?' and Abdul Rahman answered: 'No, I wasn't killed.'

"Rejoice, for God, may He be glorified and exalted, said in His Koran: 'Do not consider those who died for God's sake dead—but alive.'"

Abdul Rahman was "among those whom God used in the jihad. He was raised on the jihad and became a martyr on its course," the eulogy said.

"We will never forget you, O guiding martyr. Nor will the families [to] whom you gave their grants. The brothers who lived with you and whom you taught will never forget you. May you receive award and compensation, with God's help."

"Farewell, martyr."

* * *

Canadian consular officials in New York broke the news to Mohammed during one of their regular visits to the Metropolitan Correctional Center. He found a newspaper and read about the details of the Saudi shootout. Later, in a phone call, his parents informed him that it was true. "He was very sorry. This hurt him very, very much," Mansour says.

All their lives, the brothers had been close, sharing the same school and friends. They had survived the Iraqi invasion of Kuwait together. What's more, they had trained together in Afghanistan, fought together on the frontlines with the Taliban and prayed to die for God. It must have been comforting for Mohammed and Abdul Rahman, as they followed the wretched path of the martyr, to have a brother by their side. Together with Al Kandari, they were their own little gang of thugs for God.

The world of the martyr is filled with contradictions. If Al Kandari and the Jabarah brothers wanted nothing more than to die for the cause, why was Abdul Rahman saddened by Al Kandari's death? Isn't that what he wanted? Likewise, in the logic of martyrdom, Mohammed should have been contented by his brother's killing, but he wasn't.

"He really got hurt about Abdul Rahman," Mansour says.

Mohammed had tried to protect his older brother by giving the CSIS and the FBI false information about him, but it hadn't helped. Isolated in his prison cell in New York, his partners in jihad falling one after another, his twisted visions of glory and martyrdom crashing around him, Mohammed vented his emotions the same way his hero Antara had done centuries ago: in verse. He sat down and wrote a poem in Arabic.

> *My beloved is gone and I am captured.*
> *Is it true what happened?*
> *Did all my friends leave me?*
> *And I remain alone in captivity.*

17

INMATE 06909-091

HE sleeps no more than six hours a night. He spends his days exercising and studying. He has a daily fitness routine and passes the remaining hours reciting the Koran and reading books about history and Islam. Every few weeks, an official from the Canadian Consulate in New York stops by to visit him, and he complains about his imprisonment. The consular officials note that he looks well but remains discontented, and they send an update back to headquarters in Ottawa.

"He's not a happy camper," one official says.

The books he has read in captivity include *Six Days of War*, the definitive account of the 1967 Arab–Israeli conflict, which ended in an embarrassingly swift and decisive defeat for Israel's Arab neighbors. "This is a book which I recommend you to read so that you benefit from history," Mohammed writes to his mother. He has read several books on Islamic thinking, *The Fundamentals of Belief between the Mind and the Heart*, by Sheikh Mohammed Al Ghazaly, whose writing attacked Zionists, missionaries and Western ideas, *The Scientist of Magic and Black Magic*, by Omar al Ashqar, and *The Medicine and the Disease*, by Ibn Quim.

The discipline of his daily itinerary would be comforting and familiar for a graduate of the training camps of Afghanistan, and it helps the time pass.

In a letter to his mother he writes:

A month goes by and it feels like a day. I keep reading and getting knowledge in many fields. Learning has no age limit. Whoever wants good destiny must read in religion and its principles.

Guantanamo Bay may be the best-known prison in the United States for those captured in the war on terror, but some of the most senior Al Qaeda operatives have been held further north, at the Metropolitan Correctional Center. MCC, as it's known, is a pre-trial detention facility in lower Manhattan, at the corner of Park Row and Pearl, across the street from the federal courthouse. Almost every major Al Qaeda terrorist put on trial in the United States has been a guest of MCC. Few of them, however, were as young as Mohammed Jabarah.

The jail must seem all the more confining to Jabarah because of his youth. When he first went into U.S. custody, he was only 20 years old. In December 2004, he celebrated his 23rd birthday at MCC. He has stopped cooperating with the FBI. He talks only to his lawyer, the Canadian consular officials and his family, in the letters he writes home in neat Arabic script. He writes to his father:

Please pray for me because it has a great effect on my daily life. Don't be afraid or sad because nothing will happen to us except what is destined to happen to us by God, and because He is our Guarantor and the best support to us while our enemies have no support.

When I first read Mohammed's letters, I expected to find some expressions of remorse. He clearly did wrong, but he did right in the end. He gave himself up and talked. These were signs of a young man who had come to his senses. Freed from the grip of Al Qaeda, he had snapped out it, outgrown his youthful experiment with jihadism. Or so I thought. But when I was shown his dispatches from prison, I did not get that sense at all. His letters ooze with bitterness. They are filled with the rhetoric of his Al Qaeda masters, about "believers" and "infidels" and not being "bitten by the snake twice." He writes spitefully about his interrogators, and signs his letters using his Al Qaeda name, Abu Hafs. He compares the Americans to "when Moawiya was against the fighters and fought all governments." Moawiya was a 17th-century Arab leader who was born into a tribe that rejected the Prophet Muhammad and opposed him in battle until the conquest of Mecca. He seems to see the Americans in a similar light, a powerful political and military force that has not yet recognized the supremacy of extremist Islam.

This was not the Mohammed that the Canadian Security Intelligence Service had dealt with in Niagara Falls and Toronto, the young man led astray who was ready to face up to what he had done, to pay the price and get on with his life. What happened? Maybe the shock of losing his best friend and then his brother snapped him back into his holy warrior persona. His mood change also coincides with another shock: the realization that he was probably going to remain in jail for a good long time. His estimate that the Americans would let him off with a sentence of two to five years seems to have been wildly off base. He now wants to back out of the plea bargain, claiming he did not understand the agreement he signed. By the spring of 2005, he was seeking a new lawyer. He seems to feel he's been had.

Was he? The Americans may well have taken advantage of Mohammed's naiveté, but it is difficult to fault them for that. He was a trained killer on the side of their number-one enemy. He had tried to blow up an American embassy. Besides, the Americans did it by the book. This was not a third-country rendition of debatable legality, or even a stint at Guantanamo. Before he ever left Canada, the Department of Justice had Mohammed sign an agreement that was explicit about what was in store. It was, however, vague about the specifics of the charges and the sentence, and the benefits Mohammed would get in exchange for his cooperation. In some respects Mohammed had signed a blank check.

Mohammed's mistake may have been to misjudge the severity of the charges he would face. He was far from New York at the time of 9/11 and perhaps he did not comprehend how deep a wound the attacks had left in the United States, and how serious the Americans had become about prosecuting the war on terror. If Mohammed surrendered himself to the United States thinking he was going to get off with a slap on the wrist, he was badly mistaken. But the agreement he negotiated and signed suggests he was hardly duped. And Jabarah is not a stupid young man. "Mohammed Mansour Jabarah is one of the most intelligent terrorists we have seen," says Rohan Gunaratna, a Singapore-based scholar and renowned Al Qaeda expert who knows the case intimately. "He had the education, the contacts, the training and the motivation to become another mastermind."

There is still an argument to be made for leniency. If intelligence agencies hope to break Al Qaeda, they will have to provide incentives for its members to leave. Captured terrorists must serve an appropriate sentence, but if that sentence is not excessive, it could undermine Al Qaeda by planting a seed of doubt in the minds of those still in the field. It will remind operatives that there is an alternative to murder and martyrdom. It could sway lower-level members, and without their loyalty, bin Laden and Zarqawi are powerless, although some are doubtless too extreme for that.

There is an air of the fantastical to Mohammed's letters. He addresses his mother as "the beautiful fighter." He signs off some of his letters as "Prince," the title that was bestowed on Antara. Sometimes, he signs his letters, "your son, who is in captivity." Even as he sits behind bars, he cannot resist, in a letter home, giving religious and professional advice to his younger brother Youssef:

To my dear brother, whom I love and care for so much and no one knows how much I love you except God, Youssef bin Mansour Al-Aboussi:

How are you?

How are your studies and relationship with [not legible] and our older brother and the family? I ask God that they are all fine and in good health.

I am doing fine and in good health, thanks to God. I am also standing fast due to the support of God, who has no partner . . . You know what I want to say to you. I want you to study His book from A to Z, word for word. The reason, as I always concentrate on, is that you are at an age at which you can study more and more. This age, you will not appreciate it unless you get older. They say when you study at a younger age, it is as if you are carving on stone. This means that this carving will never go away, even if it collects dust, because you can remove dust with just a blow of air and the carving will be clear as new.

Try to benefit from everything that is of good to you during your life and at the end of your life. You are now going into the secondary school stage and I advise you that you go into the science section and excel in it. This means that you not just read what is given to you at school, but you should read and research everything at the libraries and encyclopedia.

Set your goal to be either a physician or an engineer. This is for the official field. As for the general field, your first goal must be to learn the word of God and study His religion, because it is the only knowledge that will raise your status.

You should honour your parents and grandparents, your brothers and sisters and your oldest brother.

Thank God.

Your brother, Mohammed Mansour bin Nazem Al-Aboussi, Abi Hifss Al-Bassry.

In another letter, he asks about the wedding of his eldest brother Abdullah, whom he jokes should take two wives, unlike his father, who has only the one.

Of course marrying more than one is Halal to us, but you have Om Abdullah who is worth the women of the whole world! Ha ha!

Most of his letters, at least the ones I have seen, read like postcards from summer camp. He tells his parents what he is doing and asks about his friends and relatives.

How are things with the family and the friends in Iraq and Kuwait? Please send my regards to all of them. I hope that they are all doing well.

But Mohammed's friends were not doing well at all.

* * *

The men who had been his brothers in jihad fell like dominoes after his arrest. First it was Al Kandari, then Abdul Rahman Jabarah. The two Saudis who had traveled with him to Afghanistan from Karachi, Abu Muslim and Abu Obeida, were also killed. Next came the mastermind himself, Khalid Sheikh Mohammad. When the Taliban fell in Afghanistan, KSM had run across the border into Pakistan, along with the bulk of the surviving Al Qaeda leadership. Rather than hiding in the Northwest Frontier, he made his way to Rawalpindi, on the outskirts of the capital, and moved into a large house hidden from the street by a wall. It was probably the last place anyone would have thought to look—in the upscale Westridge neighborhood, where many Pakistani military officers live. The Pakistan army base was only a short walk away. A huge manhunt was underway in the tribal areas along the Afghanistan border and here he was, hiding in plain sight. But the Americans intercepted his telephone calls and, together with the intelligence coming from human sources, investigators tracked him down. On March 1, two dozen Pakistani police officers wearing *shalwar khameez* over bulletproof vests surrounded the home armed with AK-47s. At 3 a.m., they leapt over the garden wall, pushed through the front gate and stormed inside, catching KSM fast asleep. Within days, KSM's wanted poster on the FBI website was updated: a red slash with the word "Captured" was placed over his mug shot. He was immediately put under interrogation, and he soon started to talk about his plots and his associates, among them Hambali.

After the Bali bombing, Hambali stayed in Cambodia, mostly in Phnom Penh but also in Siem Reap and Kam Phot. Even after the devastation he had just caused in Indonesia, he continued to plot more violence. He sent an operative to scout the British embassy in Phnom Penh, and also cased it himself two or three times, noting that security was lax along the main road in front. He returned to Thailand in February 2003, crossing the border at Poipet, and stayed in contact with his network by email. One operative wrote to him saying, "I want business but have no capital," which he knew meant another attack was in the works but financing was needed.

Hambali's Jemaah Islamiyah struck again on August 5, 2003. A suicide bomber hit the JW Marriott Hotel in Jakarta, killing 14 and wounding 150. Ten days later, the White House announced the capture of Hambali. In a speech to U.S. Marines in California, George W. Bush called him "one of the world's most lethal terrorists." Australian Prime Minister John Howard called the arrest "a huge breakthrough," adding, "He was almost certainly the ultimate mastermind of the Bali attack so, to those relatives and friends of the 88 Australians who died in that outrage almost a year ago, this is, I hope, some further measure of justice."

The man Jabarah knew as Mike the Bombmaker, Fathur Al-Ghozi, somehow managed a prison break in the Philippines but he was tracked by the Presidential Anti-Crime and Emergency Response Team to Pigkawayan, in North Catabato province, and killed in a shootout. His death came on October 12, 2003—the first anniversary of the Bali bombing. Southeast Asia remains a hotbed of Islamic radicalism, with violence flaring in the Philippines, southern Thailand and Indonesia. "To date Indonesia has had difficulty fighting Islamic extremist groups," a Canadian intelligence report said. "Indonesia is the largest and most populous state in Southeast Asia and has been rocked by ongoing religious and ethnic strife, an environment which fosters Islamic extremism." If Mohammed Jabarah's intent was to foment jihad in Southeast Asia, he can rest assured that he was successful, but his brothers in jihad had paid a heavy price. "The United States of America is winning this war on terrorism with unrelenting focus and unprecedented cooperation," James Comey, the prosecutor who had brought Mohammed to New York and laid charges against him, said shortly after he was named Deputy Attorney General of the United States.

Mohammed reflected on his plight in a poem from prison:

I woke up in captivity,
With tears stubborn to run through,
The iron spoke out and said,
You are weakened, you are wretched!

Depending on his mood, Mansour can be either resigned and fatalistic or wildly optimistic when he is pondering Mohammed's fate. He once told me he thought Mohammed could be home within the year, but another time he said his son could be in jail for 25 years, or that he might vanish into a witness protection program. On his good days, Mansour sees his son coming home to Canada, picking up with his studies and embarking on a professional career—a scenario that seems unlikely given the circumstances in which he now finds himself, a terrorist imprisoned by the country he terrorized.

"He has a dream to fulfill," Mansour says.

"He told me when he was young, 'I would like to continue my dream to become a doctor.'

"You can smell from his letters that he got a big lesson from what he has done before . . . that's why he is focusing on his future. He would like to rebuild his future again. He would like to come back again.

"And we are waiting for him."

In the meantime, Mansour has been waging a one-man campaign to bring his son home to Canada. He has written letters to the Department of Foreign Affairs in Ottawa, hoping to enlist the help of the government of Canada. As part of the campaign, he has translated some of Mohammed's letters. One is titled, *From POW/Abu Hafs Al Basri Mohammed Mansour Ibn Nadhem Ibn Jabarrah Ibn Saqr Al Absi.* Mansour is trying to convince the authorities that Mohammed was tricked into going to the United States, and he hopes that Canadians will rally behind his cause on the grounds that they could be next.

It is not certain, however, that Mohammed wants to return to Canada. In one letter, he urges his brother Abdullah to "leave Canada for good" and return to Kuwait. For his part, Abdullah tells me that Abdul Rahman and Mohammed "embarrassed the family." Mohammed does seem to want publicity for his case, though. He wrote a brief account of his experiences since his arrest, sent it to Mansour and said:

> *If a media company (newspaper, media broadcast) asked you for an interview, you can do that—for instance if Al Jazeera network. The news that I write to you in my letters about my case is not a private matter and there is no restriction on you telling them if you think it is of benefit.*

* * *

Mansour has some support from civil liberties and Muslim activist groups. Media reports claiming that Mohammed had been "kidnapped" by intelligence agents and taken to the United States against his will were circulated on the Internet and portrayed as an example of American security excess post-9/11. CSIS "dumped" Mohammed in the United States, Rocco Galati, a flamboyant Toronto lawyer, claimed when cross-examining agent Mike Pavlovic in a separate case. The Canadian Arab Federation referred to Mohammed in one of its press releases as a "political prisoner," and said it was disturbed by the way CSIS had dealt with him. "Is CSIS operating above the law now or have Canadians simply lost their civil rights in the post-September 11 world?" The Canadian Civil Liberties Association has also written to the Solicitor General claiming "there are reasonable concerns about the legality of the role played by the Service." The letter asks the Security Intelligence Review Committee, the oversight agency that monitors CSIS, to investigate. But the government knew something the activists did not, that Mohammed had agreed to plead guilty prior to leaving Canadian soil and that he was a self-confessed, full-fledged member of Al Qaeda.

His father pleads, "I'm asking each person, each citizen in Canada and the United States to support us, to assist us to bring our son Mohammed back to Canada, back home to be among his brothers, to be among his citizens, to be among his friends, to finish his hope to be a nice citizen, as he is. And I'm asking strongly the government of Canada to do their best."

In August 2004, Mansour sent a letter to Pierre Pettigrew, the Minister of Foreign Affairs, asking for help. Mansour wants the minister to bring Mohammed back to Canada. He also wants help getting Abdul Rahman's body out of Saudi Arabia. "My family and I are upset that my sons have not been afforded the rights one would expect from Canada," he writes. "I have heard from my son and his lawyer that he was duped into going to the United States . . . Because of the Canadian government's role in handing him to the U.S., I want you to do everything in your power to have him returned as soon as possible."

The reply sent two weeks later was written by Dave Dyet, Director of the Case Management Division in the Consular Affairs Bureau. "With regards to your request to have your son transferred [to Canada], please be informed that all Canadian citizens detained in a foreign country have the right to apply for a transfer to a Canadian penal institution. Transfer decisions are discretionary, however, and for a transfer to take place the jurisdiction where the offender was sentenced, the country of citizenship to which he or she is being returned and the offender must all agree. Once your son becomes eligible, he will be advised of the application process." He said the department was "following your son's case closely to ensure due process is taking place." Mansour sold his St. Catharines house in the fall of 2004 and bought a small townhouse near Holy Cross school for his sons Youssef and Abdullah, but Mansour seems to have little interest in returning to Canada.

It has been four years now since they saw him last, the son who set off to follow his religion and got lost. He was led astray by the bottom feeders of politics, those who seek to advance their death-cult ideology by convincing the youth of the Muslim world to commit cold-blooded murder. They turned a handsome, educated and otherwise moral young man into a killer. Bin Laden sent Mohammed off to slaughter and die for the cause while he and his sidekick Al Zawahiri stayed hidden in caves along the Afghan–Pakistan frontier. The things Mohammed did have contributed to world insecurity and the mass murder of innocents. He never detonated a bomb with his own hands but in some ways what he did was worse: He made it possible for many others to commit acts of terror by providing them with the money, logistical support and leadership they required.

"I'm asking you this question," Mansour tells me in our last discussion. "What Mohammed has done against Canada, which transferred him to the United States? And what Mohammed has done to the security of America?"

"He told CSIS," I reply, "that he was involved in plans to blow up an embassy in Singapore."

"Nothing happened!" Mansour says. "Mohammed has never done anything. I'm repeating, Mohammed has never done anything against the security, either Canada or America."

"You don't consider training in Afghanistan to be against Canada or America?" I say.

"No," Mansour says. "Why? A lot of people trained in Afghanistan, in Chechnya, in different parts of the world."

There are a lot of things we still don't know about Mohammed Jabarah, but we know enough to say that he joined a despicable cause and devoted himself to it. We also know that he did not do so entirely on his own. He was lured down that path every step of the way, beginning at a criminally young age.

There is, however, no turning back for those who have pledged the martyr's oath.

On March 23, 2004, he wrote:

I just want to say hi Salam to you and to tell you that I am all right. Thanks to Allah that I have strong spiritual feelings as usual. Concerning the legal case, they have been trying so hard, nights and days since I have been arrested convincing me and to be so cooperative with them as a betrayer. They have been trying for 15 months, to meet them, but, I insist on rejecting this which [goes] against my beliefs as a Muslim.

As I told you before, my only reason for confessing the guilt in front of the judge was because when I was arrested by the FBI and I was not in jail at that moment. They had enforced me to say what they want. They had threatened me with jail if I did not admit the guilt. Besides, David the devilish lawyer didn't make it clear to me, with fake information he gave.

In the present time, I did not want to withdraw my additions because I think it is like a film with its known end. And I don't want to waste my time with this matter. The best thing to do, which I am going to do by Allah's willing, is to ask the court to give their final decision. Remember that nothing will happen to us except what is written by Allah. So don't get upset, be patient and be happy. And remember, Allah is the only protector and the best defender against all accusation while our enemies no one will defend or protect them.
*Thanks to Allah.**

---

*The letter is reproduced here as written.

"I'm trying my best," Mansour says.

"This is our dream now. We lost one. We lost Abdul Rahman without any reason and we don't want to lose Mohammed now."

Mansour's dream of bringing Mohammed home to a normal life seems, however, unlikely to be fulfilled anytime soon. Perhaps that is as it should be, because neither will the dreams of the many killed by Al Qaeda be fulfilled.

"I have sent a letter to the prime minister to bring him home and we are waiting," Mansour says, sitting with Souad, the suffering heads of a shattered family that has brought into the world not one terrorist, but two.

"His mother, his family and myself we are all waiting for Mohammed."

Later, a letter arrives at my office from the U.S. Bureau of Prisons. Inside is the Inmate Data sheet for prisoner 06909-091. It is a printout of Mohammed Jabarah's file in the prison computer system.

Under the heading Projected Release Date, it reads, "UNKNOWN."

18

THE JIHAD FACTORY

THE fall of the Taliban robbed Al Qaeda of its land base and training ground, and brought an end to Afghanistan's dark days as the hub of global terror. Would-be terrorists can no longer fly to Peshawar and trek over the mountains to bin Laden's federation of heavily armed tent cities, as Mohammed Jabarah did not so long ago. Initially, there were expectations that this would trigger a decline in recruitment for jihad, but it has not worked out that way. Recruitment has changed due to the loss of Afghanistan as a terrorist sanctuary and the intensification of counter-terrorism efforts worldwide, but it has not stopped—far from it.

According to a confidential Canadian Security Intelligence Service study, Al Qaeda and specifically bin Laden "have reached almost mythical importance in many parts of the Arab and Muslim world." Al Qaeda has become "an ideological magnet for Sunni Islamic extremist groups worldwide," the study says. Al Qaeda has become "glocal," both global and local at the same time. With its legacy of trained terrorists, massive propaganda effort and image among many as the only organization standing up to Western economic, political, military and cultural power, Al Qaeda has become the inspiration for other radical groups that have harnessed their local causes—in Saudi Arabia, Iraq, Afghanistan and even North America—to the worldwide jihad. The burst of inhuman violence on September 11 that should have discredited Al Qaeda and brought about its demise has instead propelled it to the forefront.

This was perhaps an inevitable result of 9/11. The greatest recruiting tool of the terrorist is the act of terrorism itself. Terrorism is a form of advertising. It is a way of selling the cause. "The most important audience for a terrorist is made up of the people who are already supporters, or who could become supporters," says a Royal Canadian Mounted Police intelligence report. "The attack does not have to make sense to the victim population or government, but it does have to appeal to the population supplying the funds, assistance and recruits to the terrorist group. While terrorists want their supporters to see them as heroes, they don't care if their victims see them as villains." Terrorism feeds on itself, which is why it is essential to confront terrorist movements forcefully and put them out of business as quickly as possible. Standing idly by and hoping the storm passes will not work. Every act of terrorism that is prevented through counter-terrorist operations not only saves lives, it also robs terrorists of one of their most vital recruiting tools.

Terrorism is nothing more than a brazen grab for power and, unfortunately, it sometimes works. As Bruce Hoffman argues, this quest for power evolves in five stages: attention, acknowledgement, recognition, authority and governance. Al Qaeda has certainly succeeded in focusing attention on itself, and in winning widespread acknowledgement for its cause. And in many parts of the Arab and Muslim world, as well as among a minority of immigrants in the West, bin Laden is now recognized as the champion of the Islamic movement. As a result, even though Al Qaeda no longer has Afghanistan, and its remaining leaders are on the run, it has still managed to attract a worrisome number of fresh recruits and an even larger pool of followers who might be coaxed into terrorism if the recruiters do their jobs well.

"Certainly there is a segment of radicalized Muslims and Arabs in Europe and in Canada, in the United States that are sympathetic, supportive and even joining these groups and even willing to die for these groups, and they are educated and come from reasonably wealthy families," says Associate Professor Gunaratna, who advises governments and police forces, including some in Canada. "North America and Western Europe are safe havens for terrorist groups in terms of recruitment and fundraising."

This recruiting is now being done more discreetly, by local cells and contacts. The propaganda, rhetoric and talent-spotting have gone underground. Recruiting is being carried out more cautiously. Extremists are setting up their own mosques in strip malls and apartments and are carefully vetting who gets in as a precaution against infiltration by security agencies. It is being done in chat rooms on jihadi websites. The phenomenon of self-recruiting—that is, when someone decides on his or her own to join the cause—is far more prevalent. But even those self-recruits are being influenced by the main components of the recruiting network: radical Salafi preachers, "brothers" in the jihad movement, gatekeepers who facilitate the recruiting process and mass propaganda that portrays Islam as a faith under siege and exhorts believers to fight in its defense.

Propaganda is essential to the survival of terrorist organizations. It sustains the illusions that keep members fully devoted to the cause. Since 9/11, it has become an increasingly vital part of the recruiting equation, and much of it is, for strategic reasons, aimed directly at youths. The release of a rap music video praising bin Laden is but one example. "The youth must not wait for anybody," Ayman Al Zawahiri says in an audiotape released on October 1, 2004. "They must start their resistance now . . . Youth of Islam! This is our message to you. In case of our death or our capture, go on and follow the path after us, and do not betray God and the Prophet, or the trusts that have been consigned to you." This propaganda has long been prevalent in the Arab and Muslim mass media, but now it is on the Internet, where it can influence the minds of youths in Europe and North America. Jihadist websites now offer not only a selection of training manuals showing how to fire a shoulder-launched missile, but also the basic talking points of recruiters. "How can you become a member of Al Qaeda?" asks a message circulated on one jihadist message board. "Today, Al Qaeda is no longer simply an organization that works on fighting Jews and the Crusaders only," it says. "It has become an invitation . . . that calls upon all Muslims to rise for the support of Allah."

Al Qaeda is not the only terrorist network working on the minds of youths. Palestinian terror factions such as Hamas, and Hezbollah in Lebanon, are notorious for targeting youths by, for example, decorating elementary schools with the posters of "martyrs." In Tehran, 440 young women and men volunteered on a single day in April 2005 to carry out suicide bomb attacks against Israelis and American troops. But it is the "Al Qaeda message" of global jihad that has had the most resonance among youths, both in the Arab and Muslim world and in the West, and it is by far the most dangerous calling. "The presence of young, committed jihadists in Canada is of grave concern," a classified CSIS study says. "They represent a clear and present danger to Canada and its allies and are a particularly valuable resource for the international Islamic terrorist community in view of their language skills and familiarity with Western culture and infrastructure. As the Jabarah . . . cases illustrate, these people are fully prepared to commit support for terrorist acts, and carry out the acts themselves."

* * *

"The fight against terrorism," the United Nations counter-terrorism chief Javier Ruperez said in Vienna on October 20, 2004, "is a pre-emptive war." What he meant was that counterterrorism is not like an ordinary criminal investigation. Its goal is not to solve a crime, but rather to prevent it from occurring in the first place. The consequences of a terrorist attack are so severe that it cannot be otherwise. "Once the bomb[ing] is taking place, there is nothing much to do but mourn," he explained.

Certainly one way to preempt terrorism is to disrupt the recruitment process. If there is one fundamental challenge in the war against terror, it is to put an end to the assembly line production of terrorists. How do the responsible nations of the world stop young men like Mohammed Jabarah from joining terrorist groups? What can be done to prevent the likes of the Lackawanna Six and Muslim youths in Britain, Australia, France, Germany and the Netherlands from falling under the influence of radicals who hold the Koran in one hand and a Kalashnikov in the other? These are not questions that can be taken lightly anymore, as the Madrid bombings and the ammonium nitrate plot in the United Kingdom showed. The increasing success of recruiting efforts within the West has created a whole new set of security challenges, foremost among them how to deal with the growing number of homegrown terrorists—those "terrorists within" who live in countries like Canada but are nonetheless devoted to their destruction. On top of the problem of jihadist youth, add the rising number of Muslim converts adopting radical Islam and the jihadist returnees coming home from exploits overseas, and you have a significant extremist pool ideologically opposed to the state and society in which they live.

Curbing global terrorism, from New York to Jerusalem to Beslan to London, means not only fighting terrorism at the frontlines in Iraq and Afghanistan, but also confronting it at home, where promising young people are being drawn into violent factions that communicate their discontent by murdering bus passengers, office workers and school children. It is not an easy challenge, but once security authorities get a grasp on how this recruitment process works in their regions of responsibility, they can begin to disrupt it. We may never be able to completely stop the recruitment of terrorists into Al Qaeda and its affiliates, or any other extremist group that uses violence as a tactic, but how much grief could have been avoided had just 19 men been convinced to do something else with their lives.

During conventional wars, one of the aims of generals is to destroy the factories that arm and equip the forces of their enemies. The war on terror is not a conventional war but the same strategic thinking should be applied. The most important weapon of the Al Qaeda movement is not the AK-47 or TNT: It is recruits so devoted that they are willing to commit acts of "martyrdom" for the cause, to drive a truck bomb into an embassy, or strap on a suicide vest and detonate it in a crowd. The destruction of the global jihad factory that manufactures these terrorists must therefore be a central focus of the war on terror.

The problem, of course, is that, in the war on terror, there are no industrial buildings that can be bombed to stop the production of terrorists. That may have been possible in Afghanistan until 2001, and in Sudan until 1996, but just as Al Qaeda has become more diffuse and less visible since 9/11, so has the recruiting network. You can no longer simply fire Tomahawk missiles at a training camp. It is much more complicated than that, especially when recruitment is taking place partly through family and friendship connections.

The Khadr family in Canada is but one example. Ahmed Said Khadr was an Egyptian-born Canadian who moved his family from Ontario to Peshawar, and later to Jalalabad and Kabul, and sent his Canadian sons to Al Qaeda training camps. When an important step in the recruiting process takes place within the home, it is no easy task to stop it. "In most cases," CSIS writes of Canada's jihadist youth, "these young men are the product of an upbringing by Islamic radicals who want their sons to follow in their footsteps."

The step-by-step recruitment of Mohammed Jabarah is a case study in the classic fashion in which terrorists are manufactured through personal connections. Recruitment, Jabarah shows us, is a gradual process that takes place, as

Marc Sageman points out, through kinship, friendship, worship and discipleship. His radicalization was facilitated by modern technology—the Internet and videos—and age-old methods, notably exposure to veterans of combat. Israeli psychologist Ariel Merari calls them the "agents of influence"—the teachers, friends, parents and others that convince those close to them that the cause is worthy. Terrorism cannot be fought effectively until each of the forces pushing young people towards extremist violence are confronted. It would be an impossible—and probably highly undesirable—task to attempt to prevent anyone, especially adolescents, from developing radical views. But what governments can do is challenge the worldview of extremists and step in when radicalization crosses the line, when it becomes recruiting that materially supports terrorism.

Radical preachers must be isolated, and prosecuted if they violate hate crimes or incitement laws. Recruiters must be dealt with severely in recognition of the damage they cause: to their recruits, to the victims of terrorism and to global security. Front, cover and sympathy organizations that indoctrinate youths into jihadism and help them go off to train and fight must be shut down, bankrupted and prosecuted. And those like Mohammed Jabarah who join terrorist organizations must be prosecuted, although leniency should be considered for those who cooperate with investigators. Despite a shift in tactics, such as the rise of cyber-indoctrination and underground mosques, the recruiting process eventually reaches a stage where face-to-face contact with the recruiter must take place, and that is also where investigators can focus their efforts.

Some of these things are beginning to happen. The British have arrested most of the extremist clerics preaching violent jihad at a handful of mosques. The United States has led the way in shutting down charities fronting for terrorism, and its treatment of the Lackawanna Six was appropriately harsh. Each of the recruits pleaded guilty and agreed to cooperate with investigators, and Kamal Derwish, who recruited the young men, was killed by a missile fired from a CIA unmanned aircraft in Yemen. The members of the Virginian Jihad Network were also prosecuted and their recruiter was convicted.

In Canada, the progress has been less promising. Authorities believe there is a significant pool of Sunni Islamic extremists in the country. "We do have some extremely radical mosques," an RCMP counter-terrorism official says. Although some terrorists have been arrested for deportation to their home countries, not a single charge of hate speech has been laid against radical preachers, and not one of the many non-profit groups fronting for extremism has faced any consequence worse than losing their status as a government-registered charity. Despite more than two decades of international terrorist activity that has caused mayhem around the world, only one person has been charged with terrorism in Canada. The Sikh terrorists responsible for the 1985 Air India bombing, which killed 329 people, have not been brought to justice. Not a single charge of terror financing has been laid, although investigators claim that an estimated CDN$140 million a year is flowing through the country to terrorists. "Frankly," the RCMP officer says, "we do still have a ways to go."

Governments cannot solve this alone. Community and religious leaders can contribute by ensuring that terrorists are not romanticized but rather are exposed for the bloodthirsty killers that they are. Saudi Arabia's top cleric set a promising precedent at the 2005 Haj when he said that, "The greatest affliction to strike the nation of Islam came from some of its own sons, who were lured by the devil . . . they have spread vice on earth, with explosions and destruction and killing of innocents." The Islamic Commission of Spain, which represents 200 mosques and 70 per cent of Muslims, likewise made an important stride when it issued a *fatwa* calling bin Laden an apostate of Islam. "The terrorist acts of Osama bin Laden and his organization Al Qaeda . . . are totally banned and must be roundly condemned." In the West, worshippers must continue to alert authorities when extremists start causing problems, particularly inside mosques, which are notoriously difficult for investigators to penetrate. It may be a hopeful sign that some tips are coming in to security agencies in Canada from Muslims disenchanted with the extremists in their midst. This type of information gives intelligence agencies the early warning they need to stay on top of emerging threats and prevent acts of terrorism from occurring.

Ethnic and religious institutions must play their part by countering the propaganda of activist groups that spread false and exaggerated depictions of the plight of Muslims both at home and abroad. Over-the-top claims of religious persecution, such as those found in the press releases and email bulletins of many mainstream lobby groups in the West, are only helping to drive youths into the hands of extremists. Rather than resisting counter-terrorism, interest groups should embrace it and cooperate enthusiastically with investigators as a way of ensuring that extremists are rooted out of positions of community influence. Aside from the obvious security argument for targeting Islamic extremists, lobby groups must recognize that counter-terrorism is also a way of protecting Muslim youth from falling into the cycle of indoctrination and recruitment. Academics can do their part as well, by paying more attention to research that will shed light on radicalization and recruitment.

Since 9/11 there has been a lot of soul-searching in the West over what is driving jihadist terrorism. The West has reflexively looked inward and asked itself what it has done wrong to be so hated that terrorists eagerly die trying to kill them. Westerners eat themselves up looking in the mirror for the root causes of terrorism.

But they won't find the answers there because international jihadist terrorism is not a consequence of a particular Western foreign policy or world event. It is the product of terrorists who distort and harness these policies and events to bring followers into their movements. If the nobility of U.S. interests in Iraq are not so obvious, the reasons for Western intervention in Afghanistan, Kosovo and Somalia were far less controversial, yet they were still manipulated by Islamic extremists who depicted them as an Israeli-backed American attack on the Muslim world—and a justification for jihad.

A European politician once quipped that George W. Bush was Al Qaeda's best recruiting tool. That may have been witty, but it is not true. U.S. presidents don't create terrorists. Terrorists are created by other terrorists, by the power-hungry who demand change or else, by the bin Ladens, KSMs and Zarqawis of the world, by clerics who spew hatred in the guise of religion, by recruiters who solicit their friends, and their friends' children, by families who raise their children to be closed-minded zealots, by media outlets that see only the repression of one faith rather than the whole complex picture. All of these forces combine to radicalize youths and make them vulnerable to recruitment.

There is no shortage of psychological theories purporting to explain the terrorist mind, but none is completely convincing and the most honest are those that recognize that a wide variety of factors explains why people become terrorists. In the end, perhaps it comes down to this. We are all searching for meaning and purpose in a world of confusion. And so when someone comes along with an explanation that makes simple sense of the world and explains our place in it, and gives us something to believe in, to be a part of, it can be a powerful thing. Al Qaeda and radical Islamic jihadists offer a sense of purpose to confused young men. Look at some of the world's most notorious terrorist movements, and it becomes apparent that it doesn't seem to really matter what cause the organization is pushing. It doesn't have to be a particularly worthy cause, or even a logical one, such as Aum Shinrikyo's apocalyptic vision or even that of bin Laden. All that matters is having something to join, something to believe in and something to belong to. Add to that the sense of companionship that comes with being part of a secret brotherhood, and then throw in the excitement of it all—shooting guns, playing secret agent, blowing things up. Counter-terrorism investigators believe some of the recruits they are seeing are not religious at all. They are adolescents in it for the kicks. Mix it all together and you have a recipe for boyhood fantasy. It is a combination that has been exploited for generations by generals and revolutionaries, and now it is being harnessed by terrorists.

Mohammed Jabarah did not have to devote himself to jihad, but he did, and for that he must suffer the consequences. But if there is one thing that is apparent from his experience, it is that there were many hands guiding him to his fate.

"Those people who recruit people to fight overseas, I would like to see the old men charged, I would like to see the imams who send young people over to die charged," says Phil Rankin, a Vancouver lawyer who represents the family of Rudwan "Raider" Khalil, a 26-year-old Canadian who, according to the Russian military, was killed on October 7, 2004, while fighting with a Chechen guerrilla unit (at time of writing, DNA tests are ongoing to confirm that the body is that of Khalil).

In Kuwait and also in Canada, Mohammed's friends, his religious instructors and his mentors were all part of what influenced him to become a terrorist. "Mohammed Jabarah was recruited, financed, trained and supervised by Muslim extremists every step of the way on his path to prison," a Canadian security official tells me. "Politely looking the other way is no longer an option."

The case of Mohammed Jabarah is one of those good news/bad news stories. The good news is that through solid counter-terrorism work and the sharing of information across borders, intelligence officers and police were able to take down a rising figure in Al Qaeda and then extract useful information from him. In less than than two years, Mohammed was identified, caught, turned and prosecuted—all before he was able to complete his first violent assignment. The bad news is that he was just one solitary product of a global network that manufactures terrorists. The jihad factory that turns pliant youths into killers for God is in full production, and until it is shut down, it will continue to mass-produce terrorists who will haunt us for years to come.

Appendix 1

EXCERPTS from Canadian Security Intelligence Service reports, dated May and June 2002, based on interviews with Mohammed Jabarah in St. Catharines and Toronto.

TOP SECRET

Re: Mohammed Mansour JABARAH

My headquarters would like to apprise you of the following information regarding the activities of Mohammed Mansour JABARAH:

Quote:

* * *

According to the Service's source, JABARAH met with Usama BIN LADEN (UBL) circa July 2001 in an effort to convince UBL of his potential as an AL QAIDA operative by highlighting his excellent English language skills, his clean Canadian passport and his high standing in his AL QAIDA training courses. UBL was apparently impressed and told JABARAH to meet with 'Mohammed the Pakistani' who would give JABARAH instructions and funds for an operation. 'Mohammed the Pakistani' was identified by the source as Khalid Shaikh MOHAMMED, a Kuwaiti currently on the US's Most Wanted Terrorist list. The source also advised that 'Mohammed the Pakistani' is also apparently known as Muhktar AL BALUSHI.

The source indicated that JABARAH traveled to Karachi, Pakistan in mid August 2001 to meet 'Mohammad the Pakistani.' Apparently 'Mohammad the Pakistani' is actually Kuwaiti. JABARAH stayed with 'Mohammad' for two weeks during which time 'Mohammad' provided advice and lessons on how to handle life in a city and how to prepare himself for his AL QAIDA missions. This was necessary as he would need to become reacquainted with life 'outside' Afghanistan. 'Mohammad' told JABARAH that JABARAH'S job would be to provide money for a suicide operation in the Philippines. JABARAH would be the go-between for the local Southeast Asian operatives and AL QAIDA. JABARAH was not asked to be a driver or a suicide bomber for an operation as there were hundreds of others in Afghanistan eagerly ready to fill that role. He was considered a more valuable entity given his abilities, language capability and his clean Canadian passport. After one week (approximately the beginning of September 2001), JABARAH met a Malaysian man named HAMBALI, who later used the name Azman, at HAMBALI's apartment in Karachi. HAMBALI began giving JABARAH details regarding the planned operation in the Philippines including targets such as the American and Israeli Embassies.

* * *

Jabarah indicated that he had been in casual contact with some of the hijackers responsible for the terrorist attacks in the United States . . . He had seen four of the hijackers at a guest house in Kandahar around March 2001.

* * *

Jabarah claimed to have met UBL on four occasions. The first meeting was in Kandahar prior to the beginning of the Guerilla Mountain warfare course, circa May 2001– June 2001. . . . They met in Kandahar, and it was at this meeting that Jabarah told UBL that he wanted to join AL QAIDA. UBL told Jabarah that they must be ready to fight the enemies of Allah wherever they are and specifically mentioned the United States and 'Jews'. JABARAH indicated that UBL asked him to swear an oath to AL QAIDA. UBL asked JABARAH what courses he had taken in Afghanistan and asked if he wanted to become an active member of AL QAIDA.

APPENDIX 2

EXCERPTS from a report written by the FBI based on the interrogations of Mohammed Jabarah in New York.

U.S. Department of Justice
Federal Bureau of Investigation
August 21, 2002

INFORMATION DERIVED FROM MOHAMMED MANSOUR JABARAH

The following information concerning Father Rahman Al Ghozi, aka Saad, aka Mike, and the Jemaah Islamiyah, was obtained during FBI interviews of Mohammed Mansour Jabarah, aka Sammy. This document contains neither recommendations nor conclusions of the FBI. It is the property of the FBI and is loaned to your agency; it and its contents are not to be distributed outside of your agency.

During early September 2001, Jabarah traveled to Malaysia to meet with individuals who were planning an operation against the U.S. and Israeli Embassies in the Philippines. Jabarah advised that he (Jabarah) was in charge of the financing for the operation . . .

Jabarah stated that there were code words used by Al Qaeda. The code words were generally established by the individual cells. Some of the code words they used in Asia were:

Market = Malaysia

Soup = Singapore

Terminal = Indonesia

Hotel = Philippines

Book = Passport

White Meat = American

. . . When asked about the potential targets in Asia, Jabarah noted that the planned attack in Singapore would not have been difficult. This embassy is very close to the street and did not have many barriers to prevent the attack. An attack on the U.S. Embassy in Manila would have been much more difficult, requiring at least two operations. Jabarah added that this would most likely not [have] been successful, adding that a plane would be needed to attack this building because the security was very tough.

APPENDIX 3

AN excerpt from the Information signed by United States Attorney James B. Comey, charging Mohammed Jabarah with five criminal counts:

UNITED STATES DISTRICT COURT

SOUTHERN DISTRICT OF NEW YORK

_____X

UNITED STATES OF AMERICA

-v-

MOHAMMED MANSOUR JABARAH

a/k/a "Abu Hafs al Kuwaiti,"

a/k/a "Sammy,"

Defendant

_____X

Count One

THE United States Attorney charges:

1. From in or about January 2000, through the date of the filing of this Information, in Singapore, Malaysia, the Philippines, Pakistan, Oman, and Afghanistan, and elsewhere outside the United States and outside the jurisdiction of any particular state or district, MOHAMMED MANSOUR JABARAH, the defendant, who was first brought to and arrested in the Southern District of New York, together with Usama Bin Laden and other members and associates of the groups known as *al Qaeda and Jemaah Islamiyah*, and others known and unknown, unlawfully, willfully and knowingly combined, conspired, confederated and agreed to kill nationals of the United States.

2. It was a part and an object of said conspiracy that the defendant, and others known and unknown, would and did murder United States nationals at the United States embassies in the Philippines and Singapore.

3. In furtherance of the conspiracy and to effect the object thereof, the defendant, and others known and unknown, committed the following overt acts, among others:

   a. In or about March 2001, in Afghanistan, JABARAH, the defendant, attended terrorist training camps sponsored by *al Qaeda*;

   b. In or about May 2001, in Afghanistan, JABARAH, the defendant, made *"bayat,"* that is, he pledged allegiance to Usama Bin Laden;

   c. In or about July 2001, in Afghanistan, JABARAH, the defendant, met with Usama Bin Laden, a co-conspirator not named as a defendant herein, to convince Bin Laden of his potential as an operative for Bin Laden's terrorist group *al Qaeda*;

d. In or about August 2001, JABARAH, on instructions from Usama Bin Laden, traveled to Karachi, Pakistan and met with an individual ("Co-Conspirator #1");

e. In or about September 2001, JABARAH met another individual ("Co-Conspirator #2") in Karachi, Pakistan, who provided JABARAH with details of a terrorist operation being planned against American and Israeli targets in the Philippines, and told JABARAH that he would be working with an individual from Malaysia ("Co-Conspirator #3") and an individual from the Philippines ("Co-Conspirator #4");

f. In or about September 2001, JABARAH met with Co-Conspirator #3 and others in Kuala Lumpur, Malaysia to discuss the terrorist operation being planned in the Philippines;

g. In or about September 2001, JABARAH traveled to Manila, Philippines, where he met with Co-Conspirator #4;

h. In or about early October 2001, JABARAH met with, among others, Co-Conspirator #3, and Co-Conspirator #4 in Kuala Lumpur, Malaysia, and discussed switching the target of the terrorist operation to Singapore;

i. In or about mid-October 2001, JABARAH met with Co-Conspirator #4 and others in Singapore and conducted surveillance of numerous targets, including the American embassy;

j. In or about late October 2001, JABARAH videotaped the exteriors of the potential targets of the terrorist operations in Singapore, including the American embassy;

k. In or about late October or early November 2001, JABARAH met with co-conspirators in Kuala Lumpur, Malaysia, where it was decided that the priority targets would be the American and Israeli embassies in Singapore and that they would be attacked using explosives;

l. In or about November 2001, JABARAH met with another individual in Kuala Lumpur, Malaysia, who provided approximately $50,000 to Jabarah for the plot;

m. In or about late November 2001, in Kuala Lumpur, Malaysia, JABARAH met with Co-Conspirator #2 and another individual and they discussed shifting the operation back to the American and Israeli embassies in the Philippines;

n. In or about December 2001, JABARAH learned that Co-Conspirator #3 and Co-Conspirator #4 had been arrested and he fled from Asia; and

o. In or about February 2002, Co-Conspirator #1 instructed JABARAH to travel to Oman to assist in providing a safe haven for *al Qaeda* members/ associates traveling from Afghanistan to Yemen.

NOTES

MY primary sources of information were interviews, conducted in several countries, and my review of classified intelligence documents. I also referred to the following sources:

Prologue

Canadian Security Intelligence Service (CSIS), "Sons of the Father: The Next Generation of Islamic Extremists in Canada," Intelligence Brief 2004-5/07, Ottawa, 2004, SECRET/CANADIAN EYES ONLY.

Integrated National Security Assessment Centre (INSAC), "Al Qaeda Attack Planning Against North American Targets," Ottawa, May 21, 2004, SECRET/CANADIAN EYES ONLY.

CSIS, "Sunni Islamic Extremism and the Threat to Canadian Maritime Security," Ottawa, March 4, 2004, SECRET.

Sebastian Rotella, "Europe's Boys of Jihad," *Los Angeles Times,* April 2, 2005.

Judge Blais made his comments about associates in *Canada v. Mourad Ikhlef,* Federal Court of Canada, DES-8-01, March 8, 2002.

Mohammed T. Al-Rasheed, "The Danger of Being Half-Educated," *Arab News,* Saudi Arabia, April 7, 2005. Al-Rasheed also kindly shared his views on jihadi recruitment with me by email.

Rohan Gunaratna, *Inside Al Qaeda: Global Network of Terror,* Berkley Books, New York, 2003. The four factors of recruitment were described by Professor Gunaratna and are explained in detail in: Marc Sageman, *Understanding Terror Networks,* University of Pennsylvania Press,

Philadelphia, 2004. Sageman studied the biographical profiles of 172 jihadi terrorists, including the Jabarah brothers.

Michael Taarnby, "Recruitment of Islamist Terrorists in Europe: Trends and Perspectives," Centre for Cultural Research, University of Aarhus, Research Report funded by the Danish Ministry of Justice, Denmark, January 14, 2005.

Claude Salhani, "Politics and Policies: Euro–Islamist threats," United Press International, April 27, 2005.

"Australians are taking to terror: ASIO chief," *Sydney Morning Herald,* Australia, November 4, 2004.

Don Van Natta Jr. and Lowell Bergman, "Insurgency: Militant Imams Under Scrutiny Across Europe," *The New York Times,* January 25, 2005.

Sean O'Neill and Yaakov Lappin, "I don't want you to join me, I want you to join bin Laden," *The Times,* London, January 17, 2005.

Sebastian Rotella, "Islamic militants in Europe blend political sophistication and crude violence to influence events, as the bombings in Madrid show," *Los Angeles Times,* March 6, 2005.

Chapter 1

H.T. Norris, *The Adventures of Antar,* Aris and Philips Ltd., Warminster, England, 1980.

Michael A. Sells, *Desert Tracings: Six Classic Arabian Odes by 'Alqama, Shanfara, Labid, 'Antara, Al-A'sha, and Dhu al-Rhumma,* Wesleyan University Press, Middletown, Connecticut, 1989.

Charles F. Horne, *Sacred Books and Early Literature of the East: Ancient Arabia; The Hanged Poems; The Koran,* Kessinger Publishing, Montana, 1997.

Ignace Goldziher, *A Short History of Classical Arabic Literature,* Georg Olms Verlagsbuchhandlung, Hildesheim, 1966.

Albert Hourani, *A History of the Arab Peoples,* The Belknap Press of Harvard University Press, Cambridge, 1991.

Gilles Munier, *Iraq: An Illustrated History and Guide,* Interlink Books, Northampton, Massachusetts, 2004.

Peter Mansfield, *Kuwait: Vanguard of the Gulf,* Hutchinson, London, 1990.

Al-Mazidi's eulogy, obtained from Mansour Jabarah.

Chapter 2

Elaine Sciolino, *The Outlaw State: Saddam Hussein's Quest for Power and the Gulf Crises,* John Wiley & Sons, New York, 1991.

Micah L. Sifry and Christopher Cerf, *The Gulf War Reader: History, Documents, Opinions,* Times Books, New York, 1991.

Amnesty International, "Cases of 'disappearance,' incommunicado detention, torture and extrajudicial execution under Martial Law," October 1, 1992.

Associated Press, "Jubilation among Kuwait City rubble," *Financial Post,* February 27, 1991.

Associated Press, Canadian Press and Reuters, "Iraq offers ceasefire deal," *The Vancouver Sun,* February 27, 1991.

John King, Canadian Press, "Gulf-Kuwait-Scene," February 27, 1991.

Reuters, "Bush declares victory for mankind," *Financial Post,* February 28, 1991.

Chapter 3

CSIS, "Sons of the Father."

INSAC, "Al Qaeda Attack Planning."

Eric Hoffer, *The True Believer: Thoughts on the Nature of Mass Movements,* Harper & Row, 1951.

The CSIS testimony is from a transcript provided by the Subcommittee on Public Safety and National Security of the Standing Committee on Justice, Human Rights, Public Safety and Emergency Preparedness, Evidence Number 6, February 22, 2005.

John Gagnon, "The Psychology of Terrorism: The Multicausal Picture," distributed electronically by the Canadian Centre of Intelligence and Security Studies, Ottawa, 2004.

Richard M. Pearlstein, *The Mind of the Political Terrorist,* SR Books, Wilmington, Delaware, 1991.

Richard W. Bulliet, Fawaz A. Gerges and John O.Voll, "Producing Jihad: The Al Qaeda Recruitment Tape," Columbia International Affairs Online.

Stewart Bell, "Ontario Qaeda's exploits revealed," *National Post,* Toronto, August 26, 2004.

Stewart Bell, "Canadian admits to role in hunt for 'White Meat': Confessions to the FBI," *National Post,* Toronto, January 18, 2003.

Stewart Bell, "Canadian terrorist negotiating with U.S.," *National Post,* Toronto, January 23, 2003.

Susan Schmidt and Caryle Murphy, "U.S. Revokes Visa of Cleric at Saudi Embassy, Monarchy to No Longer be Islamic Institute's Sponsor," *The Washington Post,* December 7, 2003.

Stephen Baxter, "Jihadist's travels," Medill News Service, November 21, 2004.

"Muslims open their Mosque of Light," *The Standard*, St. Catharines, May 28, 2001.

Allison Lawlor, "Muslims mark Ramadan," *The Standard*, St. Catharines, November 27, 2000.

Marlene Bergsma, "Clerk charged in diner robbery," *The Standard*, St. Catharines, June 17, 1998.

Chapter 4

"The Sociology and Psychology of Terrorism: Who Becomes a Terrorist and Why?" Library of Congress, Federal Research Division, September 1999, Washington, D.C.

The transcript of Abu Gaith's video, "In full: Al Qaeda Statement," was posted on the BBC News Internet site, news.bbc.co.uk, on October 10, 2001.

The figures concerning Palestinian suicide bombers cover attacks from the late 1980s to 2003 and were published in: Michael Bond, "The Making of a Suicide Bomber," *New Scientist*, May 15, 2004. Bond attributes them to Princeton University economist Claude Berrebi.

The Internet posting, "How you can become a member of Al Qaeda," was obtained and translated by the SITE institute in Washington, D.C.

Chapter 6

Mohammed described his trip to Karachi and Peshawar to CSIS and the FBI.

Peter Bergan, *Holy War Inc.*, Touchstone, New York, 2002.

K.P.S. Gill et al., *Most Wanted: Profiles in Terror*, Lotus Books, New Delhi, 2002.

Chapter 7

Mohammed detailed his voyage to Afghanistan and his experience in the training camps to CSIS and the FBI.

The FBI recruiting report was reproduced in *Intel News*, an internal publication of the Illinois State Police, on March 16, 2003. A second bulletin, "Al Qaeda Recruiting," was published July 1, 2003.

Albert Bandura, "Mechanisms of Moral Disengagement," in *Origins of Terrorism: Psychologies, Ideologies, Theologies, States of Mind*, Walter Reich ed., Woodrow Wilson Center Press, Washington, D.C., 1998.

Chapter 8

Mohammed provided detailed accounts of his training at Al Farooq camp and his meetings with bin Laden to CSIS and the FBI.

The discovery of the training manual at Al Farooq camp is described in *The Interrogators: Inside the Secret War Against Al Qaeda,* Chris Mackey and Greg Miller, Little, Brown and Company, New York, 2004.

The Al Qaeda *bayat* is explained in: United States *v.* Enaam Arnaout, Government's Evidence Proffer Supporting the Admissibility of Co-conspirator Statements, United States District Court, Northern District of Illinois, Eastern Division.

The transcript of the July 24, 2003, *Frontline* interview with Sahim Alwan, which was featured in the program, "Chasing the Sleeper Cell," is available at pbs.org. I sent a letter to Alwan in prison asking whether he knew Jabarah. His lawyer called me a few weeks later and asked me not to send him any more letters as it was causing him problems.

Details of the Lackawanna case and the Al Farooq training camp are from the file: United States District Court, Western District of New York *v.* Yahya Goba, Shafal Mosed, Yasein Taher, Faysal Galab, Mukhtar Al-Bakri and Sahim Alwan; and "Statement of Fact," *United States of America v. John Lindh,* in the United States District Court for the Eastern District of Virginia, Alexandria Division, Crim. No. 02-37A.

Chapter 9

Mohammed provided the details of his dealings with KSM and Hambali to CSIS and the FBI.

The information on KSM and Hambali comes from: their interrogation reports; "Khalid Sheikh Mohammed," FBI Joint Terrorism Task Force, 2003; and Thomas H. Kean, et al., *The 9/11 Commission Report: Final Report of the National Commission on Terrorist Attacks Upon the United States,* W.W. Norton & Co., New York, 2004.

Chapter 10

Mohammed detailed his time in Hong Kong, Malaysia and the Philippines to CSIS and the FBI.

The description of CSIS targeting practices is from the testimony of Jack Hooper, Assistant Director of CSIS, at the Commission of Inquiry into the Actions of Canadian Officials in Relation to Maher Arar, June 22, 2004. (ararcommision.ca/eng/11c.htm).

INSAC, "Islamic Extremism in Southeast Asia," SABRE, Ottawa, April 21, 2004, UNCLASSIFIED: FOR OFFICIAL PURPOSES ONLY.

FBI, "Jemaah Islamiyah," *Intel News,* February 1, 2004.

Chapter 11

Mohammed gave CSIS and the FBI the details of the Singapore plot.

The Singapore government published the results of its investigation into "Sammy" in: "White Paper: The Jemaah Islamiyah Arrests and the Threat of Terrorism," Presented to Parliament by Command of the President of the Republic of Singapore, January 7, 2003.

Other Singapore government documents on "Sammy" include: "Reconnaissance of US Embassy and other Targets," Annex A, Singapore Government Press Statement on ISA [Internal Security Act] Arrests, Ministry of Home Affairs, Government of Singapore, January 11, 2002; "Video Filming of Sembawang Wharf and Changi Naval Base," Annex B, Singapore Government Press Statement on ISA Arrests, Ministry of Home Affairs, Government of Singapore, January 11, 2002; "Ministry's Response to Media Queries on 'Sammy,'" Ministry of Home Affairs, Government of Singapore, July 23, 2002; Press releases, Ministry of Home Affairs, Government of Singapore, January 5, January 11, January 18, January 24, March 1, July 23, September 19, 2002.

Robert Russo, Canadian Press, "Terror cell leader had Canadian passport," *Toronto Star*, January 17, 2002.

Tonda McCharles, "Ottawa stays mum on Al Qaeda probe; Singapore eyes Canadian," *Toronto Star*, January 18, 2002.

Chapter 13

RCMP, Criminal Intelligence Directorate, "Terrorism, Criminal Extremism and Canada: A General Introduction," Ottawa, May 17, 2004, UNCLASSIFIED.

INSAC, "Al Qaeda: Potential Threats to North American Targets," UNCLASSIFIED: FOR OFFICIAL PURPOSES ONLY, Ottawa, May 27, 2004.

CSIS, "Al Qaeda's Strategic Biological Weapons (BW) Program," Intelligence Brief 2004-5/15, Ottawa, June 28, 2004.

Security Intelligence Review Committee, Annual Report, 2004.

For a more detailed look at how terrorists use Canada as an operational base, see: *Cold Terror*, by Stewart Bell, John Wiley & Sons, Toronto, 2004. Also see: John C. Thompson and Joe Turlej, "Other People's Wars: A Review of Overseas Terrorism in Canada," MacKenzie Institute, June 2003.

Mike Pavlovic discussed his background and investigative techniques in testimony at *Republic of France v. Abdellah Ouzghar*, Superior Court of Justice, Toronto, January 20, 2003.

CSIS, "Re: Mohammed Mansour Jabarah," Ottawa, May 13, 2002, TOP SECRET.

CSIS, "Re: Mohammed Mansour Jabarah," Ottawa, June 3, 2002, TOP SECRET.

CSIS, "Re: Mohammed Mansour Jabarah," Ottawa, June 11, 2002, TOP SECRET.

Canadian Civil Liberties Association, "Dear Minister," August 2, 2002.

Chapter 14

The tactics of interrogation are discussed in the "Interrogation and Investigation" section of "Military Studies in the Jihad Against the Tyrants," which was seized by police in Britain and entered as evidence in the case against the African embassy bombers in New York.

FBI, "Information Derived from Mohammed Mansour Jabarah," Department of Justice, August 21, 2002.

United States of America v. Mohammed Mansour Jabarah, Information, United States District Court, New York, 2003.

CSIS, "Media Report Alleging that Mohamed Mansour Jabarah Arrested in Oman," House of Commons Book, Ottawa, July 18, 2002, UNCLASSIFIED.

Solicitor-General of Canada, "Canadian citizen held in U.S. custody in relation to an alleged Singaporean bomb plot," Ottawa, July 29, 2002. UNCLASSIFIED.

Solicitor-General of Canada, "Jabarah case–Update," Ottawa, August 1, 2002. UNCLASSIFIED.

Department of Foreign Affairs and International Trade, "Canadian Linked to Singapore Bomb Plot," Ottawa, July 19, 2002, PROTECTED.

Department of Foreign Affairs and International Trade, "Re. Sammy," Ottawa, July 17, 2002, UNCLASSIFIED.

The manual "The Philosophy of Confrontation Behind Bars" was posted on a jihadist message board and obtained then translated by the SITE [Search for International Terrorist Entities] Institute.

Chapter 15

The activities of Anas Al Kandari in the days before the Faylaka shooting are detailed in Enclosure 276 of the investigative file of the Office of the Staff Judge Advocate, I Marine Expeditionary Force, Camp Pendleton, California.

Details of the Faylaka Island shooting were found in: "Opening Statement, for the Release of the Judge Advocate General Investigation into the 8 Oct. 2002 Fatal Shooting of LCPL Sledd At Faylaka Island, State of Kuwait," United States Department of Defense; and "U.S. Marine Killed While

Participating in Eager Mace," U.S. Naval Forces Central Command, U.S. Fifth Fleet, Office of Public Affairs, October 8, 2002.

The Kuwaiti version of the Faylaka incident is derived from: Judgment, Kuwait Ministry of Justice *v.* Al Kandari et al.

Norma Figueroa, "An open e-mail to the president," was reproduced in the *St. Petersburg Times,* St. Petersburg, Florida, October 11, 2002.

"Bali 2002: Security Threats to Australians in South East Asia," Foreign Affairs, Defence and Trade References Committee, Autralia, August 2004.

"Interrogation Statement of Riduan Isamuddin, Also Known as Hambali," August, 2003.

David Case, "Terror in Paradise," *Men's Journal,* January 2003.

Chapter 16

The eulogy, "The Martyr Abdul Rahman Jabarah," was posted by Abdul Hadi Al-Qahtani on the Arab-language Internet message board afti.net, which is used by jihadists to distribute statements and the beheading videos of hostages in Iraq. Al-Qahtani's credibility is bolstered by the fact that he knew details about Abdul Rahman that had never been publicized.

CSIS, "Terrorist Attack in Saudi Arabia," CSIS Intelligence Brief, Ottawa, May 16, 2003, UNCLASSIFIED: FOR OFFICIAL PURPOSES ONLY.

Agence France Presse, "One dead in Saudi house blast that turns up 12 Kalashnikovs," Riyadh, March 18, 2003.

Royal Embassy of Saudi Arabia, "Press Release: Saudi Arabia foils terrorist plot," Washington, D.C., May 7, 2003.

Royal Embassy of Saudi Arabia, "Press Release: Prince Bandar's statement on the terrorist attacks in Riyadh," Washington, D.C., May 13, 2003.

Royal Embassy of Saudi Arabia, "Press Release: Saudi Arabia arrests suspects," Washington, D.C., May 19, 2003.

Royal Embassy of Saudi Arabia, "Press Release: Top Al-Qaeda fugitive surrenders to Saudi authorities," Washington, D.C., June 26, 2003.

Royal Embassy of Saudi Arabia, "Press Release: Saudi Arabia has arrested 124 suspects since Riyadh bombings," Washington, D.C., July 2, 2003.

Royal Embassy of Saudi Arabia, "Press Release: Death of top Al-Qaeda fugitive" and "Death of top Al-Qaeda fugitive (update)," Washington, D.C., July 3, 2003.

Stewart Bell, "Al Qaeda tape praises Canadian as hero, martyr," *National Post,* Toronto, December 6, 2004.

Chapter 17

Mohammed described his prison routine in letter to his mother. Parts of Mohammed's letters were blacked out by U.S. authorities prior to being mailed to his parents, who shared them with me.

Federal Bureau of Prisons, U.S. Department of Justice, "Re: Request for information, FOIA Request No. 2005-00296," October 20, 2004.

Ahmed Rashid, "Terrorists' leader was found hiding in suburb where military elite live," *The Daily Telegraph,* London, March 3, 2003.

Lely T. Djuhari, "None arrested in hotel bomb blast," Associated Press, August 18, 2003.

"Terrorist Mastermind Hambali Arrested—Fact Sheet," SITE Institute, August 14, 2003, Washington, D.C.

Associated Press, "Terrorist Suspect Believed Killed," October 12, 2003.

The final letter in this chapter was translated by Mansour Jabarah. The other letters I obtained from the Jabarahs in their original Arabic and had them translated.

Chapter 18

CSIS, "Al Qaeda and the Metamorphosis of Islamic Extremism," Intelligence Brief 2004-5/42, Ottawa, December 6, 2004, CONFIDENTIAL.

CSIS, "Canadian Converts to Radical Islam," Intelligence brief 2004-5/29, Ottawa, October 13, 2004, SECRET.

CSIS, "Is Radical Islam a Problem in Canadian Prisons?" Intelligence brief 2004-5/39, Ottawa, December 10, 2004, SECRET.

INSAC, "Sunni Islamic Extremism: Use of Converts," Ottawa, April 27, 2004, UNCLASSIFIED: FOR OFFICIAL PURPOSES ONLY.

Bruce Hoffman, "The Modern Terrorist Mindset: Tactics, Targets and Technologies," in *Terrorism and Counterterrorism: Understanding the New Security Environment,* McGraw-Hill, Connecticut, 2003.

Jeff Victoroff, "The Mind of a Terrorist: A Review and Critique of Psychological Approaches," *Journal of Conflict Resolution,* Vol. 49, No. 1, February 2005.

Ariel Merari, "The Readiness to Kill and Die," in *Origins of Terrorism: Psychologies, Ideologies, Theologies, States of Mind,* Walter Reich ed., Woodrow Wilson Center Press, Washington, D.C., 1998.

Amira Hass, "Confessions of a Dangerous Mind: Three would-be suicide bombers share their motives with a cellmate," *Haaretz Magazine,* Tel Aviv, April 4, 2003.

Reuters, "U.N. Anti-Terror Head Wants More Intelligence Sharing," October 20, 2004.

Al Zawahiri's October 1, 2004, audiotaped statement to youths was obtained and translated by the SITE Institute.

Kate Jaimet, "Ottawa imam backs jihad against U.S.," *Ottawa Citizen*, April 7, 2003.

Associated Press, "Iranian girls in search of job to die for," *The Australian*, April 22, 2005.

INDEX